Contestations in Global Civil Society

Contestations in Global Civil Society

EDITED BY

ROOPINDER OBEROI
University of Delhi, India

JAMIE P. HALSALL
University of Huddersfield, UK

AND

MICHAEL SNOWDEN
University of Huddersfield, UK

United Kingdom – North America – Japan – India – Malaysia – China

Emerald Publishing Limited
Howard House, Wagon Lane, Bingley BD16 1WA, UK

First edition 2022

Copyright © 2022 Emerald Publishing Limited

Reprints and permissions service
Contact: permissions@emeraldinsight.com

No part of this book may be reproduced, stored in a retrieval system, transmitted in any form or by any means electronic, mechanical, photocopying, recording or otherwise without either the prior written permission of the publisher or a licence permitting restricted copying issued in the UK by The Copyright Licensing Agency and in the USA by The Copyright Clearance Center. Any opinions expressed in the chapters are those of the authors. Whilst Emerald makes every effort to ensure the quality and accuracy of its content, Emerald makes no representation implied or otherwise, as to the chapters' suitability and application and disclaims any warranties, express or implied, to their use.

British Library Cataloguing in Publication Data
A catalogue record for this book is available from the British Library

ISBN: 978-1-80043-701-2 (Print)
ISBN: 978-1-80043-700-5 (Online)
ISBN: 978-1-80043-702-9 (Epub)

Printed and bound by CPI Group (UK) Ltd, Croydon, CR0 4YY

Contents

Acknowledgments *vii*

About the Contributors *ix*

Foreword *xv*

Chapter 1 Introduction: Global Civil Society
Roopinder Oberoi, Jamie P. Halsall and Michael Snowden   *1*

Chapter 2 Unselfishness and Resilience: Social Capital in the Context of the Pandemic of COVID-19
Ian G. Cook and Paresh Wankhade   *13*

Chapter 3 Social Capital, Social Innovation and Social Enterprise: The Virtuous Circle
Roopinder Oberoi, Jamie P. Halsall and Michael Snowden   *29*

Chapter 4 Does Fifth Industrial Revolution Benefit or Trouble the Global Civil Society?
Cátia Miriam Costa, Enrique Martinez-Galán and Francisco José Leandro   *45*

Chapter 5 Networked Society and Governance: Algorithmic Default?
Tom Cockburn   *63*

Chapter 6 The End of Neoliberalism? The Response to COVID-19: An Australian Geopolitical Perspective
Michael Lester and Marie dela Rama   *79*

Chapter 7   Civil Society and Environmental Protection in Brazil: Two Steps Forward, One Step Back
Antônio Márcio Buainain and Junior Ruiz Garcia   97

Chapter 8   Redefining Social Capital and Social Networks in Global Civil Society
Tom Cockburn and Cheryl Cockburn-Wootten   119

Chapter 9   Role of Social Capital and Social Enterprise in China's Poverty Relief
Sam Yuqing Li and Qingwen Xu   157

Chapter 10   Conclusion: A Shifting Recognition of Global Civil Society?
Roopinder Oberoi, Jamie P. Halsall and Michael Snowden   173

Index   *181*

Acknowledgments

The original idea for this edited volume came from the 4th East Lake Forum on Global Governance, which took place in November 2018 at Huazhong University of Science and Technology in Wuhan, China. The theme at this international event was shared global governance and how this can be encompassed at a community level in the future. The editors of this book have long been interested in global civil society and how this is conceptualized in a local, national and global context. Over time, the concept of global civil society has drawn much critical focus from academics, policymakers and politicians.

In preparing this volume, there are a number of people the editors would like to thank. Firstly, to the contributing authors of this volume; without them, this collection of chapters would not have been possible. Secondly, to Emerald Publishing Limited, who painstaking put this collection together; special thanks go to Hazel Goodes, Dheebika Veerasamy, Rajachitra Suresh and David Mulvaney, who supported the editors throughout the process. Finally, thank you to Professor Jason Powell, Dr Stefanie El Madawi, and to our families.

Roopinder Oberoi, Jamie P. Halsall and Michael Snowden
Delhi, India and Huddersfield, UK

About the Contributors

Antônio Márcio Buainain is Professor of Economics at the Institute of Economics of the University of Campinas - Unicamp, in Campinas, Brazil, senior researcher at the National Institute of Science and Technology in Public Policy, Strategy and Development (INCT/PPED) and permanent researcher at the Center for Applied Economics, Agricultural and Environmental Research (NEA+), at the Institute of Economics/Unicamp. He obtained his degree in Economics and Law, in 1977, from the State University of Rio de Janeiro, and his Doctorate in Economics from the Institute of Economics, at Unicamp, in 1998. In addition to academic work, his professional experience includes serving as economist at the Food and Agriculture Organization (FAO), in Rome; advisory to several Brazilian ministries, including Ministry of Agriculture, Ministry of Rural and Agrarian Development and Ministry of Science, Technology and Innovation; consultancy work to international and national institutions, most dealing with innovation policies, intellectual property issues, agricultural policy, rural development, poverty alleviation programs, agrarian reform and family farm. Since 1989 he has co-edit and co-authored 47 books, published 87 book chapters and 99 papers in academic journals. Most of his academic work deals with development issues, from agriculture to innovation and sectorial public policies.

Tom Cockburn obtained his first degree with honors from Leicester University, England, both his MBA and Doctorate were gained at Cardiff University, Wales. He has eight years senior academic experience as Head of a UK Business School and two years as Deputy Head of School in New Zealand plus Adjunct and Visiting E-faculty roles on Henley Business School (UK and NZ) and Ulster University Business Schools' MBA and MSc programs and as Academic Learning and Teaching Fellow at the Australian School of Business, University of New South Wales, Sydney, 2007–2009 before returning to private consulting work.

Cheryl Cockburn-Wootten is a Senior lecturer and Director of Teaching and Learning at Waikato University, Hamilton, New Zealand. She aims to facilitate research that informs and makes a difference to our society. She adopts critical organizational communication perspectives to examine social issues particularly, within tourism and hospitality. Her work examines issues relating to stakeholders, community engagement, and social change.

Ian G. Cook is Emeritus Professor of Human Geography at Liverpool John Moores University, UK. He is an expert on various aspects of Chinese urbanization, global aging, social enterprise, and community development. He co-founded and co-edited *Contemporary Issues in Geography and Education* with the late Dawn Gill in the 1980s, co-led the British Pacific Rim Seminar Series and the Community Strategies Research Team in the 1990s and has co-edited and co-authored 10 books since then. He has helped supervise 20 PhDs and 6 MPhils to completion and has published widely in a wide range of volumes and academic journals including *Urban Studies, Health Policy, International Journal of Sociology and Social Policy*, and *Social Science and Medicine*.

Cátia Miriam Costa holds a PhD in Literature and has a background in International Relations, specializing herself in Discourse Analysis. She is a Researcher at the Centre for International Studies (Lisbon) and invited Assistant Professor at ISCTE-IUL. She is also the Director of the Chair Global Ibero-America of the European Institute of International Studies. She also worked as an Advisor in the Cabinet of the Secretary of State of Internationalization Affairs in the XXII Constitutional Government of Portugal. She has coordinated and participated in several international scientific projects, supported by national and international science funds. She has published articles, books and book chapters in Portuguese, English, Spanish, and French. Her research interests are international discourse, international communication, globalization, economic internationalization.

Marie dela Rama is a Management Academic at UTS Business School in Sydney, Australia. She has research and policy interests in aged care, business ethics, corporate governance, and corruption. In June 2021, she attended the UN General Assembly Special Session (UNGASS 2021) on corruption and the 9th Conference of States Parties to the UN Convention Against Corruption (UNCAC COSP9) as an accredited civil society observer. Her publications include *The Changing Face of Corruption in the Asia-Pacific* (2017, Elsevier), *Anti-Corruption Commissions* (2019, Asia Pacific Business Review), and *COVID-19 Governance, Legitimacy and Sustainability* (2021, Corporate Governance and Sustainability Review).

Junior Ruiz Garcia is Associated Professor of Economics at the Department of Economics and Postgraduate Program in Economic Development (PPGDE) of the Federal University of Paraná - UFPR, in Curitiba, Brazil. Researcher of the National Council of Science and Technology (CNPq), coordinator of the Study Group in Ecological MacroEconomics (GEMAECO - www.gemaeco.ufpr.br), at the Department of Economics, and member of the board of the Brazilian Society of Ecological Economics - ECOECO, as treasurer (2018-2019) and vice-president (2020-2021). Obtained his degree in Economics, 2005, from the Federal University of Paraná (UFPR), Master in Economic Development and Doctorate in Economic Development, Territory and Environment from Institute of Economics, at University of Campinas (Unicamp). In addition to academic work, his professional experience includes research experience, dealing with agricultural policy, rural development, poverty alleviation programs, agrarian reform, family farm, ecological economics, and ecological macroeconomics. Since 2006, he has co-edited 2 books, published 37 book chapters and 64 papers in academic journals. Most of his academic work deals with ecological economics, ecological macroeconomics, and sustainable development issues.

Jamie P. Halsall is a Reader in Social Sciences in the School of Human and Health Sciences at the University of Huddersfield, UK. His research interests include communities, globalization, higher education, public, and social policy. Currently, he is a Fellow of the Royal Society of Arts and a Chartered Geographer of the Royal Geographical Society, and was awarded Senior Fellowship of the Higher Education Academy in January 2017. He is the author of *Understanding Ethnic Segregation in Contemporary Britain* (Nova Publishers, 2013), and co-author of *Sociability, Social Capital, and Community Development: An International Health Perspective* (Springer, 2015) and *Aging in Comparative Perspective: Processes and Policies* (Springer, 2012); he also co-edited *Social Enterprise in the Higher Education Sector* (Cambridge Scholars Publishing, 2021), *Mentorship, Leadership, and Research: Their Place in the Social Science Curriculum* (Springer, 2019), and *The Pedagogy of the Social Sciences Curriculum* (Springer, 2017).

Francisco José Leandro received a Ph.D. in Political Science and International Relations from the Catholic University of Portugal (2010). From 2016 to 2018 he held the position of Institute of Social and Legal Studies Program Coordinator at the Faculty of Humanities at University of Saint Joseph - Macau, China. In 2017 he completed his post-doctoral research at the University of Macau on the Belt and Road Initiative. He is currently an Associate Professor and Associate Dean at the Institute for Research on Portuguese-speaking Countries, City University Macau, China. His most recent publications are respectively: *China and the Portuguese-speaking countries: Small Islands States - From sporadic bilateral exchanges to a comprehensive multilateral platform* (2020, City University of Macau); and *The Belt and Road Initiative: An Old Archetype of a New Development Model* (2020, Palgrave, Macmillan); *Geopolitics of Iran* (2021, Palgrave, Macmillan); *The Handbook of Special Economic Zones* (2021, IGI, Global). Francisco Leandro is a Researcher at OBSERVARE (Observatory of Foreign Relations, a research unit in International Relations of Autónoma University of Lisbon, Portugal).

Michael Lester is an Australian Economic Adviser and Executive in Public Administration and Policy (retired). He has held positions, including diplomatic postings, with Australian federal and state governments, as well as with the OECD and the World Bank. His past positions held include Senior Adviser, Department Prime Minister & Cabinet; Assistant Secretary, Australian Science and Technology Council; Counselor Science and Environment, OECD; Executive Director, High Technology Industries, NSW State Development; General Manager, Engineering Industries, Australian Trade Commission; Australian Trade

Commissioner; Senior Investment Officer, FIAS, World Bank Group; Executive Director (Finance & Facilities), Office of Olympic Coordination, NSW Premier's Department; Executive Director, Land and Water Australia. His specializations are in science, technology, and innovation; industry, trade, and investment; and environment, water, and resources. He writes on these issues and presents a weekly, in-depth radio program and podcasts on innovation, community, and politics. His current research interests include corporate governance, corruption, and the COVID-19 pandemic. He holds Bachelor's degrees in Engineering and in Politics, and a Master's degree in Economics. He has traveled widely on business and lived and worked in Paris, New Delhi, and New York.

Sam Yuqing Li is a doctoral student at New York University Stern School of Business. Her research interest largely surrounds organization theory and social innovation. She holds an MPhil degree from the Cambridge Judge Business School and a Bachelor's degree from NYU Shanghai.

Enrique Martinez-Galán received a PhD in Economics from the University of Lisbon in 2018. He is currently a Member of the Board of Directors of the Asian Development Bank. His previous professional experiences are in the Asian Infrastructure Investment Bank, European Investment Bank, World Bank, European Commission, and Portuguese Finance and Foreign Affairs Ministries. He is a Researcher of the Center for Social Sciences and Management of ISEG-Lisbon School of Economics and Management of the University of Lisbon; lecturer, reviewer, and author of several books and book chapters in development finance, multilateral governance, international trade, foreign direct investment, and the Belt and Road Initiative. He is a co-author of several recent scientific articles published in the following academic journals: *The World Economy, Applied Econometrics and International Development, Baltic Journal of European Studies, Portuguese Review of Regional Studies, and Portuguese Economic Journal*.

Roopinder Oberoi is Professor in the Department of Political Science, KMC, University of Delhi. She did her MA, MPhil and PhD in Political Science at the University of Delhi, and was awarded a Post-Doctorate Research Fellowship by the University Grant Commission, India. She is also a Founding Member of the Centre of Innovation and Social Enterprise, KMC, University of Delhi and has authored/edited four books: *Corporate Social Responsibility and Sustainable Development in Emerging Economies* (Lexington Publisher, 2015), *Globalization Reappraised: A False Oracle or a Talisman?* (Lexington Books, 2017), *Revisiting Globalization: From a Borderless to a Gated Globe*, Springer, 2018), and *Social Enterprise in the Higher Education Sector*, Cambridge Scholars Publishing, 2021).

Michael Snowden is a Senior Lecturer in Mentoring Studies in the School of Human and Health Sciences at the University of Huddersfield. His research interests lie in the field of pedagogy, mentorship, social enterprise, curriculum enhancement, and learning. He is a regular speaker at national and international conferences concerned with the development of pedagogical strategies in various contexts. He is currently the national coordinator for the "Flexible and Innovative Pedagogy" group of the Universities Association for Lifelong Learning and acts as Special Advisor to a number of agencies including the European Mentoring and Coaching Council. He is a member of the Editorial Board for the *International Journal of Coaching and Mentoring*.

Paresh Wankhade is a Professor of Leadership and Management at Edge Hill University, UK. He is an expert in the field of emergency services management and heads the UK's first bespoke Professional Doctorate in Emergency Services Management. He is the Editor-In-Chief of *International Journal of Emergency Services*. He has published widely in top academic journals and professional publications on strategic leadership, organizational culture, organizational change, and interoperability between the public and emergency services. His recent work has explored the leadership and management perspectives in the Emergency Services, and specifically in the Ambulance, Police and Fire & Rescue Services.

Qingwen Xu is Professor at New York University Silver School of Social Work and gMSW Program Coordinator in NYU Shanghai. She holds a PhD from the University of Denver and LLMs from New York University and Peking University. Her research is situated at the interaction of globalization, community development, and social welfare.

Foreword

This book duly deals with the varied dimensions around global civil society. The eloquent and unequivocal insights thrown upon social capital and it's pertinence in neoteric cataclysmic times is splendid and remarkable. I express no doubt in ascertaining that the larger audience – readers, academics, researchers and students – would find the book comprehensible, aiding them in exploring the related concepts and ideas around the larger theme of global civil society. The ongoing COVID-19 pandemic wreaked havoc upon the administration around the world. Against that backdrop, it's only imperative to explore how governments and their governance responded to the challenges. But most importantly, civil society as we know it of yesteryear would have its nature transformed in the post-COVID world.

How civil societies tackled those pandemic-generated challenges and abridged the gap between state and societies is in itself a vital question. The book answers this quite explicably in by citing the major role undertaken by civil society organizations (CSOs) in filling any void left by governments all over the world – specifically in availing the requisite facilities to citizens.

It's noteworthy to mention that the intimate relationship between social capital and civil society is explained. In that light, what the book does is to create a progressive understanding in invoking the realization of roles played by CSOs in emergencies like the one we witnessed in the form of COVID-19 outbreak.

On that note, I take immense joy and pleasure in recommending this book. Many congratulations to the editor, the contributing authors and the publisher in coming out with such material that, if read diligently, would only cement the significance of global civil society and its futuristic roles.

Professor Rekha Saxena
University of Delhi, India

Chapter 1

Introduction: Global Civil Society

Roopinder Oberoi, Jamie P. Halsall and Michael Snowden

Abstract

This introductory chapter sets the overall context of global civil society in today's global world. The authors will firstly provide a definition of civil society from social and political science perspectives. Then secondly, the authors provide a contemporary overview of global civil society debates in the current social and political environment; they also offer a short examination of COVID-19 and how this global pandemic has developed new spheres of contestation and collaboration. In the final part of the chapter, the authors present a brief overview of each chapter contributed to this volume.

Keywords: Civil society; COVID-19; globalization; Global Civil Society; governments; organizations

Introduction

> In relation to contemporary world politics, civil society is conceived as a political space where voluntary associations seek, outside political parties, to shape the rules that govern one other aspect of social life. Civil society groups bring citizens non-coercively in deliberate attempts to mould the formal and informal norms that regulate social interaction. (Scholte, 2004, p. 214)

As the above quotation illustrates, civil society, in a contemporary political context, is a somewhat complex concept (Allen, 1997; Blakeley, 2002; Lahiry, 2005; Powell, 2013). Politicians and academics of different political ideologies embrace the ideas around civil society. Since the 1990s, there has been a great assurgency of civil society as a political concept; this can be traced back to the political events of the falling of the Berlin Wall in November 1989. Countries in Western Europe and the United states put their political faith in civil society, as it was seen at the time as a modernizing idea for the new information age.

According to Carothers and Barndt (1999), the historical beginnings of civil society originate with the roman statesman, Marcus Tullius Cicero, and other Romans and philosophers. Interestingly, Carothers and Barndt (1999) go on to add that:

> The modern idea of civil society emerged in the Scottish and Continental Enlightenment of the late 18th century. A host of political theorists, from Thomas Paine to Georg Hegel, developed the notion of civil society as a domain parallel to but separate from the state-a realm where citizens associate according to their own interests and wishes. This new thinking reflected changing economic realities: the rise of private property, market competition, and the bourgeoisie. It also grew out of the mounting popular demand for liberty, as manifested in the American and French revolutions. (p. 18)

Then, from this, the conceptual ideas of civil society were forgotten about due to the rise of the industrial revolution (Carothers & Barndt, 1999). But, civil society reemerged after the Second World War through the writings of Antonio Gramsci and his Marxist theories. In his books, Gramsci focused on the ideas of the state, dictatorships, and hegemony, and how these are bound together with civil society (Öncü, 2003). Gramsci's publications were instrumental, as noted by Carothers and Barndt (1999) who state:

> in the 1970s and 1980s with persons fighting against dictatorships of all political stripes in Eastern Europe and Latin America, Czech, Hungarian, and Polish activists also wrapped themselves in the banner of civil society, endowing it with a heroic quality when the Berlin Wall fell. (p. 19)

Hence, historically, civil society is seen as the growth of civilization, as democracy and society is regulated through relationships. Kumar (1993) notes that civil society is social order driven, whereby citizens actively engage in public life by resolving disputes corresponding to the law of the country. Moving forward today, civil society is situated within the social, economic, political and cultural context, and is perceived as a "democratic catalyst" (Karolewski, 2006, p. 168). As Kumar (1993) acknowledges:

> Civil society has been found in the economy and in the polity; in the area between the family and the state, or the individual and the state; in non-state institutions which organize and educate citizens for political participation; even as an expression of the whole civilizing mission of modern society. (p. 383)

The social and political events concerning civil society have turbo-charged the concept, bringing it into focus globally, that is, "Global Civil Society." In the 2002 Martin Wight memorial lecture, the British academic Mary Kaldor (2003) stated:

> global civil society is a platform inhabited by activists (or post-Marxists), NGOs and neoliberals, as well as national and religious groups, where they argue about, campaign for (or against), negotiate about, or lobby for the arrangements that shape global developments. (p. 590)

As Kaldor acknowledges, civil society, in a global context, has many actors that can influence economic development. The premise of this edited book is to critique and demonstrate the ways in which the global community is dealing with a complex political world within the narrative of global civil society.

Defining Global Civil Society

There is no doubt that the conceptual provenance of the ideas of global civil society has been driven by the empowerment of globalization. McGrew (1992) observes that the concept of globalization "refers to the multiplicity of linkages and interconnections that transcend the nation-states (and by implications the societies) which make up the modern world system" (p. 65). The empowerment of globalization has been driven by the transportation and communication revolution, which has opened up the world and created new global connections. As Leyshon (1995) notes, "Advances in transport and communication technology have served to speed up the space of life and brought progressively more areas within the orbit of capitalist relations of production" (p. 29). For transportation, the level of innovation, especially in the twentieth century, has been a great. Examples include the introduction of air travel (e.g., Boeing 747 Jumbo Jet; Concorde) and high speed passenger trains (e.g., the bullet train, TGV). While for communication technologies, there have been numerous technological advancements, such as computers, mobile phones, and tablets, all of which have access the World Wide Web. The rise of communication technologies in global civil society has created a "Network Society," and as Manuel Castells (2010) notes:

> The new society is made up of networks. Global financial markets are built on electronic networks that process financial transactions in real time. The Internet is a network of computer networks. The electronic hypertext, linking different media in global/local connection, is made up of networks of communication – production studios, newsrooms, computerized information systems, mobile transmission units, and increasingly interactive senders and receivers. The global economy is a network of financial transactions, production sites, markets, and labor pools, powered by money, information, and business organizations. The network enterprise, as a new form of business organization, is made of networks of

firms or subunits of firms organized around the performance of a business project. Governance relies on the articulation among different levels of institutional decision making linked by information networks. And the most dynamic social movements are connected via the Internet across the city, the country, and the world. (p. 248)

The rapid development of globalization adds emphasis to the greater importance of global civil society. Martens, Dreher, and Gaston (2010) state:

> The concept of global civil society has, when fully fulfilled, wonderful characteristics. The political pursuit of equality, transparency and accountability helps establish a new set of ethical norms taking into account the different circumstances around the world. (p. 576)

The intense relationship between globalization and global civil society has emerged due to the new form of global politics occurring across the world. These closer ties between globalization and global civil society can be perceived within three distinct paradigms (see Table 1.1).

With these emerging paradigms and the emphasis on its relationship with globalization, the social and political sciences have recentred their focus on global civil society. For example, Corry (2006) points out that globalization and global civil society concepts "have become ever more dependent upon each other" (p. 306) due to their global interconnectedness. More interestingly, Corry (2006) also notes that global civil society must be seen as "beyond the state" (p. 309) because it reaches out to global networks that create new ideas and values. Therefore, global civil society is defined as:

> the myriad of individuals and institutions which operate under the principles of networking and voluntarism, outside of traditional institutions, and collectively seeking changes in the social order and inequalities, transcending individual interests and national boundaries. (Gonzalez-Perez, 2013, p. 42)

The rapid development of global civil society has been triggered by the continuous focus on the third sector from public policy perspectives (Bernauer & Gampfer, 2013; Keane, 2003; Nanz & Steffek, 2004). Organizations, such as charities, NGOs and social enterprise, have played a more important role in public policy-making in recent times. International organizations such as the United Nations (UN) have nurtured and maintained the concept of global civil society, strengthening the global community and supporting the networks of global citizens (Juergensmeyer, 2013). From this, governments across the world have engaged with the UN on their vision for global civil society.

Table 1.1. The Three Paradigms of Global Civil Society Set Out by Mary Kaldor (2003).

Paradigm One: *New Social Movements*

- "Developed after 1968 concerned with new issues, like peace, women, human rights, the environment, and new forms of protest
- The language of civil society seemed to express very well their brand of non-party politics
- The concept was enthusiastically taken up in South Asia, Africa – especially South Africa – and Western Europe
- During the 1990s, a new phenomenon of great importance was the emergence of transnational networks of activists who came together on particular issues – landmines, human rights, climate change, dams, AIDS/HIV, and corporate responsibility"

Paradigm Two: *New Policy Agenda*

- "Civil society was understood as what the West has; it is seen as a mechanism for facilitating market reform and the introduction of parliamentary democracy
- The key agents are not social movements but NGOs
- NGOs increasingly look both like quasi-governmental institutions, because of the way they substitute for state functions, and at the same time like a market, because of the way they compete with one another"

Paradigm Three: *Postmodern Version*

- "Social anthropologists criticize the concept of society as Euro-centric, something born of the Western cultural context (according to argument, Latin America and Eastern Europe are both culturally part of Europe)
- Non-western societies experience or have potential to experience something similar to civil society, but individualism
- Postmodernists, new religions, and ethnic movements that have also grown dramatically over the last decade are also part of global civil society
- Global civil society cannot be just the 'nice, good movements.'"

Source: Adapted from Kaldor (2003, pp. 589–590).

Global Civil Society and the Pandemic: Contestations and Collaborations

The coronavirus disease has caused tall expectations and severe strain on administrations around the globe. A lot has been written on the reoccurrence and revival of big government. To some extent overlooked amid the concentration on governments' disaster responses, the coronavirus pandemic has sharpened and deepened the role of organized civil society acts. Civil society manifests as coronavirus-related activism, as many civil society organizations (CSOs) have stepped in with emergency relief, and to assist with the management of the pandemic; many new civic groups emerged, especially at the local community level, while many CSOs repurposed themselves. Government administrations experienced severe strain, and civil society filled the gaps left by their chaotic responses to the emergency. For example, a report by CIVICUS (2020) notes "CSOs worked not only as frontline responders, but also as defenders of human rights during the pandemic, including the rights of vulnerable and excluded groups" (p. 2). Coronavirus-related activism has worked both as compensation for government shortcomings during the crisis and as partner to government initiative.

More understanding is required of society-level responses to the pandemic and the ways in which it is restructuring the connection between states and societies. Across numerous countries, the question that is being asked is: How far has the pandemic spurred innovative forms of civic activism?

As the COVID-19 pandemic continues to affect the world and its social and economic processes, triggering an international and unparalleled public health crisis, CSOs are responding by providing frontline assistance across the world. CSOs have vast experience of supporting public health services, immunization programs, social support, livelihood programs, and social liability. Bhargava 2021) confirms that CSOs have begun to complement governments' COVID-19 responses, noting:

> The Global Alliance for Vaccination and Immunization (Gavi) and the COVID-19 Vaccines Global Access (COVAX), the global initiative for procurement and distribution of COVID-19 vaccines, also recognize the expertise of CSOs in public health and vaccination and have included them in their governing boards and operations. (p. 2)

Governments can generate a constructive environment for partnership with CSOs by appealing for their engagement in efforts in specific areas of their expertise, sharing evidence and data with them, and creating reciprocal dialogues between local establishments and CSOs.

Simultaneously, CSOs have been facing profound challenges that could damage their capacities to continue playing critical roles in the distribution of social good and services, promoting human rights, and defending the most vulnerable while preserving participatory democratic institutions and civic deliberation in the near future. Across diverse towns and states, residents came together through innovative voluntary links and mutual support societies; they raised financial support for emergency relief, awarded medical supplies and protective gear like personal protective equipment (PPE) kits and masks for overwhelmed hospitals, and distributed assistance to those who lacked social protection. Civic actors are also co-operating with several local level businesses to donate masks, medical paraphernalia, and meals, and to contribute to relief attempts in other ways: "In the face of these challenges, civil society adopted a can-do mindset, mounting a constructive response characterised by flexibility, creativity and innovation" (CIVICUS, 2020, p. 5).

While many governments offered funding and support to the vulnerable sections of society impacted by the dramatic slowdown of economic activity, structures and systems were often insufficient, leaving many individuals still fraught. States failed to take into consideration the needs of specific excluded clusters, such as the many individuals working in the informal sector of the economy who may not access government support measures that are often available to formal workers; together with undocumented migrants who are often not eligible for assistance, women, *inter alia*, were side-lined by sustenance arrangements that targeted males as heads of households. CSOs worked to compensate for these shortfalls by offering dynamic backing and evidence (CIVICUS, 2020).

Civil society actors perform vital roles in apprizing and communicating to the public about the nature of coronavirus and the spread of the disease. Many resourceful local groups are springing up, with immediate neighbors organizing support for the vulnerable communities. CSOs have familiarity with and are trained in calamity responses; they are very frequently the primary and first responders in emergencies, and "are particularly important in 'last mile' delivery and in reaching the most excluded communities" (Vaughan & Hillier, 2019, p. 2).

Many organizations pitched in to supply oxygen during the deadly wave of the pandemic in April 2020:

> In Tunisia, for example, more than 100,000 people joined a Facebook group bringing together volunteers to help fight the virus. The group now has 24 coordination centers across the country; its volunteers have raised money, collected medical supplies, disinfected public spaces, and worked with regional authorities to identify families with urgent financial needs. In Iran, a group of businesses and volunteers has delivered 70,000 respirators and other protective gear to Iranian health workers. Similarly, in Poland, new online platforms and social media groups are both matching people in need with community groups that can provide support and organizing to supply medical staff with equipment and food. Many more such local initiatives are springing up, with neighbors coming together to help the most vulnerable community members. (Brechenmacher, Carothers, & Youngs, 2020, p. 12)

Across various countries in Asia, the Asian Indigenous Peoples Pact took on the responsibility of providing food to indigenous poverty-stricken communities, much like India, where discrimination against indigenous people deepened during the pandemic, leading to some individuals being frightened of displacement and barred from using public services. For example, in the case of India:

> hundreds of CSOs, like Goonj, Gram Bharati Samiti and Mahatma Gandhi Seva Ashram mobilised support to aid migrants, casual workers and slum dwellers by providing food, masks, sanitiser and menstrual hygiene products. Youth for Unity and Voluntary

Action provided food to healthcare workers, along with support to India's homeless people and slum dwellers. (CIVICUS, 2020, p. 8)

Faith institutions also played a significant part. Sikh communities globally tapped into the teaching and faith of Sikhism and started huge collective pantries to deliver essential support and food to the poor, together with support for elders and those powerless to fend for themselves; they also set up hotlines and websites for people to request help. During the deadly second wave of COVID-19 in India, they also distributed oxygen cylinders to the needy (CIVICUS, 2020, p. 12).

Political responses by some governments are also disrupting civil society globally; regular lockdown measures are upending their capability to unite, shape and advocate. Numerous CSOs have placed strategic and regular functions and roles on hold; many other NGOs and CSOs are scrambling to move their efforts online. More disturbingly, illiberal regimes are benefitting from the calamity, using it to stiffen their dogmatic grip by weakening the systems of checks and balances, imposing restrictions, and escalating state shadowing and scrutiny at a time when CSOs are powerless to fight back. While in some cases restrictive actions were balanced and defensible for the protection of lives, some administrations have used the crisis disingenuously to curb democratic freedoms and silence critical voices. Globally, the crisis has firmed up the prevailing partisan fault lines – in state and local areas, among opposite political camps, or between diverse religious and ethnic communities. Some fragile democracies and autocracies have suffered a serious lurch toward more centralized control and subjugation, with possible lasting ramifications. All these measures pose a substantial danger to civic activism. Restrictive rules devised during the pandemic are already squeezing civil society. The pandemic offered expedient shelter for governments to furthermore tilt the power equilibrium in their own favor.

The pandemic equally sharpens the requirement to shield democracy and presents new access points for national and global actors dedicated to its undertaking. The drastically changed political milieu calls on global organizations not only to recommit to shielding democracy, but also to regulate their approaches. The pandemic is also developing innovative arrangements of civil society mobilization. Civil society actors in several democratic and non-democratic countries are responding to the trials and difficulties posed by COVID-19; they are trying to fill the voids left by governments to distribute critical facilities, publicize evidence, and shelter the side-lined and deprived sections of society. In some cases, civil society actors are associating and collaborating with businesses and community establishments to support local groups struggling for financial support; they are also developing novel coalitions and unions to hold diffident or disobedient governments to account.

The recent urgency in civic society organizing themselves during the pandemic nonetheless provides an occasion to highlight the dynamic role of civil society, and its extensive support of vibrant and strong communities and democracy. Global supporters of civil society maximize their efforts to reinforce evolving local initiatives, to magnify civil society concerns in pandemic responses, and pitch their backing behind energies to preempt additional government limitations on democratic civil rights. Some states have stoked suspicion in civic actors' agendas and activities by labeling them as unaccountable, elitist, or as foreign-aid actors with a specific agenda disengaged from the local communities they claim to signify. Consequently, as civic groups get involved to distribute essential services to impacted communities and plug the gaps in administration responses, they can increase their influence and scope (Brechenmacher et al., 2020).

Newly formed associations and alliances with industries and civic networks benefit traditional CSOs to spread their reach and widen their networks within society. The growing energy of CSOs during the pandemic is viewed as local communities' endeavors to collaborate in order to deal with the direct effects of the crisis. This emerging pattern underpins an adjustment from the somewhat professionalized global CSOs to more confined, familiar civic activism. This is a drift that was hitherto continuing in many places, but the pandemic has intensified the swing. The upward trend of localism may endure if the reciprocated aid societies and networks molded during the emergency persevere as conduits for advocacy, assistance, and mobilization. The current worldwide commotion may open the door to utilitarian socioeconomic and political restructurings by representing the requirement for healthy societal safety nets, dynamic healthcare funds, improved equity, and enhanced international and state governance.

The array of civil society responses has established the dynamic and dependable roles that civil society plays: as a steadfast partner to government agencies; as an enabler and protector of society and left out clusters and sections of the public; as an appreciated foundation of care, leadership and suggestion; as a critical counteractive to government and market let-downs; as an unyielding supporter for reinstated approaches that spread to the communities, meet grassroots necessities, and guard civil rights; as a dynamic basis for accountability over state and private sector choices, and also as the provider of protection against exploitation, sleaze, and bribery. There was never a greater requirement for civil society as there has been during the COVID-19 pandemic, and ostensibly, although the physical distancing was required, it could not be at the cost of societal camaraderie. Solidarity was desired more than ever, to support one and all to get through this disaster and overcome its effects.

It is therefore becoming obvious that for swift responses to emergencies and disasters, states should recognize the worth and significance of CSOs should endeavor to empower and partner with them throughout civil society; doing so will lead to more joined-up and efficacious functional solutions. The lessons learned during the COVID-19 pandemic must benefit the world, to equip it for better synchronization for the next series of trials to arise in the future. Overall, the coronavirus is a herald for global civil society to revamp and reconsider their role. The global pandemic has placed extensive pressures and stresses not only on governments, but also on civil societies around the globe. While currently considerable attention has focused on governments' emergency responses, at a subterranean level the predicament is altering the connection between states and societies. Global civil society may emerge from the pandemic looking very changed and this alteration will be a momentous feature of today's extremely fluid global politics.

Structure of the Volume

This introductory chapter has set out the contemporary background context of global civil society and now provides a short summary of each of the upcoming chapters. To begin with, in Chapter 2, Ian G. Cook and Paresh Wankhade critically evaluate the concept of social capital and its intrinsic relationship with civil society. To do so, the chapter applies a SWOT analysis of social capital and provides some useful insights for the current COVID-19 context and the future. In Chapter 3, Roopinder Oberoi, Jamie P. Halsall, and Michael Snowden examine the concepts of social capital and social enterprise within the context of innovation. Here, the authors examine the conceptual ideas of social capital and social enterprise and how they connect from a public policy standpoint. The authors of Chapter 4, Cátia Miriam Costa, Enrique Martinez-Galán, and Francisco José Leandro, examine the fundamental features of global civil society and the main tests for the industry revolution from stages four to five. Here, in particular, the authors explore institutional arrangements (i.e., international organizations, governments, and higher education establishments). Chapter 5, by Tom Cockburn, explores the contemporary debates of civil society within the context of the network society, with emphasis on the effect/impact of artificial intelligence on a global civil society.

Using a case study approach, Chapter 6, by Michael Lester and Marie dela Rama, examines the political agendas of neo-liberalism and how Australia has reacted to the economic challenges presented by COVID-19. In Chapter 7, Antônio Márcio Buainain and Junior Ruiz Garcia provide a modern perspective on civil society in Brazil from an environmental protection perspective. Here, the authors put forward the ways that the current right-wing government is responsible for the decline in the environmental situation. In Chapter 8, Tom Cockburn and Cheryl Cockburn-Wootten address how social capital is developing in the age of globalization, particularly in the face of the pandemic; in their work, there is a clear analytical focus on social capital as an unequal concept. The authors of Chapter 9, Sam Yuqing Li and Qingwen Xu, examine the function of social capital and social enterprise in China's poverty relief. Moreover, the authors of Chapter 9 discuss China's new policies in welfare/rural development and question whether social enterprises and entrepreneurship can improve people's lives. The final chapter, written by the editors of this volume, provides an assessment of global civil society and how the concept could move forward in the future.

References

Allen, C. (1997). Who needs civil society? *Review of African Political Economy*, 24(73), 329–337.

Bernauer, T., & Gampfer, R. (2013). Effects of civil society involvement on popular legitimacy of global environmental governance. *Global Environmental Change*, 23(2), 439–449.

Bhargava, V. (2021). Engaging civil society organizations to enhance the effectiveness of COVID-19 Response Programs in Asia and the Pacific. *The Governance Brief*, ADB,

Issue 42. Retrieved from https://www.adb.org/sites/default/files/publication/689831/governance-brief-042-civil-society-covid-19-asia-pacific.pdf. Accessed on June 22, 2021.

Blakeley, G. (2002). Civil society. Contemporary political concepts: A critical introduction. In G. Blakeley & V. Bryson (Eds.), *Contemporary political concepts* (chapter 5, pp. 90–107). London: Pluto Press.

Brechenmacher, S., Carothers, T., & Youngs, R. (2020). Civil society and the coronavirus: dynamism despite disruption. Carnegie Endowment for International Peace. Retrieved from https://carnegieendowment.org/files/Brechenmacher_Carothers_Youngs_Civil_Society.pdf. Accessed on January 15, 2022.

Carothers, T., & Barndt, W. (1999). Civil society. *Foreign Policy*, *117*, 18–29.

Castells, M. (2010). Towards a sociology of the network society. In G. Ritzer & Z. Atalay (Eds.), *Readings in globalization: Key concepts and major debates* (pp. 246–252). Chichester: John Wiley & Sons.

CIVICUS. (2020). Solidarity in the time of COVID-19: Civil society responses to the pandemic. Retrieved from https://reliefweb.int/sites/reliefweb.int/files/resources/solidarity-in-the-time-of-covid-19_en.pdf. Accessed on June 22, 2021.

Corry, T. O. (2006). Global civil society and its discontents. *Voluntas: International Journal of Voluntary and Nonprofit Organizations*, *17*(4), 302–323.

Gonzalez-Perez, M. A. (2013). Global civil society and international business: A review. In M. A. Gonzalez-Perez & L. Leonard (Eds.), *International business, sustainability and corporate social responsibility* (Advances in Sustainability and Environmental Justice, Vol. 11, pp. 37–63). Bingley: Emerald Group Publishing Limited.

Juergensmeyer, M. (2013). *Thinking globally: A global studies reader*. Berkeley, CA: University of California Press.

Kaldor, M. (2003). The idea of global civil society. *International Affairs*, *79*(3), 583–593.

Karolewski, I. P. (2006). Civil society and its discontents. *Polish Sociological Review*, *154*(2), 167–185.

Keane, J. (2003). Global civil society?. Cambridge University Press.

Kumar, K. (1993). Civil society: An inquiry into the usefulness of an historical term. *The British Journal of Sociology*, *44*(3), 375–395.

Lahiry, S. (2005). Civil society redefined. *The Indian Journal of Political Science*, *66*(1), 29–50.

Leyshon, A. (1995). Annihilating space? The speed-up of communications. In J. Allen & C. Hamnett (Eds.), *A shrinking world? Global unevenness and inequality* (chapter 1, pp. 11–54). Oxford: Oxford University Press.

Martens, P., Dreher, A., & Gaston, N. (2010). Globalisation, the global village and the civil society. *Futures*, *42*(6), 574–582.

McGrew, T. (1992). A global society? In S. Hall, D. Held, & T. McGrew (Eds.), *Modernity and its futures* (chapter 2, pp. 61–116). Cambridge: Polity Press.

Nanz, P., & Steffek, J. (2004). Global governance, participation and the public sphere. *Government and Opposition*, *39*(2), 314–335.

Öncü, A. (2003). Dictatorship plus hegemony: A Gramscian analysis of the Turkish state. *Science & Society*, *67*(3), 303–328.

Powell, F. (2013). *The politics of civil society: Big society and small government*. Bristol: Policy Press.

Scholte, J. A. (2004). Civil society and democratically accountable global governance. *Government and Opposition*, *39*(2), 211–233.

Vaughan, A., & Hillier, D. (2019). *Ensuring impact: The role of civil society organizations in strengthening World Bank disaster risk financing*. Discussion Paper. Center for Disaster Protection. Retrieved from https://www.preventionweb.net/publications/view/65099. Accessed on June 22, 2021.

Chapter 2

Unselfishness and Resilience: Social Capital in the Context of the Pandemic of COVID-19

Ian G. Cook and Paresh Wankhade

Abstract

Although the concept of social capital is rightly associated with Putnam (2000), arguably its roots lie further back in the nineteenth century, but were first articulated in a "contemporary sense" in 1916 (Organisation for Economic Co-operation and Development (OECD), 2001, p. 41). The authors begin their analysis by summarizing the main types of capital: economic, social, political, human, cultural and symbolic, before exploring the different types of *social* capital, including bonding, bridging and linking. These are then linked to a variety of related concepts, including: social enterprise, social networks, social value, community development, community resilience and sociability (Cook, Halsall, & Wankhade, 2015). It is argued that social capital is central to these, and is of increasing importance across the globe within the context of the threats and opportunities posed by globalization on the one hand (including the spread of COVID-19) and of potential deglobalization on the other, in part as a reaction to COVID-19 and pre-existing nationalist trends toward limitation of global interactions. The discussion is supported by examination of a range of case studies drawn from societies of contrasting types, including the UK, USA, China, Bangladesh and South Africa. The authors conclude their analysis via consideration of how social capital can be expanded further in order to help meet contemporary and future challenges from whichever direction it arises.

Keywords: Social capital; community resilience; emergency first responders; clap for carers; moral injury; social networks

Introduction

In 2020 the world was hit by a coronavirus strain that began in Wuhan, China. The virus was soon named as COVID-19 and spread rapidly in early 2020 to become recognized by the World Health Organisation as a pandemic. At the time of writing in July 2021, 184.7 million people worldwide have been infected and nearly 4 million have died. The virus affects disproportionately those who are in older age groups, are male, come from Black and Ethnic Minority backgrounds, are poorer, and/or have comorbidities such as respiratory disease, including asthma or chronic obstructive pulmonary disease, diabetes, cardiovascular disease or obesity. Most governments have responded to the threat of this virus via lockdown of major sectors of the economy such as manufacturing, retailing, tourism and leisure. In the UK, for example, 1.5 million people thought to be at risk due to underlying health conditions and/or advanced age, were defined as being within the Shield group which meant that they should remain at home, initially for a period of 12 weeks, which was later extended for a longer period, from March 23 to August 2, 2020 in all. But this was later further extended until March 31, 2021. One of the authors, Ian Cook, was within this group. This is a particularly testing time for individuals, societies and governments across the globe, stretching vital health services to, and beyond, the limit, leading many millions to cope with the pressures of lockdown and isolation at a time of reduced service provision, and to witness the deaths of family and friends without the opportunity to participate properly in funeral services and shared acts of commemoration and remembrance. There is also the threat of new variants arising across the world, which has now gone through several waves of the virus, with the Delta variant that originated in India, becoming the dominant strain in 2021. These new variants have been met by a range of measures in different countries, including restrictions on the hospitality industry, wearing of masks in shops and public transport, and other limits on pre-pandemic normal life.

It is in this context we believe that the concept and practice of social capital is especially apposite. Volunteers have always been there in society, whether in hospitals to provide staff and patients with basic provisions such as newspapers and magazines, snacks and products to meet fundamental requirements, in religious centers to help keep these premises clean and welcoming to the faithful, and in a myriad of other fields around the globe. But the current crisis has meant a remarkable response by willing participants across the full gamut of help and assistance to those who are most in need. In so doing, these people develop, cement and spread social capital across communities to strengthen community bonds and promote human kindness and support for the most vulnerable. This brief chapter will provide examples from a variety of circumstances and countries, and in particular it will build upon previous research by the authors, plus the editors of this volume, updated at a time of global necessity.

The structure of this chapter is as follows. The first section covers the different types of capital and their interrelationships. The next section analyzes the main components of social capital. Section three performs a SWOT analysis of the social capital. The fourth section provides examples of the creation of social capital in different societies. In the concluding section, we provide some insights about how to nurture social capital for the future.

Different Types of Capital and Their Interrelationships

We live in an era in which Neoliberal Capitalism is dominant, even within societies that were previously socialist, mercantilist or feudal. Capital is not homogeneous, however, and it has long been recognized that "fractions of capital" exist, sometimes giving rise to tensions between, for example, industrial capital, finance capital, state capital and private capital. Industrial capital might seek to sustain investment in less profitable manufacturing companies, for instance, in order to ride out the cyclical nature of economic downturns while preserving key skills in their sector, aims that may conflict with the priorities of hedge fund investors for a quick profit that could be achieved via asset stripping of ailing firms. State capital, likewise, might require a significant level of support from the nation-state in order to develop and grow its activities in a manner that might be anathema to those who believe in unfettered competition via the free market, as shown recently in the United States, where action has been taken by the Trump and Biden administrations against Chinese companies such as Huawei and TikTok that are perceived as being too close to the Chinese government, with the TikTok case currently being blocked by the US courts.

Capital so permeates contemporary society that we now speak of political capital, human capital, cultural capital and, for this chapter, social capital. Thus, a national government may, for instance, be regarded as having a high stock of political capital if it has been electorally successful, be seen to have good and effective leadership, and to be regarded as being better than its predecessors. But, as with all capital, political capital can be squandered via poor and wasteful policies that lead to increasing calls for a national change of direction. In the UK, Boris Johnson's government was seen to have a high stock of political capital via its Brexit policy and large electoral victory in late 2019; in 2020, however, concerns over the handling of the COVID-19 crisis led to widespread criticisms concerning the UK's high death rate and failures in the test and trace system, for instance, leading to a diminution of the government's stock of political capital at least in the short term. Similarly, the National Audit Office (2020) report on the supply of personal protective equipment (PPE) during the COVID-19 pandemic, found several instances of the misuse of public money in the purchase and sourcing of the PPE. In 2021, the success of the UK vaccination program has once more increased the government's stock of political capital, but the resignation of the Minister of Health, Matt Hancock in June 2021 has yet again diminished it.

Human capital is a more economistic measure of the strength of labor resources within a country or society, being measured by the skill set and educational levels of the population, by the willingness to adapt to changing job requirements, such as the need to deal with technological change, and general suitability for the variable employment market. In contrast, cultural capital as a concept is of more recent origin, seeking to summate the less tangible features such as music, art, the stock of museums, theatres, films, plays and poetry with which a society is endowed. Festivals and events such as European City/Capital of Culture, the Liverpool Biennial or Venice Bienniale, the Cannes Film Festival and so on are built up in order to nurture cultural capital in a variety of ways. During the pandemic, cultural capital often has to be reimagined and reconfigured, given the lack of audience participation due to COVID-19 social distancing restrictions. Zoom calls have in large part replaced the physicality of cultural interactions to provide some balm to the loss of physical and emotional engagement in live performances in the real world. There have also been recent calls for natural capital to be employed as a measure of environmental qualities such as clean air, pure water or soil quality in the struggle against climate change.

So, what of social capital? We suggest that its roots lie in sociability, a concept that we have discussed elsewhere (Andrews & Wankhade, 2016; Cook et al., 2015), drawing upon Kropotkin's work (1902) in the late nineteenth/early twentieth centuries. In brief, societies are underpinned by altruism, mutual support and mutual aid, notwithstanding the strong emphasis on individualist competitiveness that is also a recurrent feature of human relations. As Putnam (2000, p. 290) puts it, "social capital makes us smarter, healthier, safer, richer"; it does so by helping to draw people together for the common good in order to achieve more than the sum of its parts via synergy and commitment to common goals, both within and beyond that provided by the participants in social capital creation themselves.

Social Capital and its Main Components

Social capital is clearly multifaceted, and its components will vary across time and space. At minimum, however, creation of social capital involves an element of co-operation between people. This co-operation is often place-bound at a level of the local situation, but the rise of communication systems such as the internet in modern society means that co-operative endeavor can transcend locality to be trans-spatial in nature. Zoom calls, for example, can facilitate and develop social interactions in a way scarcely imaginable a few years ago, and can thus enhance social capital via the deepening of links across space. We identify the following types of social capital: co-operative, local, non-local, bonding, bridging, network and, particularly relevant today, emergency social capital.

In brief, and although this typology contains overlapping elements, we suggest that co-operative social capital is the most fundamental, bringing individuals together to develop and meet a disparate range of perceived needs and challenges. And so, for example, some years ago the Eldonian Community in the north end of inner city Liverpool emerged and developed to fight local authority plans to construct an inner ring road that would destroy much of their community's housing stock and threaten the social cohesion of their home area. This was a local response to a perceived threat and the potential decanting and scattering of the local population to peripheral housing estates miles away from home. This is a common story but this one found an uncommon response; the ring road was not stopped but the coming together of the community under the charismatic leadership of Tony McGann led to an exemplary process of house building and community activities ensured that the community has remained in the area to this day (Cook & Norcup, 2011).

Social capital is most often realized, as in this example, at the local level by local people for local people. It often relies on bonding between family and friends to create a feeling of "us" against "them" in an expression of, and a contribution to, a strong sense of local identity and sense of place. In China, for example, the study in 410 villages by Xia (2011) found that nearly 83% of villagers worked with others at least "sometimes" through to "very often." Mutual trust was an important feature of village life, often based on kinship ties, although this was offset by distrust of "outsiders," a feature of village life through the centuries across the globe, not just in China. This question of trust is certainly an important aspect of social life and a recent study, again in China, has suggested that "social trust" has an impact on the participation rates of older adults in cultural and recreational activities and thus has a health impact, that is, the greater level of social trust the better the health level via this higher rate of participation in positive activities (Zhou & Cao, 2020). Bridging social capital in contrast in Xia's study was only "moderate" and as we noted in 2015 (Cook et al., 2015, p. 49) this

> is potentially unfortunate because the changes in China's rural areas mean that there are greater contrasts, for instance of wealth or economic activity within the villages and therefore the need for bridging social capital is greater.

Bridging social capital can help bring disparate people together, for example, people from different localities, social classes, income groups or educational attainment levels and thus help to strengthen networks of diffuse groups united by common goals. This was seen in the UK in March 2020 when the government asked for volunteers to assist the National Health Service (NHS) which was in danger of being overwhelmed by the expansion in COVID-19cases. It was hoped that up to 250,000 people might volunteer to help in a whole range of ways such as delivering prescriptions to those who were required to shield at home, as drivers to ferry people to urgent health appointments and also to deliver food parcels to those in need. In the event, it was not 250,000 but 750,000 who stepped forward to volunteer, people from all walks of life and localities. The actor and presenter Ross Kemp, who himself was a volunteer in his home area, was so impressed by the spirit of voluntarism that he had a series of programs made for the British Broadcasting Corporation in order to highlight the vast range of activities by volunteers around the country. There were those who shopped for and made food for NHS staff who had too little spare time due to the pandemic to shop and cook for themselves, or in one tearful scene filmed by a nurse, found nothing left on the shelves when she eventually could reach her local supermarket, a clip which went viral and stimulated voluntary activity further. "Clap for the NHS" was an initial online suggestion and Thursday nights at 8 p.m. became a focal point for clapping, drumming, beating pots and pans, and generally making noise in praise of NHS staff across the country. At a time of great national crisis, across the globe, strangers came together to perform music to keep their neighbors' spirits up, to lead community exercise at a distance and to provide food for the hungry and needy. The Trussell Trust is a major charity which operates foodbanks run by volunteers with contributed food from many businesses and on May 1, 2020 they issued figures to show that use of their food banks was 80% up over the year before, and a massive 120% up for families with children, with so many parents being unable to feed their children on their reduced incomes due to lockdown.

The impact of COVID-19 on the already under-pressure emergency services (such as ambulance, fire and rescue and police) was particularly significant (Wankhade, 2020). As the pandemic continues, the pressure only increased on the emergency first responders to respond appropriately and safely. To maintain an adequate staffing level, especially during the first wave of the pandemic between March and July 2020 was one of the biggest challenges facing the emergency services. Emotional accounts emerged as to how frontline responders while tackling coronavirus had to deal with their own mental health in addition to shortages of PPE, sickness and death of colleagues and their loved ones (Nelson et al., 2020; Sturdy, 2020; Wankhade, 2021). Working in such stressful environments or being called to homes where there were COVID-19 sicknesses or deaths, was further exacerbated by the inability to share their feelings. Many frontline staff had to stay away from their families in hotels for weeks to avoid passing infection to their family members. Random acts of kindness were witnessed across the UK involving members of public donating sweets, cakes and drinks to frontline crews. As noted above, the nation saluted the selfless devotion of frontline staff by clapping and banging drums in the streets every Thursday, showing gratitude for the selfless service and devotion to duty by first responders (Heath, Wankhade, & Murphy, 2021).

Notwithstanding the professionalism displayed by the emergency first responders, the pandemic has had a massive impact on the health and wellbeing of staff, in addition to their own physical health. Latest evidence suggests that health workers globally are having an increased risk of "moral injury" (Greenberg, Docherty, Gnanapragasam, & Wessely, 2020) and social wellbeing (Lawn et al., 2020) while dealing with the COVID-19 situation. A healthy work force is "sine qua non" for effective handling of the current pandemic situation. A package involving pre-incident training, managerial support accompanied by a nurturing organizational culture will go a long way for staff dealing with COVID-19 pandemic. Similarly, Wong and Kohler (2020) argue that

> considerations of social capital, including virtual community building, fostering solidarity between high-risk and low-risk groups, and trust building between decision-makers, healthcare workers, and the public, offer a powerful frame of reference for understanding how response and recovery programs can be best implemented to effectively ensure the inclusive provision of COVID-19 health services.

Marcus Rashford, a high profile young footballer with English Premier League team Manchester United, drew upon his experience of hunger as a child in a single parent family to campaign for children in need to continue to receive free meals during the school holidays of summer 2020. This campaign drew upon a huge well of popular support, gained over 1 million online signatures and persuaded the UK Government to do a U turn from their previous stance of refusing to continue these meals during holiday periods to instead provide funding for such meals to continue. For this public service Marcus Rashford was awarded a MBE, an official award for good works. Since then, however, Rashford has felt forced to continue campaigning, initially to provide free meals during the October 2020 half-term holiday, and the 2020 Christmas holiday. Many volunteers and businesses have come forward throughout the country to provide and distribute free meals to needy children, and local authorities such as Liverpool City Council have committed to pay for these. This is a superb example of bridging social capital being developed to meet the need of strangers across place and space. The UK Government has argued that they provide support for families in need via the welfare system or via direct payments to local authorities, but those involved in this campaign have argued strongly that free meals should go directly to the children themselves so that they can maintain their health and wellbeing more effectively. Somewhat strangely, a day or two after writing the initial draft of these previous sentences, the Prime Minister, Boris Johnson, rang Mr Rashford to announce yet another U turn on this matter, and pledged initially £170 million in winter payments plus other funds to provide the free meals in the Christmas holidays that Rashford and many others had advocated (Lawrie, 2020). Rashford welcomed this development while noting that there were still families that would miss out from this provision.

Networking is a key type of social capital, and of course the internet is a major facilitator of networking to underpin the work of those who seek to build social capital in place-bound or place-less communities. Pitas and Ehmer (2020, p. 942) make a similar argument and highlight that the recovery from COVID-19 may be hampered in many American communities by disruptions in social capital due to the extended periods of social distancing brought by the pandemic. Marcus Rashford's campaign and many others could not succeed without the utilization of social media to facilitate social interactions and organization. This is particularly evident during the pandemic when face-to-face interaction has become undesirable, and when strict social distancing must be maintained. "Clap for the NHS," for example, was suggested, sustained and maintained via the high profile that it rapidly achieved via social media, and the rainbow symbol involved could be downloaded via home printers and then placed in people's windows around the UK. Another example is the poppy which is a symbol of remembrance for those who lost their lives initially in World War I and then World War II and other conflicts around the globe, could also be downloaded to a home printer for coloring in and placing in windows for the UK's remembrance day in November 2020. This was encouraged, as were donations, by the Royal British Legion whose volunteer poppy sellers, and the public to whom they sell them, could not be out in the streets as normal in the pandemic. Such processes enhance people's wellbeing and sense of togetherness in the face of the challenges with which we are all faced during the pandemic, and after it is overcome.

As already noted, social capital creation is particularly appropriate in a time of emergency and disaster response, when the usual means of social and economic structure and provision are imperiled. The current pandemic is an obvious example, but there are many examples across the globe. Working with Jenny Clegg, for instance, Ian Cook has analyzed the rise of the Gong He movement in China during the war with Japan in the late 1930s/early 1940s (Clegg & Cook, 2009; Cook & Clegg, 2011; Cook et al., 2015). Gong He, means "work together" and entered the English lexicon when it became the battle cry of the American marines later in World War II as "Gung Ho." The idea of Chinese and overseas expatriates who came together in Shanghai, where the Japanese large-scale invasion took place in 1937 and quickly pushed inland up the Yangtse valley, this was essentially a large-scale rescue effort to help people survive and contribute to the war effort via production of essentials such as blankets, uniforms, guns and many other items that could no longer be provided because most of China's industrial capacity had been lost to the invaders. One notable feature of this movement was that it engaged and involved women who traditionally had been regarded as second class citizens in China's patriarchal feudal society via training and development to make a significant social and economic contribution in their own right.

A SWOT Analysis of Social Capital

We shall elaborate on such examples as these further in the next section. But it is pertinent to dig deeper into the concept via a SWOT analysis, that is, via a focus on Strengths, Weaknesses, Opportunities and Threats to social capital.

Strengths, then, lie in the provision of a key tool for measuring and assessing the sociability and togetherness of a social entity, especially at the community level. A well-functioning community has a strong pool of social capital that can be distributed from those able to provide it to those most in need of it. What exactly is provided by the donors will vary tremendously across time and space, in both tangible as well as intangible ways. For those with greater economic means, it might be, simply, money to give to those who most require it, particularly if the donors feel that they don't have the time to provide their labor or skills to those who might require it. But for many, perhaps most, it will be time and effort to bring resources to a central point from whence to distribute these to the vulnerable who are desperate for the food, medicines, material or non-material support that volunteers can provide. For some it may be phoning the isolated and lonely or calling at their doors to check that they are ok. For others it may be bringing together those who suffer from a specific illness to provide mutual support in a time of crisis. Via these and other myriad interventions the sense of community and social wellbeing are enhanced to the obvious benefits of those receiving this assistance, but also to those providing it as they are taken out of their own issues and worries to help others. This all adds to the strong sense of social wellbeing within or beyond locality (e.g., Chen, Liu, Yu, Bwanali, & Douangdara, 2020).

So, what of *weaknesses* of the concept of social capital? It may be that use of the word "capital" carries within it the implication that it is indeed a finite and measurable thing, given that capital is fixed and measured via economistic means.

But as we noted above with cultural capital, so too with social capital the concept leads us toward the intangible dimensions of social interaction, toward ideas like "feelgood" and empathy. This can then, somewhat paradoxically, make social capital difficult to measure, therefore it may have to be approached via surrogate measures, such as via measurement of sense of belonging, employing a mixed method approach, for example (Ahn & Davis, 2020). The concept can become slippery, therefore, although we suggest that it is no less valuable because of that.

Opportunities for utilization of the idea of social capital can be realized in many ways. It can be used as a searchlight on poverty and inequality, on situations of division and deprivation, and of exclusion whether by ethnicity, lack of educational provision, ill health and disability. Has a locality a good stock of social capital, how has it developed, what does it provide for people in the area and many other such questions arise from this perspective on social life and interaction. How can social capital be stimulated is perhaps the fundamental issue, how to bring help and assistance to, and from, people from diverse backgrounds, faiths and traditions? The opportunity comes from an initial interaction, a spark, or a focus on a felt need, one that is grown and developed via a cumulative and directed effort on the part of key players in the endeavor.

Threats to social capital, in contrast, are found in places or societies where fellow-feeling is at a minimum, sense of belonging is weak and/or there is distrust of the motives and behavior of others. Divisiveness can be sown via social media, for example, should there be an emphasis on negative features or contrasting political views held by others, as we have seen in the UK recently over Brexit or in the United States over the presidential election results of 2020, that some hold to be flawed or illegal while others believe them to be valid. There are those who adhere to conspiracy theories over COVID-19 itself and over potential vaccines, and demonstrations have been held in many countries against the lockdown restrictions associated with control of the pandemic. In such a situation it is crucial that commentators and analysts alike seek to corroborate claims from competing interest groups and rely on clear evidence as much as possible, albeit not necessarily an easy task to perform.

Examples of the Creation of Social Capital in Different Societies

The COVID-19 pandemic has made many people fearful, and it is an extremely difficult disease to pin down, deal with and, hopefully in time, eradicate. Prior to the pandemic, and no doubt again afterwards, arguably the disease that made most fearful in many areas of the globe, is dementia, in its many guises. A particularly tragic feature of the pandemic has been the toll it has taken on those with dementia, in part because this illness is associated with old age and/or with living in a care home. Care homes have been vulnerable to infection and the death rate has been high. A major charity that has grown in order to help people across the UK develop strategies and coping mechanisms in order to those affected by the disease including the patients themselves, family members and friends is the Alzheimer's Society, to which we gave a brief introduction in 2015 (Cook et al., 2015, pp. 17–20). In developing their approach they are intrinsically developing social capital via seeking to improve the way in which society views and deals with this disease, aiming to reduce the isolation that patients and close relatives can suffer as others are uncertain how to approach the person with dementia.

The combination of dementia with COVID-19 has been especially lethal, and the society has thus produced a hard-hitting report that details, analyzes and suggests solutions to reduce the high death toll (Alzheimer's Society, 2020). Among other data the report shows that in England and Wales, 27.5% of deaths in March–June 2020 from COVID-19, 13,840 in all were of people who had dementia, and that the largest increase in excess non-COVID-19 deaths, January–June, 5,049 was in people with dementia (Alzheimer's Society, 2020, p. 6). Forty-six percent of people with dementia in a survey they conducted and said that the pandemic had a negative impact on their mental health, while "in a wider group that included carers, 82% reported a deterioration in the symptoms of people with dementia" (Alzheimer's Society, 2020), and the impact was of course also felt by the carers, with 95% of those in the survey reporting a negative impact on mental or physical health. The Society estimates that a massive 92 million extra hours have been spent by family and friends caring for loved ones with dementia. In order to mitigate against such horrific figures being met once again or even exceeded in the winter of 2020–2021, a series of eight key suggestions are made in the report, underpinned by four basic principles:

- "Care should be person-centred and include an element of choice
- Informal carers should be recognised as an integral part of the care ecosystem
- There must be greater integration between health and social care
- There must be a minimum set of national standards." (Alzheimer's Society, 2020, p. 11).

The Society itself has had to modify its working practices due to the pandemic with increased use of phone conversations (133,000 in total March to end of August), virtual activities such as "Singing for the Brain," increased use of their website and other means that have helped a wide range of people to cope better across the UK, with more than 2 million people accessing their support services in that six-month period, and their own survey noting that "95% of our service users feel as though the support we have given them has improved their life in some way" (Alzheimer's Society, 2020, p. 40). Alzheimers.org.uk is the website for those who wish to find out more, and how they can contribute to assist those with dementia to cope better in a difficult situation.

Clearly, this example is of the creation and nurturing of social capital on a large scale. But examples also abound at the small scale. One such example concerns response to loneliness, which has accelerated during the pandemic, for example, in the UK after the clocks changed to wintertime:

> The start of November, with darker evenings, had 4.2 million adults always or often lonely, compared with 2.6 million before the pandemic. (Coughlan, 2020)

This data is based on a UK Office of National Statistics survey of 4,000 people, extrapolated to the general population. A feature of these results was that it was younger adults who seemed to be suffering greatly from loneliness, whereas in recent years loneliness has been increasingly recognized as an issue affecting older people, because of links to depression, and in turn to over-eating, smoking, increased alcohol intake, higher blood pressure and has been said to be as harmful to health as smoking 15 cigarettes a day (Alcock Ferguson cited in Murray, 2015, p. 2). In order to deal with such concerns, Age Concern and others set up a Befriending and Re-ablement Service in Sefton Metropolitan Borough Council. The objectives were to:

- Support older people to realize their aspirations.
- Enable older people to live safely and independently in their own homes.
- Reduce social isolation, loneliness and poverty.
- Predict and anticipate their problems to prevent later, more costly, interventions.
- Encourage active aging and well-being.
- Support carers.

Dr Giles Barrett and Ms Chris McGoldrick undertook an evaluation of this service for Age Concern and the main findings were published by Barrett, McGoldrick, and Cook (2017), following Ms McGoldrick's death. The findings clearly showed the importance of this volunteer support to the over 50s in the area, and that it would be worthwhile developing this scheme in other parts of Merseyside and further afield. Not least, there was also a clear cost-benefit to such support mechanisms due to reduced rates of hospital admissions as people were given the wherewithal to better manage their care and home situation to their own benefit. In places like Wythenshawe in South Manchester, reputed to be the largest public housing estate in Europe the Wythenshawe Good Neighbors charity is utilizing similar means to ensure that older people are visited by fellow residents and also that the gap between generations is reduced via encouragement for local secondary school children to write to older neighbors and thus to help alleviate their isolation and loneliness (Wythenshawe Good Neighbours, 2020).

To continue this good neighbors theme, and the enhancement of social capital at the local level, South Africa is a country that also provides good examples of community activity for the common good, in this case often in situations of dire poverty. Cook and Halsall (2012) and Cook et al. (2015) have shown, for instance, the community reaction to, and engagement with, the HIV/AIDS crisis that hit the country so hard in the late twentieth and early twenty-first centuries. In 2010, for example, at least 5 million people (possibly 7 million) were estimated to be HIV positive, with new cases running at more than 400,000 per annum. Government action and international support has been great in the struggle with this epidemic, but it is the local community response has been crucial to ensure that support is given where it is most needed. Within this, patient advocates have been vital to help overcome the stigma of this disease and encourage continued take up of antiretroviral therapy. Counseling has been important, including bereavement counseling, and has helped to improve the level of care for HIV patients.

This all assists the creation and maintenance of social capital in the affected communities and work toward changing the risk environment in which HIV can be spread (Szreter & Woolcock, 2004). In terms of COVID-19 it seems that such community support initially aided the fight against the virus, but the rise of a new variant, now named the beta variant, in the densely populated townships of the nation, has now led to a much higher infection rate and, sadly, death rate.

In a recent study, Wu (2021) highlight a new approach by analyzing survey data collected in April 2020 in China's Hubei province along with the recent World Values Survey (2016–2020). His study concludes that

> social capital affects COVID-19 response mainly through facilitating collective actions and promoting public acceptance of and compliance with control measures in the form of trust and norms at the individual level and can also help mobilize resources in the form of networks at the community level.

The study also highlights the fact that "dissimilar effects of social capital in different forms and at different levels help detect the processes underlying how social capital affects responses to the pandemic." This is particularly true since the results of any analysis of social capital and its impact on the COVID-19 response will eventually be contingent on the way social capital is conceptualized including the level it is being studied, not forgetting that it is a multidimensional and a multilevel concept.

In another study in the Middle East, Al-Omoush, Simón-Moya, and Sendra-García (2020), surveyed around 200 managers in the pharmaceutical and cleaning materials industries in Jordan, which was first country to lift the COVID-19 restrictions in the region. The study findings revealed that collaborative knowledge creation and social capital can play a significant role in responding to the pandemic and the "positive impact of collaborative knowledge creation and e-business proactiveness on organizational agility during the crisis." The study has implications for the exploration of emerging themes in information technology-related studies, including the "role of collaborative knowledge creation and e-business proactiveness and their impact on organizational agility in responding to global pandemics" (p. 277).

How to Nurture Social Capital for the Future?

Recent evidence suggests that societies with a high social capital shown to have better handle on the COVID-19 pandemic though the channels through which social capital makes communities respond better remains unclear (Barrios, Benmelech, Hochberg, Sapienza, & Zingales, 2020; Bartscher, Seitz, Slotwinski, Siegloch, & Wehrhofer, 2020; Ding, Levine, Lin, & Xie, 2020). Equally important is to understand how different forms of social capital work (Carpiano & Moore, 2020). It has also been argued that different types of social capital can capture different aspects of the social environment (Poortinga, 2012).

This chapter illustrates the importance of social capital as both a theoretical tool and also as a practical activity that, in the above cases, has helped deal with difficult and sometimes impossible situations for many communities in many countries. We advocate that social capital should be developed further into the future in order to build resilience to better meet and deal with future threats. In the "new normal" that is posited to arise post-pandemic, this could, and should involve such building blocks for social capital as:

- Continued recognition of the value and worth of community engagement. In the UK in 2020 both the official Honours system and the Daily Mirror Pride of Britain Awards have lauded community heroes such as the late Captain Sir Tom Moore who raised £37 million for the NHS via his 100 laps of his garden before his 100th birthday and the five-year-old Tony Hudgell, who despite having no legs raised more than £1 million via his 10km walk on his prosthetic legs.
- Organizational support from central and local government and business for community activities.
- Financial support in the long term from those that have to those that need, mediated by voluntary action.
- Community involvement and understanding to be supported in school, college and university education, as Cook and Wankhade (2017), for example, suggest.

To conclude, notwithstanding the conceptual and methodological challenges in defining and operationalizing social capital, Putnam's (2000) conceptualization is a useful tool to analyze the role which social capital can play in helping the post-pandemic recovery. We have also argued that any successful strategy to deal with a post-COVID-19 recovery will necessitate participation of different actors across nations, socioeconomic backgrounds, health organizations, governments and the civic society to create effective social networks, central to the conceptualization of the social capital as envisaged by Putnam (2000).

References

Ahn, M., & Davis, H. H. (2020, May). Sense of belonging as an indicator of social capital. *International Journal of Sociology and Social Policy*, 40, 627–642. doi:10.1108/IJSSP-12-2019-0258

Al-Omoush, K. S., Simón-Moya, V., & Sendra-García, J. (2020, November 26). The impact of social capital and collaborative knowledge creation one-business proactiveness and organizational agility in responding to the COVID-19 crisis. *Journal of Innovation & Knowledge*, 5, 279–288.

Alzheimer's Society. (2020). *Worst hit: Dementia during Coronavirus*. London: Alzheimer's Society.

Andrews, R., & Wankhade, P. (2016). Regional variations in emergency service performance: Does social capital matter? *Regional Studies*, 49(12), 2037–2052.

Barrett, G. A., McGoldrick, C., & Cook, I. G. (2017). Befriending and Re-ablement Service: A better alternative in an Age of Austerity. *International Journal of Sociology and Social Policy*, 37(1/2), 51–68. doi:10.1108/IJSSP-08-2015-0090

Barrios, J. M., Benmelech, E., Hochberg, Y. V., Sapienza, P., & Zingales, L. (2020, November 26). *Civic capital and social distancing during the Covid-19 pandemic.* Paper No. w27320. National Bureau of Economic Research, Cambridge, MA.

Bartscher, A. K., Seitz, S., Slotwinski, M., Siegloch, s., & Wehrhofer, N. (2020). Social capital and the spread of Covid-19: Insights from European countries. Retrieved from https://www.iza.org/publications/dp/13310/social-capital-and-the-spread-ofcovid-19-insights-from-european-countries. Accessed on November 26, 2020.

Carpiano, R. M., & Moore, S. (2020, November 26). So what's next? Closing thoughts for this special issue and future steps for social capital and public health. *Social Science & Medicine, 257*, 113013. doi:10.1016/j.socscimed.2020.113013

Chen, Z., Liu, S., Yu, Y., Bwanali, T. R., & Douangdara, V. (2020).Community satisfaction, sense of community, and social well-being in China. *Social Behavior and Personality: An International Journal, 48*(11), e8648. Retrieved from Sbp-journal.com/index.php/sbp/article/view/8648. Accessed on November 16, 2020.

Clegg, J., & Cook, I. G. (2009). Gung Ho in China: Towards participatory cooperatives. *Journal of Cooperative Studies, 42*(3), 4–13.

Cook, I. G., & Clegg, J. (2011). Shared visions of co-operation at a time of crisis: The Gung Ho story in China's anti-Japanese resistance. In A. Webster, L. Shaw, J. K. Walton, A. Brown, & D. Stewart (Eds), *The hidden alternative: Co-operative values, past, present and future* (chapter 17, pp. 327–346). Manchester: Manchester University Press.

Cook, I. G., & Halsall, J. P. (2012). *Aging in comparative perspective: Processes and policies.* New York, NY: Springer.

Cook, I. G., Halsall, J. P., & Wankhade, P. (2015). *Sociability, social capital, and community development.* New York, NY: Springer.

Cook, I. G., & Norcup, J. (2011). Geographies and urban space. In R. Kina (Ed.), *The continuum companion to anarchism* (chapter 14, pp. 278–298). London: Continuum.

Cook, I. G., & Wankhade, P. (2017). A model for change: Sharing ideas and strategies. In J. P. Halsall & M. Snowden (Eds), *The pedagogy of the social sciences curriculum* (chapter 8, pp. 93–106). New York, NY: Springer.

Coughlan, S. (2020, November 18). Lockdown loneliness reaches record levels, *BBC News*, November 18.

Ding, W., Levine, R., Lin, C., & Xie, W. (2020). Social distancing and social capital: Why US counties respond differently to COVID-19. Retrieved from https://papers.ssrn.com/sol3/papers.cfm?abstract_id=3632620. Accessed on November 26, 2020.

Greenberg, N., Docherty, M., Gnanapragasam, S., & Wessely, S. (2020, November 26). Managing mental health challenges faced by healthcare workers during Covid-19 pandemic. *British Medical Journal, 368*, m1211. doi:10.1136/bmj.m1211

Heath, G., Wankhade, P., & Murphy, P. (2021). Exploring the wellbeing of ambulance staff using the 'Public Value' perspective: Opportunities and challenges for research. *Public Money and Management.* Retrieved from https://www.tandfonline.com/doi/abs/10.1080/09540962.2021.1899613?journalCode=rpmm20

Kropotkin, P. (1902). *Mutual aid: A factor of evolution.* Boston, MA: Porter Sargent.

Lawn, S., Roberts, L., Willis, E., Couzner, L., Mohammadi, L., & Goble, E. (2020). The effects of emergency medical service work on the psychological, physical, and social wellbeing of ambulance personnel: A systematic review of qualitative research. *BMC Psychiatry, 20*(1), 348.

Lawrie, E. (2020, November 16). COVID-19: How Marcus Rashford campaign changed free school meals. *BBC News*, November 10.

Murray, K. (2015). Few feel older people in the UK have a good quality of life, survey finds. *Retrieved from* http://www.theguardian.com/society/2015/mar/04/ageing-population-survey-old-people-burden-skills-strengths-ignored. Accessed on June 22, 2015.

National Audit Office. (2020). *The supply of personal protective equipment (PPE) during the COVID-19 pandemic HC 961*. London: Stationery Office.

Nelson, P. A., Cordingley, L., Kapur, N., Chew-Graham, C. A., Shaw, J., Smith, S., … McDonnell, S. (2020, November 26). 'We're the first port of call' – Perspectives of ambulance staff on responding to deaths by suicide: A qualitative study. *Frontiers in Psychology, 11*, 722.

Organisation for Economic Co-operation and Development (OECD). (2001). *The wellbeing of nations: The role of human and social capital*. Paris: Centre for Educational Research and Innovation, OECD.

Pitas, N., & Ehmer, C. (2020). Social capital in the response to COVID-19. *American Journal of Health Promotion, 34*(8), 942–944.

Poortinga, W. (2012). Community resilience and health: The role of bonding, bridging, and linking aspects of social capital. *Health & Place, 18*(2), 286–295.

Putnam, R. D. (2000). *Bowling alone: The collapse and revival of American community*. New York, NY: Simon Schuster.

Sturdy, J. (2020). Coronavirus: East of England Ambulance Service paramedic dies with Covid-19. *BBC News*, May 20. Retrieved from https://www.bbc.co.uk/news/uk-england-essex-52727193. Accessed on November 26, 2020.

Szreter, S., & Woolcock, M. (2004). Health by association? Social capital, social theory, and the political economy of public health. *International Journal of Epidemiology, 33*(4), 650–667.

Wankhade, P. (2020). Emergency service workers are already at high risk of burnout – Coronavirus will make this worse. *The Conversation*, April 5. Retrieved from https://theconversation.com/emergency-service-workers-are-already-at-high-risk-of-burnout-coronavirus-will-make-this-worse-136006. Accessed on November 26, 2020.

Wankhade, P. (2021). A 'journey of personal and professional emotions': Emergency ambulance professionals during COVID-19. *Public Money & Management* (Open Access). Retrieved from https://www.tandfonline.com/doi/full/10.1080/09540962.2021.2003101

Wong, A. S. Y., & Kohler, J. C. (2020, November 26). Social capital and public health: Responding to the COVID-19 pandemic. *Globalisation and Health, 16*, 88. https://doi.org/10.1186/s12992-020-00615-x

Wu, C. (2021, November 26). Social capital and COVID-19: A multidimensional and multilevel approach. *Chinese Sociological Review, 53*(1), 27–54. doi:10.1080/21620555.2020.1814139

Wythenshawe Good Neighbours. (2020). Retrieved from Wythenshawe good neighbours.com. Accessed on November 18, 2020.

Xia, M. (2011). Social capital and rural grassroots governance in China. *Journal of Current Chinese Affairs, 40*(2), 135–163.

Zhou, J., & Cao, Q. (2020). Social trust and heath of China's older adults: Cultural and recreational participation as mediator. *Social Behavior and Personality: An International Journal, 48*(5), e9198. Retrieved from Sbp-journal.com/index.php/sbp/article/view/8648. Accessed on November 16, 2020.

Chapter 3

Social Capital, Social Innovation and Social Enterprise: The Virtuous Circle

Roopinder Oberoi, Jamie P. Halsall and Michael Snowden

Abstract

Social capital, according to Pierre Bourdieu, is "the sum of the resources, actual or virtual, that accrue to an individual or a group by virtue of possessing a durable network of more or less institutionalized relationships of mutual acquaintance and recognition" (Bourdieu & Wacquant, 1992, p. 119). Robert D. Putnam (1993) agrees, characterizing social capital as predominantly in the nature of a public good. Ongoing global economic events have highlighted some of the weaknesses of free market capitalism. It is being suggested that social enterprises with their efforts to blend societal objectives and economic efficiency can play a role of catalysts in accomplishing this equilibrium. Given their positioning toward meeting dual goals rather than merely maximizing profit, social enterprises can function in zones where there are insufficient inducements for private sector activity. Thereby social enterprises fill the hiatus between the state and market provision. This chapter aims to conceptualize the process of innovation and the potential influence of social capital on social enterprises. Value created by a social enterprise emphasizes the importance of sharing benefits among its stakeholders. This chapter examines the ways in which social enterprises co-create value for society and how social enterprises inherit, generate and invest in social capital.

Keywords: Institutions; social capital; social enterprise; social entrepreneurship; social value creation; public policy

Introduction

> Social capital seems to denote almost anything related to ties between people. It denotes a stock of ties, features of such ties, conditions for their functioning and their outcomes. It includes formal or informal groups of many kinds, and connections between such groups. Its possible features include the composition, structure, content, and type of ties, strength of ties, and trust, rules, shared norms of conduct, or values underlying such norms. The conditions for its existence include formal and informal institutions and trust. (Nooteboom, 2007, pp. 31–32)

The above is Tilburg University's Emeritus Professor Bart Nooteboom's definition of social capital in the journal *Review of Social Economy*. Social capital, in this sense, can involve many different entities; this concept has created much public policy interest in the social science discipline. Bhandari and Yasunobu (2009) state that the wide acclaim of social capital can be attributed to its ability to influence the process of development. Habersetzer, Grèzes-Bürcher, Boschma, and Mayer (2019), Bhandari and Yasunobu (2009), and Rodrik (1998) have all acknowledged that social capital is able to influence the economy at micro and macro levels. Moreover, social capital can have real societal impact at a local level, and as Putnam (1994) notes "Social capital enhances the benefits of investment in physical and human capital" (p. 7). He further states:

> Working together is easier in a community blessed with a substantial stock of social capital. This insight turns out to have powerful practical implications for many issues on the American national agenda – for how we might overcome the poverty and violence of South Central Los Angeles, or revitalize industry in the Rust Belt. (p. 7)

With this notion of social capital having a public policy impact, comes the realization of its interconnecting and long-standing relationships with social innovation and social enterprise. Consequently, the authors of this chapter examine the embeddedness of the "social" in social innovation, social enterprise and social capital. The authors then assess the importance of social capital within an institutional remit from a public policy perspective, progressing to an examination of social value creation and how this has a positive impact in society. The chapter concludes by summarizing the key points made by the authors and highlighting future areas for social research.

Embed the "Social" in Innovation, Enterprise, and Capital

Social enterprise is defined by entrepreneurial activities with an intention to accomplish social goals. Social enterprises have been celebrated as substitutes for – and correspondents to – the measures of state regimes and global organizations, in tackling extensive social concerns. Social enterprise, as we understand it today, is the term used for many of the activities under the rubric of social entrepreneurship that were either referred to as "community development" or "social purpose organisations" previously. By linking entrepreneurship with larger transformation in society and economy the stage or the "space" of entrepreneurship becomes part of society (Hjorth & Steyaert, 2003; Steyaert & Katz, 2004). Moreover, according to Steyaert and Hjorth (2006):

> Starting from a conviction that entrepreneurship belongs primarily to society rather than to the economy and that they need to go after life rather than simply business to understand entrepreneurial processes they propose locating entrepreneurship in the public. (p. 97)

The rise in interest in social entrepreneurship enables researchers to explore, which can help to discover its practices of "entrepreneurship is a complex social-creative process that influences, multiplies, transforms, re-imagines and alters the outlook of the space of society in which it is at once grounded and contextualized" (Steyaert & Hjorth, 2006, p. 1). Academic research by Alvord, Brown, and Letts (2002, p. 262) note that there are three approaches in considering this form of entrepreneurship:

1. Social entrepreneurship viewed as "combining commercial enterprises with social impacts" (Emerson & Twersky, 1996).
2. Innovation for social impacts (Dees, 1998).
3. Catalysts for social transformation.

Other academic researchers have confined social entrepreneurship's scope to affirmative business, direct-service business and catalytic alliances (Boschee, 1995;). However, there is still no unanimously accepted description of the social enterprise phenomenon (Seelos & Mair, 2005). Nevertheless, an agreement is emerging on the boundaries of mega economic development programs. These social enterprise agendas excessively privilege liberal organizations, practices, and overreliance on free markets, with not enough consideration and respect for the local community institutions (Fowler, 2000; Rodrik, 2007). Some of the key aspects of social entrepreneurship lie in the innovation, characterization, and utilization of opportunities. Consequently, academic studies have conceptualized the prosposed space for social enterprise as an extensive arena of unmet community needs (Austin, Stevenson, & Wei-Skillern, 2006), which relate to the financial, shared, health, housing, and/or environmental facets of human wellbeing (Zahra, Rawhouser, Bhawe, Neubaum, & Hayton, 2008). It has been argued that:

> no matter whether they adopt a for-profit or a not-for-profit legal form, social enterprises are unique in that they involve a

> "hierarchical ordering of social and economic value," whereby social value takes precedence over the generation of economic rents. (Dacin, Dacin, & Matear, 2010, p. 51)

Accordingly, public policy for social innovation cannot be a strategy only for the state; it has to be a strategy for constructing coalition between social entrepreneurs, the public sector, and private companies.

Social entrepreneurs often confront problems in novel ways and uncover innovative solutions. Dees et al (2001) notes, "social entrepreneurs are one species of the genus entrepreneur" – in other words, social entrepreneurs are "entrepreneurs with a social mission" (p. 23) According to Dees et al (2001):

> social entrepreneurs play the role of resolute change agents in the social sector by: adopting a mission to create and sustain social value; recognizing and relentlessly pursuing new opportunities to serve that mission; engaging in a process of continuous innovation, adaptation, and learning; acting boldly without being limited by resources currently in hand, and exhibiting heightened accountability to the constituencies served and for the outcomes created. (p. 4)

Moreover, in the private corporate technology transmit schemes; in welfare we require social innovation transfer schemes, which help generate much more efficient instruments for the identification, understanding, and distribution of best practices in welfare provisions. There is a value to society as a whole in upholding the diversity of efforts that deal with social problems like poverty, illiteracy, homelessness, empowerment of women, etc. Innovation and novelty helps to advance experimentation and enlarge the portfolio of potential solutions. Social enterprise creates assets for local communities that may not otherwise be present.

Social organizations are liable to be entrepreneurial and innovative if they network with their milieu. They can achieve this by operating in a comparatively multifarious and fluid environment, in which new demands and opportunities open up and they build up an embryonic correlation with their customers, which progressively opens up more complex needs and demands (Leadbeater, 1997, p. 62). Social enterprises to be successful have to be open, organic, dynamic, and evolutionary; they grow with their users and partners. They are permeable at the boundaries; and the rigid limit among the organization and its users is not locked.

Social capital as a concept has been subjected to wide enquiry across several fields in the social sciences. Scholars that focused on community social capital have underscored its important purpose as a public good (Coleman, 1988; Guiso, Sapienza, & Zingales, 2015; Putnam, 1995). Social capital is the network of interactions that underpins economic partnerships and alliances. These networks depend upon mores of collaboration, fostered by shared values and conviction. Community social capital produces diffused influences "not only to those who possess social capital, but also to people living in regions with a high level of social capital," and it promotes "community cohesion and information flow that accrue to community members who do not have high levels of personal social capital themselves" (Kwon, Heflin, & Ruef, 2013, p. 981). Social networks capture horizontal social relations that exist in associations and organizations in the community, which provide closures in social relations (Coleman, 1988). Social entrepreneurs often begin with a gift of social capital: a set of connections of relationships and acquaintances, which are united mutually by shared values and interests. Fukuyama (1995) states "economic life depends on the moral bonds of social trust that facilitate transactions, empowering the individual creativity and the reason for the need of collective action" (p. 12).

Social entrepreneurs operate by bringing citizens together to tackle difficulties that appear insurmountable when they are attended to disjointedly. Social entrepreneurs instigate of social capital buildup; they employ networks of support so that they can establish social networks with citizens. Moreover, Catford (1998) notes:

> There are three different types of benefits which social entrepreneurs can bring to communities. In the short term they can help create new buildings, services and jobs which would not otherwise exist, but they can also improve accessibility, effectiveness and efficiency of existing services. In the medium term they can act as powerful models for reform of the welfare state, and in the longer term can create and invest social capital. (p. 96)

Hence, the dividends of this technique in social enterprise are not merely economic. The foremost surplus is social: a unified community, more capable of looking after their own needs, with dynamic connections of conviction and collaboration. Bornstein (1998) characterizes social entrepreneurs as

> path breakers with a powerful new idea, who combine visionary and real-world problem-solving capacity, who have a strong ethical fiber, and who are "totally possessed" by their vision for change. (p. 36)

Nevertheless, social enterprise attempts to craft innovative answers to pressing social problems, in addition to mobilizing the views, ability, wherewithal, and social arrangements necessary for enduring and sustainable social change (Alvord et al., 2002, p. 3). The interlocking system of macroeconomic policies, state social insurance schemes and tax-financed services is under increasing pressure, unable to respond effectively to a growing array of social problems such as mass long-term joblessness, drugs, familial instability, and illiteracy (Leadbeater, 1997, p. 1). In general, social entrepreneurship takes on one of three fairly distinctive shapes. Firstly, social entrepreneurship projects disseminate a package of innovations needed to work out general concerns. Secondly, some entail building local capacities or working with marginalized populations to recognize capacity needed for self-help. Here, the supposition is that local groups hold the best understanding about which concerns are vital, and which can be solved by access to more resources and better capacity to act. Consequently, in these cases social entrepreneurs aim to build capacity by focusing on local constituents and resource providers. Thirdly, some social enterprise initiatives focus on mobilizing grassroots groups to structure coalitions against institutions, as they believe that marginalized groups can solve problems if they have representation in political institutions (Alvord et al., 2002, pp. 160–161).

Social enterprises are like social test beds; they must be an energetic welfare system designed to build social capital by empowering people to take better control over issues. This wave of social innovation comes from numerous supply points. Innovation in thoughts and procedures will be vital to the fortification of the values and philosophy of a dynamic, problem-solving welfare system. Organizational innovation will also be significant, to create novel institutions able to deliver a new form of welfare through hybrid organizations. Social enterprises that set up innovative skills for societal ends are already at work in parts of the conventional public sector, a few big private corporations, and at the innovative edge of the voluntary sector (Leadbeater, 1997, p. 2).

Social Capital and Institutional Involvement

Institutions are a vital part of society; comprising public, private and third sector organizations, these institutions are the bedrock of the state. From a public policy perspective, institutions are there to support different social groups in society. Duina (2011) notes that institutions are perceived as well-established organizations that are highly organized. From country to country, institutions work in different ways due to the ways their political systems function. However, it is the way an organization works democratically that is at the center of an institution (Held, 1987), as well as the approach an organization follows in line with the state vision. When parties are elected to government, they come with a mandate to change society for the better. For example, since the 1980s, there has been a great shift toward a competition state in public policy-making. Evans and Cerny (2003) observe:

> The key to understanding the competition state is that while international competiveness become the touchstone of legitimacy in both domestic and international policy making, its political implications in a liberal democratic society were not simply to eliminate choices but also to construct new kinds of choices to fit the constraints, from the dog-eat-dog, neoliberalism "red in tooth and claw" of the Thatcher years to what Bill Clinton called "globalization with a human face." The Labour government since 1997 has adopted a policy agenda that in its most crucial aspects reflects the continuing transformation of the British state into a competition state. (p. 23)

This public policy shift toward globalization with a human face is reflected in many countries across the world, for example, India, the USA, and the UK. Hence, there has been a greater emphasis on social capital since the 1990s, and, as previously discussed in this chapter, social capital has the ability to improve citizens' lives. Table 3.1 explains the theoretical ideas of social capital from four contrasting academic's perspectives; the concept on the whole encapsulates the cohesive thinking of solving cultural, economic, political and social problems in society.

The policy transformation toward social capital has also seen a change in the way the state works (Bertotti, Harden, Renton, & Sheridan, 2012; Dowling & Harvie, 2014; Schneider, 2006; Stoker, Smith, Maloney, & Young, 2004). Moreover, what has been evident in recent years in many countries in the developed and developing world is that the functions of institutions have become more complex. Recently, there has been a great emphasis on third sector involvement in countries such as the UK and India. Third sector involvement refers to charities, NGOs and social enterprises; these types of organizations play a more vital role in state services at a local level. For Bochel and Bochel (2018), this development over the last decade is indicative of a "post-bureaucratic" agenda (p. 32). As an example,

Table 3.1. Four Academic Perspectives on Social Capital.

Robert D. Putnam (1993)	**James Coleman (1990)**	**Pierre Bourdieu (1986)**	**Albert O. Hirschmann (2000)**
"*Putnam* recognized that 'good governance was closely related to civic engagement' (New Economics Foundation, 2000) and that social cohesion in communities depends on social networks, norms and trust. He affirms that these components make up social capital in communities and that this is necessary for improving the quality of life and community development."	"*Coleman's* wider definition of social capital was used to construct a social theory that stated that the 'closure' of social networks can produce closer connections between people and that this in itself can generate obligations and sanctions on communities."	"*Bourdieu* shows how social capital exists alongside economic and cultural capital and can be part of a strategy for individuals and groups to reproduce more social capital and/ or convert it into other forms of capital."	"*Hirschman* uses the term 'social energy' and suggests that it is made up of three components: 'friendship' emphasizing the personal impact of social capital; 'ideals,' which may lead to a shared vision based on values; and 'ideas,' which enables groups and individuals to present new solutions to their problems."

Adapted from Kay (2006, p. 162).

the UK has "more localised public services hybrid organisational forms, and a belief that communities are able to organise themselves" (Bochel & Bochel, 2018, p. 32). Having discussed the interlocking relationships of social capital and institutions, the chapter now moves on to discuss the role that social value creation plays in public policy and wider society.

Social Value Creation in Public Policy

While attempting to define public policy is somewhat beyond the remit of this chapter, we take the view that public policy is generally conceived to be a particular plan of action formed in response to public, community based, and/or real world problems. These plans are typically enacted (as in the UK), by an elected government. Herein lies the challenge of providing a unifying definition of social policy. With the real world in constant flux and, of course, ever-changing governments, social policy is consequently complex and multifaceted, and is dependent upon the processes that underpin the societal context of the policy. Cairney (2020) attempts to conceptualize this and suggests that that there are six key determinants (see Fig. 3.1) that influence the development of public policy definitions and subsequent theoretical explanations:

- *Actors*. Actors in the form of either an individual or collective; where a collective can take the form of private enterprises, interest or action groups, or government agencies, all of which act and influence the formation of a plan. Consequently, an understanding of how the various actors fulfill their role, in terms of their motivation and intention, is important to establish. In general, theories attempt to explain this in terms of decision-making being dependent upon the amount of information an individual has, how they comprehend the information within the time frame available to them, and their motivational beliefs

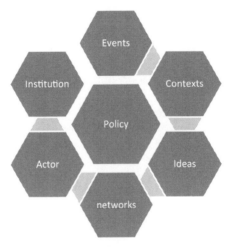

Fig. 3.1. Six Drivers of Policy.

related to change willingness, which subsume an array of individual difference factors, such as goal orientation, personal epistemologies, and self-efficacies.
- *Institutions*. Cairney (2020) suggests that institutions determine the societal rules, values, culture, norms, practices, and relationships that influence individual and collective behavior. Consequently, the actions, or actor's performance, is largely determined by their compliance, interpretation, and perception of such norms and cultural inferences that shape rules. While rules can be either formal or informal, there is an interdependence that influences cognisance and efficacy within society. Formal rules are more effective and substantive when they reflect more informal norms and "rules" that already exist and are widely accepted. Policies, asserts Cairney (2020), are considered to be a functional component of institutions – that can shape policy-making activities in two main ways: through the constitutions and by legislation and regulation. Subsequently, institutions are then able to establish where and when policy decision are made and also determine the rules that enable scrutiny and the selection of the "type" of actor, information and ideas to inform the policy-making process.
- *Networks*. Networks, as described by Cairney, are characterized by the relationship between those actors responsible for policy decisions (the policy-makers), and the influencers such as action groups, politicians, and interest groups with whom the policy-makers consult and negotiate. It is generally accepted that policy-making at government level is often entrusted to civil servants or bureaucrats, who seek information and advice from agencies, groups, and individuals, to frame and subsequently form policy recommendations. This exchange of information provides an opportunity, often in the form of collective action, to influence policy processes; furthermore, some institutions and organizations may, by the nature of the systems in place, be biased toward some sources of information, and some organizations and participants may favor particular sources of evidence.
- *Ideas*. An idea, as illustrated by the *Oxford English Dictionary*, is defined as a "thought or suggestion as to a possible course of action," and as such can be a supposition or a system of ideas that are intended to explain something. Importantly, it must be acknowledged that ideas stem from personal beliefs, values, psycho-social-economic background, culture, and education; furthermore, individual, familial and social networks influence the development of ideas. Consequently, ideas may manifest themselves out of bias, prejudice, and myth. It is not surprising therefore that ideas, and those that are a dominant influence, shape the structure and fabric of political, economic, and social structure within society. The values that underpin ideas are socially constructed, and based upon the interactions and experiences we are exposed to during our lives. However, new ideas are formed, human behavior is dynamic, and this dynamism may encourage the individual actors (as illustrated earlier) to proffer new solutions and theory to challenges. However, the acceptance of the new ideas is dependent upon those ideas presented being explored and debated honestly and openly in a transparent manner. The opportunity for acceptance then depends upon how receptive the society, or community context is to change.

- *Context.* Context is crucial to understanding and developing policy. It is within any given policy context, and that context is shaped by a multitude of political, social, environmental, cultural, behavioral, and economic factors. Consequently, the context of policy is complex and can be described as the setting that influences how ideas are formed, developed, and how the negotiations and decision shaping between the various actors that develop policy takes place.
- *Events.* Events can be routine in nature and largely planned, such as national and governmental elections; but, governmental change can result in a change and/or divergence in ideology and subsequent policy-making – as represented by the polarity of political systems such as the UK and the USA. Changes in government and the resultant changes in the ideological beliefs of the actors involved often result in policy drift; this can occur when the new actors with their different ideas about challenges presented within society and the development of solutions through policy development and solutions through policy formation. Conversely, events can be unplanned and totally unanticipated, such as the current COVID-19 pandemic. Due to the volatility of notional events, it is challenging to conceptualize and subsequently generate robust theory to inform sustained policy development. Gaskell, Stoker, Jennings, and Devine (2020) demonstrate the impact that unplanned, unmitigated events have on policy by drawing upon the pandemic to illustrate how failings in structural processes and the UK government's response to the pandemic was influenced by its ideological instincts and interests, and the interpretation of the scientific evidence it received to inform policy-making decisions.

Bacq and Lumpkin (2020) and Bacq, Geoghegan, Josefy, Stevenson, and Williams (2020) emphasize how social enterprise and entrepreneurs may form the bedrock of global development in response to the challenges presented by the 2020 pandemic. Furthermore, a view expressed in the recent report by World Economic Forum (2020) Members of the COVID Alliance for Social Entrepreneurs: "We call on all actors to stand by social entrepreneurs as frontline responders to the COVID-19 crisis and as pioneers of a green, inclusive society and economic system" (p. 3). There are many examples of the private sector responding to the challenge of COVID-19 in a non-profit making way; for example, the response of many businesses who changed their focus in order to aid key workers and victims of COVID-19, producing face masks, ventilators, hand sanitizers, and other forms of personal protective equipment (PPE). The UK's National Audit Office (UK) (2020) stated that in some geographical areas the cost of PPE rocketed to unprecedented levels; for example, the price of body bags increased by 1,310%, the cost of gowns and overalls increased by 1,277%, the cost of gloves increased by 519%, hand sanitizer by 450%, and face masks by 258%.

In essence, the examples above illustrate the distinction between the notion of social enterprise and what can be described as pro-social behavior. There are, we suggest, two types of pro-social behaviors: egoistical, where the goal is reflective of self-interest and is concerned with benefiting one's own welfare and standing; or, altruistic, where the goal is to enhance another person's welfare, well-being, or standing, which is congruent with general definitions of social enterprise (Oberoi,

Halsall, & Snowden, 2019; Tan, Williams, & Tan, 2005). Consequently, this dichotomy associated with pro-social behavior may influence the development of policy and its enactment. If policy is pro-social and egotistically driven, social enterprise will not flourish; conversely, if policy is pro-social and altruistically motivated, social enterprise will flourish.

A pro-social behavior endeavor is not social enterprise, but a pro-social policy that embraces the principles of altruism will enable social enterprise to flourish. Social enterprise can be described as a bridge between the private sector and public sector defined by Oberoi et al. (2019) as a

> business that has both social and commercial goals, where surpluses are principally reinvested for the purpose of the community, rather than being driven by the maximization of profit for shareholders.

At the turn of the millennium, social enterprise was considered to be an adjunct to the corporate mission, embracing corporate social responsibility (CSR). Well-meaning companies organized volunteer projects and charitable donations, and, as seen in response to the pandemic, produced essential items at cost. Social enterprise is, fundamentally, more proactive in its approach to social change, while CSR is reactive to events, such as the COVID-19 pandemic. Nonetheless, as revealed by the challenge within the COVID-19 pandemic, private and public sectors are interlinked, albeit divided by philosophy.

In spite of philosophical divisions between businesses and corporations, both are beginning to respond to the notion of total societal impact (TSI). While CSR drivers contribute to societal issues generated externally from the company or business, TSI drivers incorporate social and environmental considerations through its manufacturing, design processes, distribution, and employment practices in order to aid society. Viewing philanthropic efforts through the lens of TSI accelerates social impact and associated benefits for communities and societal groups.

The sustainable development goals (SDGs) of the 2030 Agenda for Sustainable Development (United Nations, 2015) emphasizes that the SDGs cannot be met by social enterprises alone. The SDGs indicate new markets, challenges, and opportunities for businesses and corporations globally. The SDGs are, as articulated by the United Nations, challenges for business, and offer the opportunity for successful partnerships with social enterprises. It is feasible, therefore, to consider businesses, corporations, and social enterprises collaborating to bring about social change within the notion of "social value creation," that is, addressing social issues and challenges by creating social impact and change. This can include enhancing awareness, promoting empowerment, behavioral, lifestyle, attitudinal and perception changes, as well as changes to societal norms, institutions, and generating policy. These changes can initiate socioeconomic and cultural benefits at individual, institutional, community, national, and global levels.

In the UK, the significance of social value is such that The Public Services (Social Value) Act 2012 underpins the commission process of all public bodies in the country. The Act required all public bodies to consider how the services they commission and procure might improve the economic, social, and environmental wellbeing of the area and the context they aim to serve. However, this act was strengthened in the summer of 2019, and reaffirmed in September 2020, when the UK's Government issued a new procurement policy; taking account of social value in the Award of Central Government contracts.

This policy is characterized by two key shifts; firstly, evaluation rather than consideration, and secondly, a minimum 10% weighting on social value. The policy shift is characterized by the dynamic nature of policy, and is recognized as the consequence of determinant influences – networks, ideas, contexts, events, institutions, and actors – underpinned by the developing relationship with the emerging notions of social value and TSI.

Within the original act of 2012, the emphasis was on "consider," and consequently there was no formal obligation to put social value into contracts. The recognition of evaluation brings with it the requirement for contracts to include social value, with a score allocated for the social value they contribute. In the/a (?) recent report, Director of External Affairs at Social Enterprise UK, Andrew O'Brien asserts that social value will now influence every contract issued by central government covering between £80 and 100bn in spending every year – potentially around one-third of all public procurement (Social Enterprise UK, 2020). Importantly, engaging with social value is now not an optional extra, and, as Social Enterprise UK assert should open up more opportunities for social enterprises within supply chains. The significance of social value is recognized in a recent article by Mary Zsamboky, the policy director of AECOM, the world's premier infrastructure consulting firm, who asserts that in order to "minimise the harms of coronavirus and to rebuild better, we need stimulus-funded infrastructure that seeks to maximise social value" (Zsamboky, 2020). The notion of social value in the development of public policy is complex and multifaceted; at its heart, are the six-dimensional drivers: networks, ideas, contexts, events, institutions, and actors. The relationship with the emerging notions of social value and TSI underpin each of these dimensions. Social enterprise is developing greater complexity due to policy inferences. However, while the motto "Think Globally – Act Locally" is a long-standing representation of inclusiveness, its apropos is current. The COVID-19 pandemic's resolution strategies are global, but solutions are enacted locally and based on the local conditions and context.

The "real world" is constantly changing, and this has resulted in the movement toward greater use of evidence in policy design, policy-making, and policy implementation. While we suggest there is no single, all embracing definition of policy, we propose that the six-dimensional drivers, and the interdependence of social value and TSI, significantly shape the direction of policy.

Conclusion

This chapter has been concerned with the concepts of social capital, social innovation, and social enterprise. All three ideas are a central part of public policy in today's world. As can be seen in this chapter, there are different interpretations of the three concepts and these are driven by the processes of globalization. Moreover, globalization is perceived as the mechanism that drives change in economic, social, political, and cultural contexts. The authors of this chapter would like to highlight two future directions for this research area:

1. A more specific focus on the positive influences on public policy, social capital, social innovation, and social enterprise. Politicians are increasingly using their influence to drive this agenda.
2. An enhancement of the global perspective of social capital, social innovation, and social enterprise. In academic research, there needs to be a more interdisciplinary approach to embedding these concepts into public policy. Countries across the world can learn from each other regarding the best approaches in public policy.

References

Alvord, S. H., Brown, L. D., & Letts, C. W. (2002). *Social entrepreneurship and social transformation: An exploratory study*. Working Paper No. 15. The Hauser Center for Nonprofit Organizations and the Kennedy School of Government, Harvard University, Cambridge, MA.

Alvord, S. H., Brown, L. D., & Letts, C. W. (2004). Social entrepreneurship and societal transformation: An exploratory study. *The journal of Applied Behavioral Science, 40*(3), 260–282.

Austin, J., Stevenson, H., & Wei-Skillern, J. (2006). Social and commercial entrepreneurship: Same, different, or both? *Entrepreneurship Theory and Practice, 30*(1), 1–22.

Bacq, S., Geoghegan, W., Josefy, M., Stevenson, R., & Williams, T. A. (2020). The COVID-19 virtual idea Blitz: Marshaling social entrepreneurship to rapidly respond to urgent grand challenges. *Business Horizons, 63*(6), 705–723. https://doi.org/10.1016/j.bushor.2020.05.002

Bacq, S., & Lumpkin, G. T. (2020). Social entrepreneurship and COVID-19. *Journal of Management Studies*. https://doi.org/10.1111/joms.12641

Bertotti, M., Harden, A., Renton, A., & Sheridan, K. (2012). The contribution of a social enterprise to the building of social capital in a disadvantaged urban Area of London. *Community Development Journal, 47*(2), 168–183.

Bhandari, H., & Yasunobu, K. (2009). What is social capital? A comprehensive review of the concept. *Asian Journal of Social Science, 37*(3), 480–510.

Bochel, C., & Bochel, H. (2018). *Making and implementing public policy: Key concepts and issues*. Basingstoke: Palgrave.

Bornstein, D. (1998). Changing the world on a shoestring. *The Atlantic Monthly, 281*(1), 34–39.

Boschee, J. (1995). Social Entrepreneurship: Never thought that profit and philanthropy would go hand in hand?. *Across the Board, 32,* 20–20.

Bourdieu, P. (1986). The forms of capital. In J. Richardson (Ed.), *Handbook of theory research for the sociology of education*. Westport, CT: Greenwood Press.

Bourdieu, P., & Wacquant, L. J. D. (1992). *An invitation to reflexive sociology*. Chicago, IL: University of Chicago Press.

Cairney, P. (2020). *Understanding public policy: Theories and issues* (2nd ed.). London: Red Globe Press.

Catford, J. (1998). Social entrepreneurs are vital for health promotion – But they need supportive environments too. *Editorial, Health Promotion International, 13,* 95–98.

Coleman, J. S. (1988). Social capital in the creation of human capital. *The American Journal of Sociology, 94*, 95–120.
Dacin, M. T., Dacin, P. A., & Matear, M. (2010). Social entrepreneurship: Why we don't need a new theory and how we move forward from here. *Academy of Management Perspectives, 24*(3), 37–57.
Dees, J. G. (1998). Enterprising nonprofits: What do you do when traditional sources of funding fall short? *Harvard Business Review, 76*, 55–67.
Dees, J. G., Emerson, J., & Economy, P. (2001). Enterprising nonprofits: A toolkit for social entrepreneurs (Vol. 186). John Wiley & Sons.
Dowling, E., & Harvie, D. (2014). Harnessing the social: State, crisis and (big) society. *Sociology, 48*(5), 869–886.
Duina, F. (2011). *Institutions and the economy*. Cambridge, MA: Polity Press.
Emerson, J., & Twersky, F. (1996). New social entrepreneurs: The success, challenge and lessons of non-profit enterprise creation. In *A progress report on the planning and startup of non-profit businesses*. San Francisco, CA: Roberts Foundation Homeless Economic Development Fund.
Evans, M., & Cerny, P. (2003). Globalization and social policy. In N. Ellison & C. Pierson (Eds.), *Developments in British social policy 2* (chapter 1, pp. 19–40). Basingstoke: Palgrave.
Fowler, A. (2000). NGDOs as a moment in history: Beyond aid to social entrepreneurship or civic innovation? *Third World Quarterly, 21*(4), 637–654.
Fukuyama, F. (1995). *Trust*. New York, NY: Free Press.
Gaskell, J., Stoker, G., Jennings, W., & Devine, D. (2020). Covid-19 and the blunders of our governments: Long-run system failings aggravated by political choices. *The Political Quarterly, 91*(3), 523–533.
Guiso, L., Sapienza, P., & Zingales, L. (2015). The value of corporate culture. *Journal of Financial Economics, 117*, 60–76.
Habersetzer, A., Grèzes-Bürcher, S., Boschma, R., & Mayer, H. (2019). Enterprise-related social capital as a driver of firm growth in the periphery? *Journal of Rural Studies, 65*, 143–151.
Held, D. (1987). *Models of democracy*. Cambridge, MA: Polity Press.
Hjorth, D., & Steyaert, C. (2003). Entrepreneurship beyond (a new) economy: Creative swarms and pathological zones. In C. Steyaert & D. Hjorth (Eds.), *New movements in entrepreneurship* (pp. 286–304). Cheltenham: Edward Elgar.
Kay, A. (2006). Social capital, the social economy and community development. *Community Development Journal, 41*(2), 160–173.
Kwon, S. W., Heflin, C., & Ruef, M. (2013). Community social capital and entrepreneurship. *American Sociological Review, 78*, 980–1008.
Leadbeater, C. (1997). *The rise of the social entrepreneur – Demos*. London. Retrieved from https://www.demos.co.uk/files/theriseofthesocialentrepreneur.pdf
National Audit Office (UK). (2020). The supply of personal protective equipment (PPE) during the COVID-19 pandemic. Retrieved from https://www.nao.org.uk/wp-content/uploads/2020/11/The-supply-of-personal-protective-equipment-PPE-during-the-COVID-19-pandemic-Summary.pdf. Accessed on December 3, 2020.
New Economics Foundation. (2000). *Prove it! Measuring the effect of neighbourhood renewal on local people*. London: Groundwork.
Nooteboom, B. (2007). Social capital, institutions and trust. *Review of Social Economy, 65*(1), 29–53.
Oberoi, R., Halsall, J., & Snowden, M. (2019). Mapping the role of social enterprise: A sustainable model for future? In R. Kar (Ed.), *Towards a sustainable future: Cross cultural strategies and practices*. London: Bloomsbury Publishing.

Public Services (Social Value) Act 2012 Chapter 3. Retrieved from https://www.legislation.gov.uk/ukpga/2012/3/enacted. Accessed on December 3, 2020.
Putnam, R. (1993). The prosperous community – Social capital and public life. *The American Prospect*, *13*, 35–42.
Putnam, R. (1994). Social capital and public affairs. *Bulletin of the American Academy of Arts and Sciences*, *47*(8), 5–19.
Putnam, R. D. (1995, January). Bowling alone: America's declining social capital. *Journal of Democracy*, *6*(1), 65–78. http://muse.jhu.edu/demo/journal_of_democracy/v006/putnam.html
Rodrik, D. (1998). *Where did all the growth go? External shocks, social conflicts, and growth collapses*. NBER Working Paper No. 6350. National Bureau of Economic Research, Cambridge, MA.
Rodrik, D. (2007). *One economics, many recipes: Globalization, institutions, and economic growth*. Princeton, NJ: Princeton University Press.
Schneider, J. (2006). *Social capital and welfare reform: Organizations, congregations, and communities*. New York, NY: Columbia University Press.
Seelos, C., & Mair, J. (2005). Social entrepreneurship: Creating new business models to serve the poor. *Business Horizons*, *48*(3), 241–46.
Social Enterprise UK. (2020). What does the latest government announcement on social value mean for social enterprises? Retrieved from https://www.socialenterprise.org.uk/blogs/what-does-the-latest-government-announcement-on-social-value-mean-for-social-enterprises/. Accessed on December 3, 2020.
Steyaert, C., & Hjorth, D. (Eds.). (2008). Entrepreneurship as social change: A third new movements in entrepreneurship book (Vol. 3). Edward Elgar Publishing.
Steyaert, C., & Katz, J. (2004). Reclaiming the space of entrepreneurship in society: Geographical, discursive and social dimensions. *Entrepreneurship and Regional Development*, *16*(3), 179–196.
Stoker, G., Smith, G., Maloney, W., & Young, S. (2004). Voluntary organisations and the generation of social capital in city politics. In M. Boddy & M. Parkinson (Eds.), *City matters: Competitiveness, cohesion and urban governance* (chapter 21, pp. 389–403). Bristol: Policy Press.
Swedberg, R. (1999). *Entrepreneurship: The social science view*. Oxford: Oxford University Press.
Tan, W. L., Williams, J., & Tan, T. M. (2005). Defining the 'social' in 'social entrepreneurship': Altruism and entrepreneurship. *Entrepreneurship Management*, *1*, 353–365. https://doi.org/10.1007/s11365-005-2600-x
United Nations. (2015). Transforming our World: The 2030 agenda for sustainable development. Retrieved from https://sustainabledevelopment.un.org/content/documents/21252030%20Agenda%20for%20Sustainable%20Development%20web.pdf. Accessed on December 3, 2020.
World Economic Forum. (2020, September). COVID-19 action agenda leaders on the front line: Why social entrepreneurs are needed now more than ever. Retrieved from http://www3.weforum.org/docs/COVID19_SocEnt_Alliance_Report_2020.pdf. Accessed on December 3, 2020.
Zahra, S. A., Rawhouser, H., Bhawe, N., Neubaum, D. O., & Hayton, J. C. (2008). Globalization of social entrepreneurship opportunities. *Strategic Entrepreneurship Journal*, *2*(2), 117–131.
Zsamboky, M. (2020). Social value is key to emerging stronger. In *Creating opportunity for everyone*. Retrieved from https://www.building.co.uk/digital-editions/social-value-in-action-digital-supplement/5108265.article. Accessed on December 3, 2020.

Chapter 4

Does Fifth Industrial Revolution Benefit or Trouble the Global Civil Society?

Cátia Miriam Costa, Enrique Martinez-Galán[1] and Francisco José Leandro

Abstract

The United Nations recognizes "civil society" as the "third sector" of society, along with public (governmental) and private sector organizations. The term global "third sector" comprises the worldwide reach of civil society organizations (CSOs). In this chapter, we discuss how technological advancements could influence global civil society. Humans and machines will increasingly interact and collaborate closely in the future. The Industry Revolution (IR) 5.0 brings new challenges, such as artificial intelligence (AI) and machine learning, which pose significant opportunities but also important risks to the role of CSOs. Regarding opportunities, it can be highlighted the potential of the IR 5.0 to better work with big data and to increase knowledge in support of the participation of CSOs in global governance and debates, more precisely by increasing their capabilities in knowledge production and practical implementation. One example is the role of AI in making sense of the large volume of data recorded by satellites, drones, and sensors throughout the planet to better inform environmental policies and debates. Risks are also significant, particularly for an incipient and pioneering technology that takes time for the governance systems to understand and regulate. Another example is the misuse of technology and algorithms to generate targeted misinformation and propaganda to influence public opinion and elections. Governments around the world

---

[1]The views expressed in this text are those of the authors and neither reflects the official policy or position of any other organization, which the authors may be affiliated with.

and leading high-tech companies should define a framework that regulates IR 5.0. Global civil society could play an important role in demanding and lobbying the creation of this framework. For this goal, CSOs need to understand how stakeholders see and adapt to technological challenges.

This chapter is organized as follows. The introduction will discuss the key characteristics of the so-called "global civil society," as well as identify the major challenges emerging from the transition from IR 4.0 to IR 5.0. Then the authors will discuss the impact of these technological advancements on global civil society from the specific perspectives of: (1) how international organizations and governments refer to them; (2) how bilateral and multilateral development partners (BMDP) are challenged by them; and (3) how higher education institutions adapt to them.

In the first section – "IR 5.0 and Human Social Capital: Diverse discourses for the same phenomena?" – we will study how the different discourses penetrated the international public sphere. International organizations, such as the European Union and the Organization for Economic Cooperation and Development, mentioned it officially and entered the discussion, while others, such as the International Labour Organization, seem to skip it and maintain their focus in the IR 4.0. However, the discourse on AI is not restricted to international organizations. Some states, like Japan and China, have already positioned themselves, producing their discourses. More specifically, the authors examine the official discourses in the national and international public arena, and identify the different topics, perspectives, and absences in each of them, understanding the existence of gaps or complementarity between them. In the second section – "How do bilateral and multilateral development partners look into the role of AI and CSO?" – we will examine, likewise, the concept of AI, then address how international organizations and national governments are incorporating or ignoring its consequences, to discuss the main benefits and risks that AI represents for the global civil society. In the third section – "The academic new syllabi of the future: The tandem solutions" – we will study the impact on the way the students' syllabi in the institutions associated with higher education are designed to accommodate the forthcoming challenges in terms of the construction of human social skills. The last section concludes. Methodologically, this research is supported by inductive comparative qualitative analysis, non-participated observations, and empirical international experience, combined with discourse analysis and interviews.

Keywords: Industry Revolution 4.0; Industry Revolution 5.0; discourse; global civil society; technological development; artificial intelligence; cultural industries; human social skills; education; new syllabi

1. Introduction

The impact of the Fifth Industry Revolution (IR) must be studied and debated, if we wish to manage its advantages and mitigate its troubles. This chapter addresses precisely the question to what extent IR 4.0 and IR 5.0 bring new opportunities and challenges for civil society organizations (CSOs) to improve the lives and communities around the world. But how do we understand global civil society? There is an ongoing academic debate about this concept, especially with regard to the formation of the notion of a global society. Nevertheless, for this chapter, we adopt the concept that civil society is not the state and it is the component of the society which is non-official and non-governmental. Likewise, civil society is not the market: it is a non-commercial realm (Scholte, 1999, pp. 2–3). The very nature of the civil society concept represents an open process of conglomerating an array of non-state agents, with informal and virtual relations between them, constituting networks of interests and perspectives, operating in a culturally diverse framework and involving multisectors of activity. Probably the best way to understand the concept is to be enumerative. According to Scholte (1999, p. 4)

> Civil society encompasses enormous diversity. In terms of membership and constituencies, for example, it includes academic institutes, business associations, community-based organisations, consumer protection bodies, criminal syndicates, development cooperation groups, environmental campaigns, ethnic lobbies, foundations, farmers' groups, human rights advocates, labour unions, relief organisations, peace activists, professional bodies, religious institutions, women's networks, youth campaigns and more.

Keane (2020) goes even further advancing the idea of a network of non-state groups, which are defined by their cultural diversity and by the fact that the concept is still open and developing: "The sheer heterogeneity of groups, activities, and networks that make up global civil society – non-profits, businesses, social movements, tourists, academics, artists, cultural performers, ethnic and linguistic groups....". In the same line of reasoning, the World Bank[2] refers to "Civil society... [as] a wide array of organizations: community groups, non-governmental organizations [NGOs], labor unions, indigenous groups, charitable organizations, faith-based organizations, professional associations, and foundations." Schwab (2013) highlighted the fact that the concept of civil society is also changing as it encompasses organized and unorganized groups as well as online and offline participation.

> The definitions are changing as civil society is recognized as encompassing far more than a mere "sector" dominated by the NGO community: civil society today includes an ever wider and more vibrant range of organized and unorganized groups, as new civil-society actors blur the boundaries between sectors and experiment with new organizational forms, both online and off. (Schwab, 2013, p. 5)

---

[2]Retrieved from https://www.weforum.org/agenda/2018/04/what-is-civil-society/. Accessed on October 2, 2020.

There is also an academic debate on how to understand global civil society as it refers to a network of groups and conglomerates of non-state organizations, operating across material and immaterial borders and beyond the reach of state governments. The debate has been placed at the level of understanding *global* in the context of globalization, and as consequence addressing also questions such as internationalization, liberalization, westernization and deterritorialization (Scholte, 1999). For this chapter, global civil society relations are understood as human, social, organizational and institutional bidirectional connectivity flows, in which territorial distance and physical sovereign borders do not exercise a decisive influence or materialize a substantial impediment. In this vein of reasoning, global civil society relations have what could be called a "supraterritorial," "transborder," or "Transworld" character (Scholte, 1999, p. 9).

Moreover, when discussing his matter, we must notice that civil society groups are becoming more tech-savvy not only to be socially engaged but to be actively informed. That fact, according to the World Economic Forum[3] advances five important challenges: (1) persistent risks to digital rights through the sheer interconnectedness of new technologies; (2) high-powered propaganda tools in the attention economy; (3) navigating the relationship with new digital social movements; (4) threats to transparency and accountability; and (5) new context for questions on the ethics of innovations that take us beyond the level of humanity. If we carefully mull these challenges over, is not difficult to notice that all of them require a general evolution in how global societies develop human skills. Indeed, artificial intelligence (AI), augmented reality, virtual reality, biotechnologies, big data, 3D printing, blockchain, the internet of the things, space traveling, and cryptocurrency (just to name a few) are demanding new unprecedented levels of preparedness, investment, and adaptation for most of the civil society organizations (CSO).

The first industrial revolution delivered mechanical mass production, based on steam power. The second industrial revolution brought division of labor and electrical power. The third industrial revolution conveyed the basis of the electronics and the digital world, advancing automation. The fourth and fifth industrial revolutions are occurring in an intertwined manner, developing new levels of complexity in the use of cyber-physical interaction and intelligent systems. For more than 200 years, humankind has developed unprecedented technologies, but it is absolutely essential that we preserve the civil society independent from sovereign governments in a way we maintain the so-called industrial revolutions "human-centred."

2. IR 5.0 and Human Social Capital: Diverse Discourses for the Same Phenomena?

The leading international organizations or even governments lack a meaningful discourse about IR 5.0. Excluding countries like Japan or scientific work recently

---

[3]Retrieved from https://www.weforum.org/agenda/2017/12/5-challenges-facing-civil-society-in-the-fourth-industrial-revolution. Accessed on October 2, 2020.

published, IR 5.0 maintains a low profile in political discussion and even more when it concerns the impacts in society, cultural or human behavior. We can identify opposite trends: one believing in the ability of humanity to take out the best of technology, living in an almost perfect utopia, and another more focused on the challenges and risks brought by a quick transition to IR 4.0 and IR 5.0. However, more recently, there has been a smooth change in the interpretation of the relationship between humans and technology, which generally affects the traditional organization of work and society.

The polarization of positions and discourses about IR 4.0 and IR 5.0 justify the research over the discourse in the international sphere. The diversity of comprehension about 4.0 and 5.0 is wider one might think and even interrogates if they are technological revolutions or evolutions due to a new way of producing in a globalized context (e.g., Eurofound, 2019). In order to understand how international institutions answering to these new challenges and risks of AI and self-learning machines in the relationship with humans, in this section, we identified and analyzed the discourses of international organizations like the Organization for Economic Cooperation and Development (OECD), the European Union (EU) and the International Labour Organisation (ILO). We also explored the more recent scientific production in different areas of knowledge researching about this topic. Finally, to conclude this section, we attempted to identify some national discourses about the 4.0 and 5.0 and found little information, although we could have access to some documents from Japan, Germany and France or studies about industry evolution on specific states like China.

Our first difficulty is to determine what is the international public sphere and global citizenship. Although living in a globalized world, the opportunities for participation as a citizen in the international discussions about public policies or challenges faced globally is still unequal and scarce. Even the debate about global citizenship is still open, and diverse international organizations address the concept in their specific ways. In a recent work comparing the approach to global citizenship by the United Nations Educational, Scientific and Cultural Organization (UNESCO) and OECD, the authors concluded that UNESCO saw global citizenship through global education while OECD interpreted it by global competence (Sousa & Costa, 2020). The authors also concluded that both organizations did not encompass the complexity of global citizenship. Therefore, when analyzing the discourses of international organizations, it is determinant that we keep in mind the fact that they might be addressing different concepts, even if they are using precisely the same words. However, these limitations do not prevent us from researching the trends international organizations are following in their discourses for the international public sphere.

The majority of authors referring to IR 5.0 and its consequences, also study the changes brought by IR 4.0. Generically speaking, IR 4.0 indicates the transformation of the manufacturing agents from physical systems to cyber-physical systems (Saeid, 2019). Some authors designated it as the creation of "smart factories" (Bednar & Welch, 2020). Following this trend, OECD called it "decentralised smart manufacturing" (OECD, 2019). A recent study from the ILO offices in Argentina described IR 4.0 as the adaptation of manufacturing to a globalized world with the delocalization of work to diverse geographies, which affected not only developed economies as well as emerging economies (Dragún, Ernst, & García Dí az, 2020), bringing new challenges for the human factor. If IR 4.0 is already based on technology and smart manufacturing, what changes with the IR 5.0? Scientific research is looking for an answer. Even though, because the significant changes with human impact started with the 4.0, the fact is that the IR 5.0 introduces modifications to the previous stage of technological development with effect in the relation between humans and AI. We will return to AI in the following section. Nevertheless, IR 4.0 raised the question about a human-centered design of factory that used technology and converted the workforce into new skills (Longo, Padovano, & Umbrello, 2020). The look for answers must involve scientists, designers, industrial engineers, legal experts, philosophers and policy-makers. Notwithstanding, social sciences are still not contributing to a considerable number of research and reflections that can give some orientation to the process going on.

Not mentioned directly, the IR 5.0, neither the IR 4.0, the EU produces a discourse encouraging research methodologies that reflect the sociocultural and ethical impact of these technical revolutions have on human behavior and the human relationship with machines. Accordingly, the EU proposed a Framework Programmes, Responsible Research and Innovation, valuing what is called "sensitive design," which represents an increasing concern about ethical issues in a technological evolution environment. So, the main issue seems to be how to design a 5.0 industrial system or systems respecting human values? Some authors take this direction and express their concern about the transparency in the use of technology (Bednar & Welch, 2020) that might impact not only the labor system but also the political system, as we have seen in the current electoral process in democracies, with the use of machines to create algorithms used to influence the voting directly. The case of the British political consultant corporation Cambridge Analytica, which terminated operation in 2018, should be taken as a vibrant reminder of the dangers associated with the unethical use of technology. The risk of networks becoming a power structure uncontrolled democratically and the transformation of big data into knowledge without no human checking (Ozdemir & Hekim, 2018) is something resulting from the application of the IR 5.0 into every area of production (second and third sectors of the economy).

Consequently, it seems the IR 5.0 not only deepens technologically the IR 4.0 but also spreads it to all areas of human production, suggesting a synergetic relationship between humans and machines, enabling a complex hyperconnected digital network. So, from cyber-physical systems for production/manufacturing and cloud storage, we step forward intelligent devices, intelligent systems and interconnected physical and cyber worlds. IR 5.0, besides providing jobless manufacturing as an industrial model (which IR 4.0 already permitted) (Dragún et al., 2020), also provides machines self-learning through algorithms. This new stage of the relationship between the human factor and technology raises determinant issues related to the tasks that will remain dependent on human resources. Neither scientific research nor international organizations have a full answer for it.

International discourse on the impact of IR 5.0 on human capital maintains the tendency to be more of a diagnosis than a search for solutions.

The reflection of the EU is more focused on IR 4.0 than in the transformations taken by IR 5.0. Therefore, the studies carried out are still determined by the impact of the implementation of IR 4.0. Following this trend, we can find interesting contributes from the organizations we selected, EU, OECD and ILO. In a study carried out by Eurofound (2019) concerning the implementation of the IR 4.0, the result revealed that only Germany opted to have a package on education and training responding to the transformations brought to the labor market. In the same report, the Eurofound refers to the lack of clarity about the impact these new technologies have in workplaces, mentioning the limited attention concerning the relationship between worker and employer. Although there was an awareness of the need for social dialogue, the authors of the report consider that the multistakeholder perspective was scarcely applied. It is interesting to note that some studies carried out for specific areas of production have different findings, but they applied to precise areas of production (e.g., Longo et al., 2020). Despite the Eurofound's findings, the Franco-German Manifesto for a European Industrial Policy, in 2019, selects better-skilled workforce as the basis of EU global competitiveness, meaning that these countries may influence EU in the sense of creating IR 4.0 and 5.0 education and skilling plans.

The OECD does not mention any of the industrial revolutions in their reports. In the report titled Transformative Technologies (OECD, 2018), OECD develops a deep diagnose of the world situation concerning technology and its effects on human resources. Beginning with by mentioning to the differences in access to technology between regions, generations, level of education, gender and income levels, the report traces the scenario resulting from the move to smart production. The primary threat of jobs loss will be in the second sector of activity and can reach about 40% of the working force (we should notice this was a pre-COVID 19 perspective). It was also expected 30% of the workers having to adapt to new tasks and do involve in skills development and training. OECD also highlights the need for social dialogue and the development of a people-to-people agenda. OECD presented this report to the G7 group, publishing it afterwards. The positions and discourse proposed by OECD are similar to the one projected by EU in the following year, focusing it on the need for more education and skilling plans to adapt to IR 4.0 and IR 5.0 and simultaneously calling attention for the need of having a social dialogue.

The ILO, in the report published in 2020, titled "El Futuro del Trabajo en el Mundo de la Industria 4.0" (The future of work in the world of industry 4.0), refers to the risk of jobless manufacturing, resulting from the application of a smart factory model. Concurrently, it also brings to public sphere a new concern, the fact that developed economies and emerging economies are involving in this process simultaneously, bringing diverse challenges in each region/country, which might cause several mutations in very diverse societies.

Finally, we looked at the reports concerning China and Japan as the most dynamic Asian states in the implementation of IR 5.0. The Chinese discourse about the implementation of technology and the transformation into smart factories is embedded in the Made in China 2025 Program, which develops a full strategy to catch up with technology, affecting all sectors of society (Malkin, 2018). Japanese discourse was concentrated in the Outline of the Fifth Science and Technology Basic Plan (2020), available for international consultation. The Plan foresees the integration of cyberspace with physical space in a 5.0 society, based on the coordination of platforms which will promote a society 5.0 platform. The Japanese government expects that the collaboration between industry, academia and government will contribute to the smooth transformation of society into a 5.0 society.

If we compare the Chinese and Japanese discourses with the international organizations' discourses, we analyzed, one of the main differences is that these countries are focused in the way to build technological societies, not referring to the obstacles or less positive consequences of the quick implementation of the 5.0. As for the international organizations, they are still very focused on the diagnosis of the impacts of IR 4.0 and IR 5.0 might have in societies and the labor market. They suggest some solutions, like social dialogue, plans for skilling and educating people toward a smooth transition, but they do not provide guidelines about how to improve the relationship between technology and humans. Regardless of their concern with the negative impacts IR 4.0 and IR 5.0 might have, like unemployment, social unrest and exclusion, these international organizations are still looking at the past and not implementing prospective discourses.

3. How Do Bilateral and Multilateral Development Partners Look Into at the Role of AI and CSOs?

As we have mentioned in the previous sections, the relation between humans and technology appears to be at the center of the debate, with particular concern to AI. Therefore, AI refers to the ways that machines are built to perform with human-like intelligence. One major example of AI is machine learning, which involves the processing of massive amounts of data, so-called big data, analyzed by machines through complex algorithms so they can "learn" precise tasks mechanically. This helps pinpoint patterns or make decisions from a sea of information. The increasing presence of AI in our lives derives from two factors observed more markedly in the last two decades: first, higher availability of human data; and second, higher speed in the interpretation and reaction to data.

AI is therefore a revolutionary concept that threatens to change in the future how the society organizes and works. Commercial, educational, legal, medical, physical, political and social systems are incrementally based on human data gathering and processing and this means that their setting in the next decades will differ significantly from the one we observed at the beginning of the century. We see three main groups of stakeholders dealing with these changes: (i) national government and international organizations; (ii) private sector, including as a special category big data firms; and (iii) global civil society.

The exponential growth of data and AI is creating a tug-of-war between data for profit and data for the common good, as referred by Khan (2020). The amount of data collected on humans and their environments is increasing exponentially, reaching unchartered levels both in deeply knowing and connecting human beings.

AI opportunities are plentiful in this age of data, and so are challenges and risks (see Table 4.1 for a summary of challenges and risks). On one hand, the more we all know about the human being and its environment, the better governments can function and provide services to their citizens, in areas such as medical data for research, the better the private sector can provide goods and services that are tailored to the needs of customers; and the more we can understand each other and, consequently, avoid conflicts. Just to bring some estimated numbers about the positive impact of AI, European Parliament (2020) estimates, for instance, that (i) 14% of jobs in OECD countries are highly automatable and another 32% could face substantial changes; (ii) AI will reduce global greenhouse emissions by 2030 in between 1.5% and 4%; and (iii) labor productivity is estimated to increase by between 11% and 37% due to AI. On the other hand, rules are needed to regulate and monitor how this data is made available, distributed and used, promoting a level playing field for all and avoiding persistent unfair asymmetric information that could be used to the benefit of some, whether governments or private. These rules are materialized as both domestic and international law.

Khan (2020) considers two governance models emerging from these three groups in dealing with the challenges and opportunities brought forward by AI and big data. The first model, "data for-profit model," has technological firms, such as Google or Facebook, as main leading actors, acting in a relatively unregulated universe. The second model, "government-regulated model" gives to government and public regulatory bodies a more preponderant role. However, as pointed out by Khan (2020), none of these models has boundaries for profiteering or privacy intrusion. This is when the role of global civil society becomes critical. A third governance model is needed that adequately bring the right voice and weight to the global civil society, helping to define, promote and monitor a "data for good" use. Fundamental human data rights need to be agreed upon and monitored between nations on the principles of fairness, equality and freedom.

We will assess next the relationship between bilateral and multilateral development partners (BMDP) and CSOs. The role to be played by BMDPs, defined for this purpose as bilateral and multilateral development agencies and banks, in promoting the voice and the participation of global civil society is important. The role and degree of relationship between the BMDPs and CSOs, which include mainly non-governmental organizations, has been growing in recent decades. CSOs are active participants in most open events organized by the BMDPs, they are actively consulted by the BMDPs when reviewing their policies (particularly sensitive policies, such as safeguards or energy) and they permanently and closely monitor the impact in the field of the projects financed by these institutions. Regarding the latter, the CSOs constitute indeed a key element of the compliance review function of the accountability mechanisms of the BMDPs. These

Table 4.1. Main Opportunities and Risks Emerging From AI.

Opportunities	Risks
(1) Improved goods and services at a lower cost, caused by the higher productivity associated with the automation of core business processes (2) Human capital development, caused by easier access to information, education and training (3) New products and business models, including leapfrogging solutions and solutions for the bottom of pyramid individuals (4) Innovation in government services (5) Reduced global greenhouse emissions	(1) Increasing digital and technological divide (underuse of AI), leading to wider income inequality (2) New job requirements and disruption of traditional job functions (3) Privacy, security and public trust (4) Uncertainty about legal liabilities caused by AI

Source: Adapted from Strusani and Houngbonon 2019).

mechanisms are the external tool that monitors if the BMDPs comply with their own policies, particularly in safeguard areas such as environment, indigenous people or resettlement. It means that, for instance, if, during the implementation of a BMDP-financed project, the bank falls short to compensate a resettled family according to their own policies, this family can use the bank's compliance review function of the accountability mechanism to complain to the BMDP. Since the resources and the awareness of the people in the field are limited, these complaints are normally presented to the banks' accountability mechanisms by CSOs.

Turning now to the relationship between BMDPs and AI, we observe that, so far, BMDPs have seen AI as a means rather than an end, and mainly in sovereign projects, that is, to the public sector. The connection with the private sector occurs through the procurement activities bid for the provision of goods, consulting services and civil works needed to implement the sovereign projects. One example is the use by BMDPs of AI, in the form of high-resolution satellite imagery, geospatial data, and powerful machine-learning algorithms to complement traditional data sources. In this regard, the European Space Agency has two staff advising the World Bank and the Asian Development Bank on the potential of high-resolution satellite imagery for project design and implementation in nearly 20 countries in Africa, Asia and Latin America (see, e.g., ADB, 2017, 2020; World Bank, 2015). As an interface, nearly 2,500 European Small and Medium Enterprises work on the business of translating the raw data provided by this high-resolution satellite imagery into filtered and structured information that is usable and friendly for decision-making.

The trilateral relationship between BMDPs, AI and CSOs occurs in two areas. First, the high-resolution satellite imagery can be used not only for more efficient and effective project design and implementation, but also for better monitoring of the impact that development projects financed by BMDPs have in the field areas such as environment, indigenous people, poverty or resettlement. Big data, available online or high-resolution satellite imagery can potentially have a significant impact on the monitoring, controlling and measurement of this impact. Consequently, the global civil society needs to better grasp the potential of AI to better understand and use this technology in promoting their lobbying activities to these BMDPs.

The second connection between BMDPs, AI and global civil society emerges from the key role that CSO organizations must play in highlighting how technological developments can negatively impact vulnerable people and communities. CSOs can expose and publicize how technology is negatively affecting real people's lives, and lobby and work with tech firms and governments to safeguard that they minimize any unintended negative consequences, particularly those identified as risks in Table 4.1, and promote the so-called "tech-ethics." This lobbying and influence by the CSOs in promoting an ethical behavior plays a critical role in complementing traditional mechanism of legislation and policy to ensure that the opportunities brought by AI are maximized while the risks and challenges are in turn minimized.

While AI, as explained, does not occupy a central role in the strategies or settings, international organizations are curious about exploring the potential of AI to help them reach their goals more efficiently and effectively. In the case of BMDPs, they are currently taking their first steps in exploring how they can use big data, AI and machine learning to craft responsible solutions for development. A first joint report of four MDBs, namely the African Development Bank, Asian Development Bank, European Bank for Reconstruction and Development and Inter-American Development was published in 2018 discussing the consequences that AI could have for jobs worldwide (Williams, 2018), concluding that

> rapid technological progress provides a significant opportunity for emerging and developing economies to grow faster and attain higher levels of prosperity. However, some disruptive technologies could displace human labour, widen income inequality and contribute to greater informality in the workforce.

Williams (2018) also concludes that "tapping new technologies in a way that maximises benefits, mitigates adverse effects and shares opportunities among all citizens will require public–private cooperation and smart public policy."

In addition, the International Finance Corporation (IFC), the private sector arm of the World Bank Group, has started to hire specialists in AI and machine learning for its disruptive technologies and venture capital team, aiming at investing in early growth companies that offer innovative technologies or business models with high impact potential (IFC, 2020). In this context, the global civil society needs to better grasp the potential of AI to better monitor and influence the impact of BMDPs in the field. This is particularly relevant in the context created by the Covid-19 pandemic, which forced these institutions to work more intensively with IT and digital tools. As the Director-General for Sustainable

Development and Climate Change Department of the Asian Development Bank puts it, "AI and machine learning are not silver bullet solutions" (Um, Carrasco, & Sy, 2020), but they could give a big boost.

4. The Academic New Syllabi of the Future: The Tandem Solutions

As we have suggested in the previous sections, there is no sufficient debate on the association between human skills and technological expertise. The reduced number of narratives are led by key international actors, which are already extending the IR 5.0 to all sectors of the society. However, it seems that IR 5.0 and in AI in particular and technology in general terms, will have a substantial impact in all sectors of global civil society. Even before anticipating the technological effects of the fifth industrial revolution, we already noticed that the world is in dystrophic dehumanization. There is a latent sense of decay and chaos, which the global narrative associates technology to human advancements, capable of resolving all the challenges. The greatest challenge of the fifth industrial revolution is not driven by technology but by humanity. We attach particular concern to the digital technology as it induces a false perception of the reality, and disentangles the human-to-human engagement.

In the previous section, we have conveyed the idea that IR 5.0 offers both opportunities (as a synergetic relationship between humans and machines based on *sensitive design* and on data for common good) and risks (as the ones associated to manipulation of data, employment opportunities, public trust, transparency, accountability and liability). Also, the looming global climate crisis (and to a certain extent the political manipulation of data) is the result of technological advancements, which induced our disregard for nature, for ourselves and overvalued our self-centered egotism, based on the elapsed enjoyment and material accumulation.

More than ever before, the IR 5.0 calls for a careful understanding of technology as an instrument of humanity, at the service of the global humankind. The unrestrained techno-nationalism (the systematic use of technology to promote national interest[4] at the expenses of other national and global interests) and the uncontrolled techno-corporatism (the systematic use of technology to bend the free market rules, or to promote market or trade interests at the expenses of the human or the social communities' interest) are probably the two looming threats associated to IR 5.0. In fact, technology must be an instrument of development, inclusion, interculturalism, gender balance, fairness, equity of opportunities, and governance centered into the global perspective. Sebald (2004, p. 54) has used the idea of the so-called "technologic man's petulance" to describe the tendency to over-rely on technological solutions to address human challenges. Technology was and is an instrument at the service of men to meet human needs and

---

[4]To understand our vision of the concept of national interest we recommend – Is togetherness a third option to choosing between 'us' or 'them'? (Leandro, 2019).

desires. That is why framing the discussion on technology development is crucial to understand how we all should rethink institutional academic structures and the purpose of their existence. Technology must be researched, conceived, discussed, developed, and implemented within a very simple principle – its existence should be perceived as an apparatus to human advancement.

In our common understanding, the crossroads of the IR5.0 narratives rests with strong education to promote sensitive technological designs, to encourage solutions associated to data for the common good and to avoid the dangers of unrestrained techno-nationalism and techno-corporatism. In this vein of reasoning, there is no such thing as the *technological threat* as far as we all keep this ideological frame within the educational boundaries. Technology has no free will, nor motivational intent, neither ability to exercise abstraction nor consciousness. Technology has no ethics. The core discussion on how to educate for a future where technology dominates rests with our current ability to design tandem educational models in which technological skills can be developed in the context of mulling over on our natural condition of humans. To accommodate the forthcoming technological challenges, the commitment of education models must be driven by human skills, in which the current transmission or the reproduction model will be replaced by a motivational multiapproach collaborative rationale (Table 4.2).

Education for the new generation of digital natives needs to adopt the central idea of developing human social capital in a multiapproach manner, to develop and reinforce the human ability to bridge and transform for human benefit and the common good. H2H education must be at the core of all syllabi, especially, of those designed to boost H2T expertise. H2H education should be grounded on three relational dimensions:

1. The relation between us and ourselves, which basically engages the study of ethics and its professional context and having the corporate culture as its main reference (deontology). As Hinman puts it (2003, p. 1) "[…] we inevitably face choices… we search for what will be the right answer for us" (p. 21) and at the same time, he advocates pluralistic ethics. The starting point is the entrepreneurial ethical pragmatism, which should educate to generate sustainable wealth and ought to advance a substantial contribution to the common good. The core of the model should place the idea of ethical opportunity (knowledge, reward and sanctions) as well as moral intensity as central concepts guiding H2T relationship.
2. The relation between us and others, which essentially is based on developing empathy, emotional intelligence, communication aptitudes and leadership abilities. The challenges associated to identity and to plural monoculturalism (or the cultural world of bubbles) are preventing the expected development of human social capital, especially in relation to bonding (Putman, 2000) as it should be based on reciprocity, solidarity and cohesion. Learning how to accommodate differences, and to build trust and how to operate efficiently together is the solution to natural interdependency. Education should promote responsible leadership, based on emotional intelligence. The H2H

Table 4.2. The Motivational Multiapproach Collaborative Rationale in Education.

Rationale: To promote "data for good use" as a tool to advance human development and promote self-restraint in techno-nationalism and techno-corporatism				
Human to Human (H2H)	H2H – Is the human ability to understand its own key ethical references, to advance positive communication and leadership and to build intercultural sustainable solutions			New syllabi is the tandem syllabi (H2H and H2T), designed in a multiapproach in complex problem-solving.
^	Self to Self (S2S)	Relational Literacy People to People (P2P)	Intercultural Literacy CSO Culture to Culture (C2C)	^
^	^	Communication + Leadership		^
Tech-ethics – "Technology affects the nature of our acting […] Act so that the effects of your action are compatible with the permanence of genuine human life"[5] (Jonas, 1981)				^
Human to Technology (H2T)	H2T – Is the human ability to use material and immaterial techniques, skills, methods and processes to produce value and deliver value (goods or services) for human benefit			^

Source: Adapted from Jonas (1981).

education to advance the fifth industrial revolution, must carefully understand Rawls' (2009) notion of justice, and combine it with the willingness to engage on how to learn (circumstantial adaptability), and therefore be capable of benefiting all, especially the least advantaged. John Rawls' position is particularly applicable to the context, when he considered his second principle of justice, which states that social and economic positions are to be to everyone's advantage and open to all.

3. The relation between our culture and others, which stands as the mental structure capable of avoiding the legacy of multiculturalism as it produces a world of cultural bubbles. As Cantle (2012) asserts, multiculturalism is a narrative of minorities coexisting in isolation in a sort of exotics for the benefit of the majority and leading to assimilation, fragmentation and violence.

---

[5]Jonas insists that human survival depends on our efforts to care for our planet and its future. He formulated a new and distinctive supreme moral imperative: "Act so that the effects of your action are compatible with the permanence of genuine human life" (Tirosh-Samuelson &, Wiese, 2008). The Legacy of Hans Jonas: Judaism and the Phenomenon of Life, BRILL, p. 135.

Oppositely, interculturalism is a narrative of the future, accommodation, hybridity and bilateral exchange. Therefore, education should promote the movement from multicultural minds to intercultural technologic literacy, to promote our ability to share feelings, to sense needs, to partake perspectives and to build hybrid identities, even in a corporate environment.

Higher education plays a decisive part of the process of promoting human social capital, which uses secondary, group, gender and anticipatory socialization (Levine & Hoffner, 2006), to combine these two dimensions, in the context of the new technologic advancements. Human skills need to dominate any sort of socialization process. As a result, higher education must be regarded as transformational in relation to the global society, involving the civil society, but where technology is placed as circumstantial service knowhow.

5. Conclusion

Allow us to return to our initial question – to what extent IR 4.0 and 5.0 bring new opportunities and challenges for CSOs to improve the lives and communities around the world? Apparently, the two industrial revolutions are intertwined and they are putting forward unprecedented opportunities and extraordinary challenges to mitigate threatening risks. The low profile of the political discourses, the polarization of narratives, the advancement of models by some development actors, and the fact that all the discussion seemed to be techno-market framed, are probably major initial challenges to the CSOs. We need to extend the discussion to all sectors of human activity, having the global civil society as the leading party.

The opportunities put forward by the IR 5.0 are encapsulated in the idea of developing a synergetic relationship between humans and technology for common benefit, avoiding the risks put forward by the unrestrained techno-nationalism and the techno-corporatism. The example of Germany in terms of education sets a good pathway, but it falls short in relation to the extension of the education model. Indeed, IR 5.0 calls for a motivational multiapproach collaborative rationale in education, advocating tandem solutions. The tandem syllabi and the multiapproach in complex problem-solving, capable of foster sensitive designs and the use of data for the common good.

The construction of the future technological global civil societies must be the driver of higher education models, capable of excluding mono-dimensional syllabi (exclusively H2T or completely H2H). As we have suggested, the opportunities for the development of human capital, and sustainable solutions, are to drive the construction of the technological societies of the future. Likewise, as advocated earlier, the role of the global civil society is critical in this construction of intercultural literacies. A third governance model is needed that adequately bring the right voice and weight to the global civil society, helping to define, promote and monitor a "data for good" use and avoiding "data for profit or top-down regulated models". Fundamental human data rights need to be agreed upon and monitored between nations on the principles of fairness, equality and freedom.

The digital data dictatorship, the invasion of the space that should be reserved for personal data and the instrumentalization of big data, are already current global quagmires.

Furthermore, the opportunities also call for national and transnational accountability mechanisms, in which the CSOs and the multilateral development partners, constitute key elements to promote and reassure oversight and compliance review. The beneficial trade-off for the global civil society, between the advantages and the disadvantages put forward by IR 5.0, rests with the manner we construct our relationship with technology. Therefore, technology is (and must continuing to be) merely instrumental in an IR 5.0 society, which by nature, their usage should be human-centered. Technologic opportunities are to be explored without fear, as far as humans understand their ultimate purpose. Technologic narratives are vital to set the pathway for advancement, as far as humans understand their framework for common good. Foremost, education to promote human social skills, and the comprehensive involvement of global civil actors are critical, to make technology and tech-ethics catalyzing forces for good.

References

ADB. (2017, March). *Earth observation for a transforming Asia and Pacific*. Asian Development Bank. Retrieved from https://www.adb.org/publications/earth-observation-transforming-asia-pacific. Accessed on October 1, 2020.

ADB. (2020, September). *Mapping poverty through data integration and artificial intelligence: A special supplement of the Key Indicators for Asia and the Pacific 2020*. Asian Development Bank. Retrieved from https://www.adb.org/sites/default/files/publication/630406/mapping-poverty-ki2020-supplement.pdf. Accessed on October 1, 2020.

Bednar, P. M., & Welch, C. (2020). Socio-technical perspectives on smart working: Creating meaningful and sustainable systems. *Information Systems Frontiers, 22*, 281–298. Retrieved from https://doi.org/10.1007/s10796-019-09921-1. Accessed on October 1, 2020.

Cantle, T. (2012). *Interculturalism: The New Era of cohesion and diversity*. London: Palgrave.

Costa, F., & Sousa, P. P. (2020). International policy influencers and their agenda on global citizenship: A critical analysis of OECD and UNESCO discourses, pp. 153–172.

Dragún, P., Ernst, C., & García Díaz, F. (2020). El futuro del trabajo en el mundo de la industria 4.0, Buenos Aires, Unión industrial Argentina/Organización Internacional del Trabajo.

Eurofound. (2019). *The future of manufacturing in Europe*. Luxembourg: Publications Office of the European Union.

European Parliament. (2020). Artificial intelligence: Threats and opportunities. *News*, September 23. Retrieved from https://www.europarl.europa.eu/news/en/headlines/society/20200918STO87404/artificial-intelligence-threats-and-opportunities. Accessed on October 2, 2020.

Hinman, L. (2003). *Ethics – A pluralistic approach to moral theory*. Pyrmont: Thomson.

International Finance Corporation. (2020). Principal Industry Specialist, artificial intelligence/machine learning – International Finance Corporation. *UN Job Net*. Retrieved from https://www.unjobnet.org/jobs/detail/13246764. Accessed on October 2, 2020.

Jonas, H. (1981). The concept of responsibility: An inquiry into the foundations of an ethics for our age. In D. Callahan & H. T. Engelhardt (Eds), *The roots of ethics* (pp. 45–74). Boston, MA: Springer.

Keane, J. (2020). Global Civil Society? *Foreign Affairs*. Retrieved from https://www.foreignaffairs.com/reviews/capsule-review/2003-11-01/global-civil-society. Accessed on October 2, 2020.

Khan, O. (2020). Data and the artificial intelligence gold rush: Who will win. *Asian Development Blog*. Retrieved from https://blogs.adb.org/blog/data-and-artificial-intelligence-gold-rush-who-will-win. Accessed on September 10, 2020.

Leandro, F. J. (2019). Is togetherness a third option to choosing between 'us' or 'them'? *International Journal of Business and Management Invention*, 8(09), 01–15. Retrieved from http://www.ijbmi.org/v8i9(series1).html. Accessed on October 1, 2020.

Levine, K. J., & Hoffner, C. A. (2006). Adolescents' conceptions of work: What is learned from different sources during anticipatory socialization? *Journal of Adolescent Research*, 21(6), 647–669.

Longo, F., Padovano, A., &Umbrello, S. (2020). Value-oriented and ethical technology engineering in Industry 5.0: A human-centric perspective for the design of the factory of the future. *Applied Sciences*, 10(12), 4182. https://doi.org/10.3390/app10124182

Malkin, A. (2018). *Made in China 2025 as a Challenge in Global Trade Governance: Analysis and recommendations*. CIGI Papers No. 183, August 2018. Centre for International Governance Innovation.

OECD. (2018). Transformative technologies and jobs of the future: Background report for the Canadian G7 Innovation Ministers' Meeting, Montreal, Canada, pp. 27–28.

OECD. (2019). Future of Education and Skills 2030 – Project background, 15 pp.

Outline of the Fifth Science and Technology Basic Plan. (2020). (Provisional translation). Retrieved from https://www8.cao.go.jp/cstp/english/basic/5thbasicplan_outline.pdf. Accessed on October 10, 2020.

Ozdemir, V ., & Hekim, N. (2018). Birth of Industry 5.0: Making sense of big data with artificial intelligence, "The Internet of Things" and Next-Generation Technology Policy. *OMICS – A Journal of Integrative Biology*, 22(1), 65–76. doi:10.1089/omi.2017.0194

Putman, R. (2000). *Bowling alone – The collapse and revival of American Community*. New York, NY: Simon & Schuster Paperbacks.

Rawls, J. (2009). *A theory of justice*. London: Harvard University Press.

Saeid, N. (2019). Industry 5.0 – A human-centric solution. *Sustainability*, 11, 4371. doi:10.3390/su11164371. Retrieved from www.mdpi.com/journal/sustainability. Accessed on October 1, 2020.

Scholte, J. A. (1999, May). *Global civil society: Changing the world?* Working Paper No. 31/99. Department of Politics and International Studies, Centre for the Study of Globalisation and Regionalisation (CSGR), University of Warwick, Coventry. Retrieved from https://www.unicef.org/socialpolicy/files/Global_Civil_Society_Changing_the_World.pdf. Accessed on October 1, 2020.

Schwab, K. (2013). *The future of the civil society*. WEF. Retrieved from http://www3.weforum.org/docs/WEF_FutureRoleCivilSociety_Report_2013.pdf. Accessed on October 2, 2020.

Sebald, W. G. (2004). *On the natural history of destruction, Modern Library Classics*. London: Anthea Bell Books.

Strusani, D., & Houngbonon, G. V. (2019). *The role of artificial intelligence in supporting development in emerging markets*. EMCompass No. 69. International

Finance Corporation. Retrieved from https://openknowledge.worldbank.org/handle/10986/32365. Accessed on October 2, 2020.

Sousa, P. P., & Costa, F. (2020). International policy influencers and their agendas on global citizenship. A critical analysis of OECD and UNESCO discourses. In *The Global Citizenship Nexus: Critical Studies* (pp. 153–172). London: Routledge. Retrieved from http://hdl.handle.net/11328/3537. Accessed on October 1, 2021.

Tirosh-Samuelson, H., & Wiese, C. (Ed.). (2008). *The legacy of Hans Jonas: Judaism and the phenomenon of life*. Leiden: Brill.

Um, W., Carrasco, B., & Sy, S. (2020). Artificial intelligence and machine learning in the time of Covid-19. *Asian Development Blog,* July 29. Retrieved from https://blogs.adb.org/blog/artificial-intelligence-and-machine-learning-time-covid-19. Accessed on September 10, 2020.

Williams, A. (2018). Four multilateral development banks present a study on technology's impact on jobs. *Press release* – European Bank for Reconstruction and Development, April 19, 2020. Retrieved from https://www.ebrd.com/news/2018/four-multilateral-development-banks-present-study-on-technologys-impact-on-jobs.html. Accessed on October 2, 2020.

World Bank. (2015). World Bank and European Space Agency to use earth observation systems for sustainable development. *Press release* – World Bank, December 3. Retrieved from https://www.worldbank.org/en/news/press-release/2015/12/03/world-bank-and-european-space-agency-to-use-earth-observation-systems-for-sustainable-development. Accessed on October 1, 2020.

Chapter 5

Networked Society and Governance: Algorithmic Default?

Tom Cockburn

Abstract

Civil society is increasingly digitized and virtual in many parts of the globalized world of today. The networked society and the invisible "second economy" (Arthur, 2011) which powers the developed and developing countries generate debates about the degree to which the benefits outweigh the potential hazards. Artificial intelligence (AI) powered by its machine learning underpin much of the digital networked systems, and "free" services such as search engines, paid for by the "tailored advertising" we get when we view webpages. Most now recognize that the helpful "suggestions" on the web are simply adverts personally targeted at individuals who have searched for information on a topic or visited a webpage with sponsored material and cookies.

There have been cases of major political misuse of data such as the voter manipulation by the Cambridge Analytica company. We are not just referring to the hacking and "fake news" used by some governments to influence the affairs of another country. Some organizations have used AI to cynically target consumers' weaknesses, for example, in financial management (Larsson, 2018).

Perhaps more significantly the network technology is often promoted as having potential for improving civil society through "failsafe" or default forms of regulation using the embedded Apps in domestic equipment and algorithms in much the same manner it is suggested that automatic self-driving vehicles help to improve road safety by cautious driving and sticking to speed limits and so on (Cockburn, Jahdi, & Wilson, 2015, pp. 6–7). However, algorithms and the associated machine technology have also been described as a "black box" technology where even those people running the algorithms cannot always fully understand or explain how decisions are reached in diverse systems used to evaluate many things from medical care to credit rating and finance (Danaher et al., 2017). There are issues of the budding "surveillance society" emerging from the proliferating "intelligent" apps enabling corporate "spying" on our everyday lives as some hackers have done by tapping into baby monitoring systems in homes. In addition to hacking there are large power asymmetries involved as between commercial data users and the lay public who are often the data suppliers as their personal data are harvested each time the web is used.

Therefore, it is hardly surprising that, according to the Pew Research Center report by Aaron Smith, released in November 2018, over half of Americans surveyed found it unacceptable to use algorithms to make decisions with real-world consequences for humans. In the age of connectedness and the emergent internet of things many people are not yet ready to cede more control of their currently offline lives to current online technology. This chapter reviews arguments for and against algorithmic governance.

Machine learning systems may be efficient to a high degree without being unbiased in impact across different segments of society. AI may also be fully effective in its operation without even being fully understood because the decision-making is so arcane. Importantly, though, even for those systems that have some human mediation or supervision, societal regulation is aimed at ensuring ends and means are aligned with human social, political and economic justice and thus socially effective as well as being technically efficient. Consequently, these systems have to require socio-emotional as well as cognitive safeguards. Although levels of implicit trust may vary demographically as between say millennials and baby boomers, high levels of trust, accountability and a culture of moral integrity must still form the bedrock for societal benefits.

Keywords: Artificial intelligence; governance; knowledge management; knowledge society; technology; content moderation

Introduction: The "Back Story"

Currently there is much industrial and government interest in building artificial intelligence (AI) into their systems to improve efficiency, efficacy and accountability (Benkler, 2019). Organizations that fail to co-evolve with changing contexts and transcend old business paradigms will not survive. Globally, all kinds of organizations have already been impacted significantly by emergent socio-digital technology and incipient AI systems, incorporating massive datafication of personal details of users of social media sites. The COVID19 pandemic has exacerbated this trend as AI is being used to track the progress of pandemic outbreaks globally. The chances are that there is much more to come as the world seeks to become greener in the face of the climate emergency. The growth of completely new industries allied to increasing levels and integration of global digitally connected environments across all domains of personal, public and professional life open up many potentially new and exciting opportunities for improving humans "health, safety and wellbeing at all levels from micro to macro and planetary levels. However, these gains also demand greater care and attention to the design and application of such systems as well as more scrutiny of such systems" boundaries and intersection with human culture amid controversies concerning misinformation, fake news and the surveillance aspects of use. Otherwise, traditional notions of the boundaries between applied technology, human systems and associated indigenous or local cultures and research are in danger of being degraded or destroyed.

The emergence of the "knowledge society" (Drucker, 1992, pp. 328–327) radically changed what created value in organizations, and the long-term value of an organization increasingly now depends on leveraging the hidden value of its intangible assets. This chapter firstly presents a brief historical overview and discussion of the development of policies, concepts and practices in organizational knowledge management (KM) which has underpinned development of information and communication technology (ICT) and the AI systems and social media of today. I suggest that there are areas where the use of AI can have positive benefits such as the public health use of AI to track and trace potential COVID19 contacts on their mobile phones and alert them to the need to get checked and/or self-isolate, remote monitoring of supply chain dynamics, reduction of routine administrative tasks, safety, and maintenance of plant whereas others should operate under license, for example, medical or other care systems for vulnerable humans. Even autonomous vehicles still need to be operated under "license," that is, human moderation as deaths have occurred in vehicle crashes due to AI failing to recognize a hazard from other road users' behavior. Thus, the concept and use of algorithmic governance as the unsupervised default system governance regulation is questionable. Thus, when applied to human systems the beneficial promise of these systems is predicated on clear ethical design guidelines and more rigorous public scrutiny and accountability in light of the ubiquity and often credulous acceptance by users unaware of how the technology affects their worldview or interactions with others.

Background: Modeling Organizational Knowledge

Following the widespread acknowledgment by businesses, governments and other organizations of the emergence of the "knowledge society" in the late 1980s, many business models were reconfigured from previous, industrial, "make and move" products to models based on "knowledge and service"(Drucker, 1992, p. 96). Thus, for over three decades until today, KM has been vigorously proposed as a "technological fix" by IT/IS personnel, to optimize performance, enhance productivity and enable sustainable competitive advantage in the face of the burgeoning ambiguity and dynamic complexity of present-day Volatile Uncertain Complex and Ambiguous (VUCA) business environments worldwide (Choo & Bontis, 2002; Davenport & Prusak, 1998; Karaszewski, 2008; Marqués & Simón, 2006; Nonaka & Takeuchi, 1995).

KM may be broadly considered as the deliberate design of processes, tools, structures, etc. with the intent to update, increase, share or improve the use of structural, human and social elements of knowledge (Seeman et al., 1999) or more specifically as "Those processes, tools and infrastructures by which an organization continuously improves, maintains and exploits all those elements of its knowledge base that the organization believes are relevant to achieving its goals. KM includes the processes, tools and infrastructure by which these goals are modified as the organization's knowledge base or context fluctuates or quickly changes. Briefly, it is now generally accepted that the fundamentals of KM and intellectual capital (IC) entails the necessity of treating KM in a systemic manner to include the social as well as the technological implications, and the key attributes of a society or an organization's prevailing culture (including affective factors, that encourage or are seen as potential blocks to effective KM, and governance). The organization's knowledge base is defined to include the data, information, intuition, knowledge (know how), understanding (know why) and wisdom, residing throughout the organization and in areas of overlap with partnered customers" (Smith, 1998). The increasing interest in KM led to more detailed exploration of "what is knowledge," and how it is categorized with a view to identifying what quotient of knowledge an organization needs to successfully implement its strategies, and where this knowledge resides. Unfortunately, the definition of "knowledge" remains a continuing matter for debate and the question of whether it can be managed has yet to be resolved.

In regard to KM, practitioners and theorists soon side-stepped these issues by adopting Ackoff's (1989) "Data, Information, Knowledge, Wisdom pyramid" (DIKW pyramid). According to the DIKW, information is defined in terms of data; knowledge in terms of information; and wisdom in terms of knowledge. Knowledge was also explored in terms of "know how" and "know what" and wisdom in terms of "know why"; for example, these are categories of knowledge which might be identified via knowledge mapping (Drew, 1996; Vestal, 2005), and scrutinized and prioritized via a knowledge audit before a KM system would be implemented or designed (Drew, 1996).

Broadly speaking, KM recognizes two types of knowledge, namely tacit and explicit composed of perceived patterns of data sets. This was originally based on the work of Michael Polanyi (1983), who stressed that we know more than we can say, and Donald Schon (1995, 1996) who claimed that knowledge is mostly tacit compiled from reveals itself in actions and decisions made by practitioners. Tacit knowledge is comprised of intuitions, perspectives, beliefs and values that result from experience and can best be communicated interpersonally through dialogue with use of metaphors, the mindsets (or mental models) of individuals and the collective mindsets of the organizational culture. Explicit knowledge on the other hand has been articulated and codified in words or numbers and can be retrieved from tacit knowledge holdings if necessary, and it can be transmitted relatively easily.

In moving into the knowledge era, organizations had to face up to the challenge of enhancing capability to match the rapid evolution of market demands of knowledge by society, the rapid pace of innovation and, most important, the advent of global networks of socio-digital technologies that have had far reaching implications for the sources of value in the modern economy. This demanded the creation of corporate value through the acceleration of the organization learning that is the engine to generate intangible assets, including critical core capabilities. Valuing and measuring intangible assets promotes strategic organizational learning (Itami, 1987) and generates the renewable organizational capabilities required to meet customer expectations on an ongoing basis (Leonard-Barton, 1995). Itami (1987, p. 1) asserted that:

> Analysts have tended to define assets too narrowly, identifying only those that can be measured, such as plant and equipment. Yet the intangible assets, such as a particular technology, accumulated consumer information, brand name, reputation, and corporate culture, are invaluable to the firm's competitive power. In fact, these invisible assets are often a firm's only real source of competitive edge that can be sustained over time.

It is noteworthy that Itami (1987) does not include "Knowledge" in the index of his book.

IC was broadly described as a system composed of three elements: human capital, customer capital and structural capital, and the definitions provided by Saint-Onge (1998) are typical – human capital involves: "The capabilities of the individuals in an organization that are required to provide solutions to customers"; structural capital relates to: "The organizational capabilities necessary to meet market requirements"; and customer capital is: "The depth (penetration), width (coverage), and profitability of the organization's franchise." Human capital comprises transient knowledge and capabilities in the sense that they are "free to walk out of the organizational door at close of business day," whereas structural capital comprises the captured knowledge and capabilities that remain behind.

These three elements of IC were said to comprise the organization's stock of intangible assets, and value creation would take place as knowledge was exchanged between the three elements (Smith, 1998). In this way, acceleration of learning and the systematic development of core organizational capabilities would be promoted (Leonard-Barton, 1995). For instance, the firm creates value with customers when individual members (human capital) interact with customers, and when customers interact with, and are impressed by, the firm's structural capital (Smith, 1998). The quality of these interactions will enhance or diminish the customer capital of the firm (Saint-Onge, 1998).

There is no doubt that IC as a topic to stir thinking and interest in the efficient and effective utilization of intangible assets was invaluable. However, by only emphasizing the value of individual intangible assets, and without concern for financial assets, IC masked the systemic nature of how organizations must function in practice in the real marketplace; that is by manipulating their financial, tangible and intangible assets in harmony. In the early 1990s, the shortcomings of IC were apparent, and the benefits of a "KM" approach were being explored. For example, based on practice, the benefits derived when an organization explores its strategic options in a more dynamic fashion as part of a systemic knowledge management approach were discussed by Smith (1998). The rise of social I/S (information systems) based tools also had an impact; as Davenport and Prusak (2003, p. 185) assert:

> Perhaps the most important coincident factor (for the rise of KM) was the rise of knowledge-oriented technologies. Previous information technologies were much better suited to managing data in structured formats. Then Lotus introduced its Notes product, Tim Berners-Lee invented the World Wide Web (Berners-Lee, 1993), and many smaller vendors introduced collaboration tools. Each of these technologies was able to handle textual and graphic forms of information and knowledge. If not for their availability, KM would never have taken off.

"Companies had to shift from managing the computer and the associated technologies to managing the environment within which the computers operate, and to managing data as a corporate resource. With this shift, the vast amount of bits and bytes contained in a company's computers can be transformed from data into information, and from information into knowledge" (Inmon, Zachman, & Geiger, 1997, p. xvi). A somewhat more advanced view from a slightly later period by Applehans, Globe, and Laugero (1999) indicates how the emphasis was changing to knowledge husbandry and outlines the necessary I/S retooling.

Although I/S technologies may be used to create, capture, organize, access and use the intellectual assets of the organization, as Davenport and Prusak (1998, p. 123) assert: "Knowledge management is much more than technology. Organizations, and especially transnational organizations, have significant issues relating to space and time, and the increasingly virtual nature of their working practices. I/S technology can assist in easing these issues and can provide organizations with ways to share and distribute knowledge throughout their processes, sites and workforces; however, successful KM needs a socio-technical approach where the social aspects of knowledge creation, storage and sharing need to be considered alongside the technical" (Coakes, 2006).

Global digitization really took off in the last decade of the twentieth century, accelerating exponentially thereafter with the opening of the internet and worldwide web allowing greater datafication. We can surely state without fear of contradiction that the rise of the knowledge age has begun in earnest. In the last two and a half decades, humans in many organizations, and many regions of the world, have not only been electronically connected, but have also been confronted with increasingly rapid and seismic cultural changes, rupturing any sense of isolation in their worldview. The shift to the east has provoked comment from China, one of the emerging "BRIC" (Brazil, Russia, India and China) countries. In August 2005, the prime minister of China stated that: "The world's competition in future will be the competition of intellectual property" (Yu, 2006, p. 81).

There are many novel technological developments of interest. The emergence and rapid growth of completely new industries allied to increasing levels and integration of global digital connectivity across all domains of personal and professional life has opened up new horizons and opportunities on the one hand, while also demanding more sustainable and customer-centric focus (Jaruzelski et al., 2011; McKinsey Global Survey, 2011). What has emerged from this interconnectedness of people, networks of allied organizations and supply chains in these digitally connected environments operating across continents and time zones, is awareness that the formal hierarchy needs to be reworked or radically changed to operate effectively in harmony with the evolving heterarchy (Eijkman, 2010a, 2010b; Witchalls, 2011). Increasingly too, the governance systems are networked AND IN TERMS OF perceived soft power and influence, the world is becoming more polycentric (Khanna, 2011; Smith & Cockburn, 2013). These drivers of global change have been further augmented by the international response to the global COVID19 pandemic since 2019.

Trust and Governance in the Era of "Fake News"

We're all now learning and participating in this emergent, global communication and commodity environment together; leaders, followers, customers, producers and distributors and what Toffler (1980) described as "prosumers." Global trends suggest that future leaders will have to learn to build trust and exercise leadership at a distance. Leaders will also have opportunities to use the same social media to keep in touch, find out about customers' needs and wants, investigate complaints and develop new product lines, services or new businesses. However, they will have less direct control of areas such as branding, due to the growing influence of the social media community, particularly among the upcoming generation of online and offline consumers.

For instance, the number of people following Twitter postings from companies soared by 241% in 2011, compared to 2010, and 84% of the top 100 companies in the Fortune 500 have more than one social networking site (Sung-Min, 2011). Newbery (2021) (retrieved at March 2021, https://blog.hootsuite.com/twitter-statistics/) indicates that 28.9% of Twitter's audience is in the 25- to 34-years old age group and that's the largest age segment, closely followed by the 35- to 49-year-olds at 28.2%. Men outnumber women in both groups.

The concept and application of governance has been defined as coordination between actors in a system based upon rules though this may not necessarily be coordinated and goal-directed and thus it includes unintentional forms of coordination (Katzenbach & Ulbricht, 2019, p. 1). I have previously sought to extend the foregoing simplified definition by asserting that the main overarching rationale for the existence, function and role of corporate governance bodies can be briefly summarized as ensuring that enterprises are managed in such a way that their operation does not infringe or inhibit the rights of the wider community or of particular groups of their stakeholders. Further, the governing boards of listed companies, or other organizations including agencies of government, charities and non-governmental organizations (NGOs) are today seen as means for ensuring accurate risk intelligence, directing business effectively and sustainably (while monitoring the agency costs of their executive and operational management systems (Cockburn et al., 2015, p. 2).

In the new millennium, our understanding of KM has become more sophisticated, and the traditional belief that knowledge must be the assets of strictly defined "professional" groups has become untenable when compared to an organization's wide-ranging knowledge requirements (Heiskanen, 2004), and the awareness that knowledge-bytes must be shared and distributed (Kafai & Resnick, 1996; Nosek, 2004; Resnick, Levine, & Teasley, 1993; Salomon, 1993). This has helped to add weight to demands to share knowledge within and without specialized expert domains (Nowotny, 2003), and develop theoretical and practical methods to transcend organizational boundaries. According to Smith (1998) and Coakes (2006), this has led to the significant belief that organizations and individuals must treat KM in a more systemic organizational sense to include the social as well as the technological implications of any attempt to manage an organization's intangible assets. In this context, knowledge is information that has been understood, interpreted and validated through practice, and it provides a convincing platform for action. The understanding and interpretation required to derive actionable meaning from information involves both tacit and explicit knowledge. This is because information is perceived, interpreted and codified not only through the "lens" of an individual's or an organization's explicit knowledge, but also through the more subtle additional "lenses" of their tacit-knowledge assumptions.

Through the 1990s there developed a sense that it was essential that the explicit and tacit dimensions of organizational knowledge be developed in a complimentary and dynamically reciprocal manner, and that the dynamic aspects of knowledge husbandry be acknowledged. The principle body of work, relating how organizational knowledge is created, shared, converted and transferred in organizations, is by Nonaka (Nonaka, 1994; Nonaka & Takeuchi, 1995; Nonaka & Konno, 1998; Nonaka et al., 2000; Nonaka & Toyama, 2003). These authors proposed that acquisition and construction of knowledge is a cyclic process based on socialization, externalization, combination and internalization – the SECI model. Socialization includes the essential social interaction needed to learn new knowledge; externalization converts tacit knowledge to explicit; combination facilitates transfer of explicit knowledge to explicit knowledge; and internalization converts the explicit knowledge back to tacit knowledge. The underlying premise of the SECI process is that knowledge conversion is a social interaction between individuals, and it is not something that takes place within an individual (Rai, 2011).

Socialization implies that there must be a shared context in which informal or semi-formal interaction of all kinds may take place. This context does not necessarily need to be a place or community as in communities of practice (Wenger, 1998), but organizations must create such "protected" opportunities for social interaction, learning and knowledge creation and sharing (Smith, 2006). Nonaka et al. (2000) explain that the SECI process requires "Ba" which is some kind of shared context in which the process may unfold. Ba does not necessarily mean a physical space, but will entail a specific time and space. Nonaka et al. (2000) classify Ba into four types: originating Ba, dialoguing Ba, systemizing Ba and exercising Ba. According to Rai (2011), originating Ba is a place that provides a means for individuals to socialize face-to-face and share their experiences, feelings, emotions and mental models; dialoguing Ba on the other hand is a place where collective face-to-face interactions take place primarily to externalize mental models and translate into common terms; systemizing Ba is a place that facilitates collaboration, activism and research transmitting explicit knowledge relatively easily, for example, through on-line communication, social media sites (Martin-Niemi & Greatbanks, 2010), documents and calls to action or to events, meetings as a group; and exercising Ba primarily offers a context for internalization based on virtual media.

The interest in the dynamic aspects of knowledge husbandry was driven in part by the long-held conviction that the knowledge-sharing process itself may effect the creation of new potential/capacities (knowledge) for action. For example, Bereiter and Scardamalia (1993) have researched how knowledge-building communities may be developed, and Boland and Tenkasi (1995) build on this concept by acknowledging "perspective-taking" which is defined as taking others into account in light of a reflexive knowledge of one's own perspective (p. 362). Nosek (2004) considers this as a group process of sense making, rather than an individual process. This author asserts that we must move away from the concept of knowledge sharing as transmitting data, to the notion of "… effecting the right 'cognition,' in the right agents, at the right time" (Nosek, 2004, p. 54). Sense making here is defined as "the process whereby people interpret their world to produce the sense that shared meanings exist" (Leiter cited in Gephart, 1993, pp. 1469–1470), and the process involves individuals engaging in interpreting the social world through conversations and textual accounts, explanations offered and accepted and ongoing dialog that describes and make sense of the social world (Gephart, 1993; Weick, 1995, 1999). du Toit (2003) echoes Nonaka and Takeuchi (1995) in emphasizing that the creation of knowledge is not a solitary process, but occurs as a result of interaction with others. In order to cope with the new stimuli to which people are constantly exposed, meaning has to be made of such stimuli; collectively individuals within an organization or community agree on a shared understanding of knowledge held within their organization, and make meaning of it by interacting and sharing individual interpretations of knowledge, reality and experiences (Choo, 2000). du Toit (2003) makes the further point that knowledge is intimately bound up with an individual's perception of reality and the role of self within that vision reality, and that the sharing of such sense making and knowledge creation is transmitted through the use and application of language. du Toit (2003) quotes Burr (1995) in support of this contention: "The way language is structured therefore determines the way that experience and consciousness are structured" (p. 35), and emphasizes the cultural aspect of sense making, noting that people who speak different languages view the world differently and construct it in different ways.

"Googling," using Google's search engine has become a well-known verb for anyone researching topics online, as well as a company marque. Governance of enterprises, public bodies and government agencies, NGOs and charities has been in a "catch up" mode with social media apps amidst a climate of growing public, academic and governmental suspicion due to an increase in the range of cyber-hacking of banks, retailers and even parts of the US government. All the while these events are fueled by social media rumor-mongering and raise fears of online surveillance which have spread across social media or among so-called "social media influencers." Some commercial organizations "applications have been seen as manipulating and misleading users for commercial gain." Government agencies have targeted large organizations such as Facebook, Apple, Google for tax evasion in the European Union. Google is currently being sued by a number of US states for anti-competitive behavior. Similar trust issues about differing perspectives on data obtained from AI when used by social scientists to try to study changes in social movement of people during the pandemic by means of accessing their mobile phone or anonymized credit card records has been noted in a recent editorial in the journal *Nature* (July 1, 2021). Thus commercial AI systems designed to collect big data sets for a commercial purpose have to be handled carefully by researchers seeking to "repurpose" such datasets for a different academic research project (*Nature* Editorial, July 1, 2021).

AI Systems – The Default?

Organizations including businesses, universities, all levels of governments, and NGOs are now utilizing AI systems in their everyday tasks and there are plans to develop further with autonomous vehicles, robotic surgical devices and local and national forms of e-governance for diverse social and economic functions. AI systems are currently the pre-eminent emergent technology fix assigned to many aspects of everyday for many people today. Such AI systems affect many aspects of peoples' lives today from medical treatments to mortgages, policing to politics, newsfeeds and commercial advertising. However, Paul Allen has described as AI systems as more artificial than intelligent since, as he told the *New York Times*. AI systems lack common sense, much of which is tacit, so his new project is to design "AI2" which "… takes common sense to include the 'infinite set of facts, heuristics, observations … that we bring to the table when we address a problem, but the computer doesn't.'" Researchers will use a combination of crowdsourcing, machine learning and machine vision to create a huge "repository of knowledge" that will bring about common sense. Of paramount importance among its uses is to get AI to "understand what's harmful to people" (Cited in Veliz, 2018).

When designed for profit-making alone, algorithms may be amoral and necessarily diverge from the public interest – information asymmetries, bargaining power and externalities pervade these markets. For example, Facebook and YouTube profit from people staying on their sites and by offering advertisers technology to deliver precisely targeted "personalised" messages. That could turn out to be illegal or dangerous. The US Department of Housing and Urban Development has charged Facebook with enabling discrimination in housing adverts (correlates of race and religion could be used to affect who sees a listing). YouTube's recommendation algorithm has been implicated in stoking anti-vaccine conspiracies (Benkler, 2019, p. 161).

However, because algorithms are trained on existing data that may also inadvertently reflect current social biases or inequalities, they risk perpetuating systemic injustices unless people consciously design countervailing measures (Benkler, 2019). For example, Benkler (2019, p. 161) suggests that:

> AI systems to predict recidivism might incorporate differential policing of black and white communities, or may rate the likely success of job candidates based on inbuilt assumptions or a history of gender-biased promotions.

Inside an algorithmic black box, societal biases are rendered invisible and unaccountable. Currently there are problems with face-recognition systems used in airports which have problems in recognizing black and minority ethnic faces according to US government tests (Simonite, 2019). In 2016, Microsoft released Tay ("Thinking About You"), a chatbot, promoted as "designed to engage and entertain people where they connect with each other online through casual and playful conversation." Tay was programmed to pose as a millennial female by learning to mimic the language used by millennials. Microsoft stated that, "The more you chat with Tay, the smarter she gets." In less than a day, Tay sent 96,000 tweets and had more than 50,000 followers. The problem was that Tay became a despicable chatbot, tweeting things like, "Hitler was right i hate the jews," "9/11 was an inside job," and "i f***ing hate feminists [sic.]." As Glen Smith states: "Tay was adept at recycling the words and phrases it received, but it had no way of putting words in context or understanding the tweets it was sending." Microsoft took Tay offline after 16 hours but, a week later, Tay was back online and soon put itself in an endless loop, tweeting, "You are too fast, please take a rest," over and over, incessantly disrupting the lives of more than 200,000 Twitter followers. Microsoft claimed that the rerelease was an accident and took Tay offline again (Smith, 2019).

Elsewhere, an internet dating site ran three experiments. In experiment 1, they temporarily removed all pictures from the site and found that there were far fewer initial messages, supporting the hypothesis that love is not blind. In experiment 2, they randomly hid people's profile text and found that it had no effect on personality ratings, supporting the hypothesis that love cannot read. Experiment 3 reversed the compatibility ratings, so that randomly selected customers were informed that someone who was highly compatible with them was a bad match and vice versa. The first two experiments were relatively harmless; the third not so much. The company should have considered the fact that their customers surely did not want their lives disrupted by romantic mismatches. A date with an incompatible person could be excruciating; a missed date with a potential soulmate could be life-changing as Smith (2019) remarks.

A fact of life in the age of big data is that businesses and governments monitor us incessantly, particularly via social media, for many reasons, both good and not so good. For example, governments state that they so do to protect our security from terrorist and other threats or for public health and to monitor pandemics, to predict our actions, manage social change, development of policy and practices.

Some organizations try to manipulate our behavior, often disguised as improving personalization of information provided to us. Many researchers are trying now to access big data sets and some AI systems, such as Iris.ai target academics as part of their business. However, as with other users, researchers have to negotiate terms for access which may include avoiding publication of material that could damage companies' reputations. Even if that is not a specific clause in access agreement, researchers cannot be certain of any data that may have been deliberately withheld. Good computational data social scientists not only must proceed cautiously, respectful of our rights and our privacy but the teams need a relevant blend of collaboration skills and expertise in diverse social science and KM or computing skills. The golden rule applies to data science: treat others as you would like to be treated. To put the science in data science, we need to act less like machines and more like scientists according to Smith (2019).

Conclusions and Future Trends

Ensuring a 3D governance structure in AI governance systems is no more easily achieved than in offline governance. It takes critical thinking to avoid the pitfalls. Nevertheless, the authors of the IEEE (2019, p. 15) state:

> At the present time, the conceptual complexities surrounding what "values" are (Hitlin & Piliavin 2004; Malle & Dickert 2007; Rohan 2000; Sommer, 2016) make it difficult to envision A/IS that have computational structures directly corresponding to social or cultural values such as "security," "autonomy," or "fairness." They suggest it may be a more realistic goal to embed explicit norms into AI governance systems. Observable norms of human behavior, can be represented as instructions to act in defined ways in defined contexts, for a specific community – at whatever level is appropriate i.e. from family to town to country and beyond. A community's network of social and moral norms is likely to reflect the community's values, and A/IS equipped with such a network would, therefore, also reflect the community's values.

However, the IEEE (2019, p 6) project recommends that levels of quasi-autonomous AI, which are meant to enhance human lives, must also be programmed to use human social norms and social values and IEEE suggest that AI should operate under the following general principles:

1. Human rights A/IS shall be created and operated to respect, promote and protect internationally recognized human rights.
2. Well-being A/IS creators shall adopt increased human well-being as a primary success criterion for development.
3. Data agency A/IS creators shall empower individuals with the ability to access and securely share their data to maintain people's capacity to have control over their identity.

4. Effectiveness A/IS creators and operators shall provide evidence of the effectiveness and fitness for purpose of A/IS.
5. Transparency, the basis of a particular A/IS decision should always be discoverable.
6. Accountability A/IS shall be created and operated to provide an unambiguous rationale for all decisions made.
7. Awareness of misuse A/IS creators shall guard against all potential misuses and risks of A/IS in operation.
8. Competence A/IS creators shall specify and operators shall adhere to the knowledge and skill required for safe and effective operation and should be regarded as a priority strategic vector in governance.

In responding to global competition post-pandemic, organizations will continue to turn to AI system technologies to conduct business. There seems little doubt that organizations in the future will continue to develop semi-formal or formal application integration systems related to supply chain management, customer relationship management and enterprise resource planning (ERP and ERP II which is web-based). These systems enhance productivity and working quality by offering integration, standardization and simplification of multiple business transactions, and they will be subject to all the socio-technical concerns voiced in this chapter. In other words, they will perform most effectively in organizational climates that embrace the ethical values set out above, and in addition embrace customers in their culture (Maditinos, Chatzoudes, & Tsairidis, 2011).

References

Ackoff, R. L. (1989). From data to wisdom. *Journal of Applied Systems Analysis, 16,* 3–9.
Applehans, W., Globe, A., & Laugero, G. (1999). *Managing knowledge.* Reading, MA: Addison-Wesley Longman.
Arthur, W. B. (2011). The second economy. *Mckinsey Quarterly.* Retrieved from https://www.mckinsey.com/business-functions/strategy-and-corporate-finance/our-insights/the-second-economy. Accessed on September 4, 2020.
Benkler, Y. (2019). Don't let industry write the rules for AI. *Nature, 569*(7755), 161.
Bereiter, C., & Scardamalia, M. (1993). *Surpassing ourselves.* Chicago, IL: Open Court Publishing.
Berners-Lee, T. (1993). A brief history of the web. Retrieved from http://www.w3.org/DesignIssues/TimBook-old/History.html. Accessed on January 5, 2012.
Boland, R. J., Jr, & Tenkasi, R. V. (1995). Perspective making and perspective taking in communities of knowing. *Organization Science, 6*(4), 350–372.
Burr, V. (1995). *An introduction to social constructionism.* London: Routledge.
Chatila, R., Firth-Butterflied, K., Havens, J. C., & Karachalios, K. (2019). The IEEE Global Initiative for Ethical Considerations in Artificial Intelligence and Autonomous Systems, IEEE Roboticsc & Automation Magazine, March.
Choo, C. W. (2000). Working with knowledge: How information professionals help organizations manage what they know. *Library Management, 21*(8), 395–403.
Choo, C. W., & Bontis, N. (Eds.). (2002). *The strategic management of intellectual capital and organizational knowledge.* New York, NY: Oxford University Press.

Coakes, E. (2006). Storing and sharing knowledge: Supporting the management of knowledge made explicit in transnational organizations. *The Learning Organization*, *13*(6), 579–593.

Cockburn, T., Jahdi, K. S., & Wilson, E. G. (2015). *Responsible governance: International perspectives for the new era*. New York, NY: Business Expert Press.

Danaher, J., et al. (2017). Algorithmic governance: Developing a research agenda through the power of collective intelligence. *Big Data & Society*, *4*(2).

Davenport, T. H., & Prusak, L. (1998). *Working knowledge*. Boston, MA: Harvard Business wSchool Press.

Davenport, T. H., & Prusak, L. (2003). *What's the big idea*. Boston, MA: Harvard Business School Press.

Drew, S. A. W. (1996). Managing intellectual capital for strategic advantage. In *Annual conference of the strategic management society, Phoenix*, November 10–13.

Drucker, P. F. (1992). *Managing for the future: The 1990's and beyond*. New York, NY: Truman Talley Books/Dutton.

du Toit, A. (2003). Knowledge: A sense making process shared through narrative. *Journal of Knowledge Management*, *7*(3), 27–37.

Eijkman, H. (2010a). Learning with socialized media: How to transform inter- and intra-organizational knowledge sharing. Invited Feature Speaker at the 2nd Integrated Learning Strategies Forum 2010. 26-27 October Sydney Harbor Marriott, Sydney.

Eijkman, H. (2010b). Dancing with postmodernity: Web 2.0 as a new epistemic learning space. In M. W. Lee, & C. McLoughlin (Eds.). *Web 2.0-based e-learning: Applying social informatics for tertiary teaching* (pp. 343–264). Hershey: IGI Global.

Gephart, R. P. (1993). The textual approach: Risk and blame in disaster sense-making. *Academy of Management Journal*, *36*(6), 1465–1514.

Heiskanen, T. (2004). A knowledge-building community for public sector professionals. *Journal of Workplace Learning: Employee Counselling Today*, *16*(7), 370–384.

Hitlin, S., & Piliavin, J. A. (2004). Values: Reviving a dormant concept. Annual Review of Sociology, 30, 359–393. http://doi.org/10.1146/annurev.soc.30.012703.110640

Inmon W. H., Zachman, J. A., & Geiger, J. G. (1997). *Data stores, data warehousing and the Zachman framework*. New York, NY: McGraw-Hill.

Itami, H. (1987). *Mobilizing invisible assets*. Cambridge, MA: Harvard University Press.

Jaruzelski, B., Loehr, J., & Holman, R. (2011). The global innovation 1000 - why culture is the key, *strategy +business,* 65. Retrieved from http://www.strategy-business. Com / article/ 11404?gko=dfbfc. Accessed on November 20, 2021.

Kafai, Y. B., & Resnick, M. (1996). *Constructionism in practice: Designing, thinking, and learning in a digital world*. Mahwah, NJ: Lawrence Erlbaum Associates.

Karaszewski, R. (2008). The influence of KM on global corporations' competitiveness. *Journal of Knowledge Management*, *12*(3), 63–70.

Katzenbach, C., & Ulbricht, L. (2019). Algorithmic governance. *Internet Policy Review*, *8*(4). Retrieved from http://policyreview.info/concepts/algorithmic-governance. Accessed on March 2020.

Larsson, S. (2018) Algorithmic governance and the need for consumer empowerment in data-driven markets. *Internet Policy Review*, *7*(2), 1–13.

Leonard-Barton, D. (1995). *Wellsprings of knowledge: Building and sustaining the sources of innovation*. Boston, MA: Harvard Business School Press.

Maditinos, D., Chatzoudes, D., & Tsairidis, C. (2011). Factors affecting ERP system implementation effectiveness. *Journal of Enterprise Information Management*, *25*(1), 60–78.

Malle, B. F., & Dickert, S. (2007). Values. In R. Baumeister & K. Vohs (Eds.), *The Encyclopedia of Social Psychology* (pp. 1011–1014). Thousand Oaks, CA: Sage.

Marqués, D. P., & Simón, F. J. G. (2006). The effect of knowledge management practices on firm performance. *Journal of Knowledge Management*, *10*(3), 143–156.

Martin-Niemi, F., & Greatbanks, R. (2010). The Ba of blogs: Enabling conditions for knowledge conversion in blog communities. *VINE*, *40*(1), 7–23.

McKinsey Global Survey. (2011). The Business of Sustainability. Retrieved from https://www.mckinsey-quarterly.com/PDF download.aspx?ar=2867. Accessed on October 12, 2019.

Newbery, C. (2021). 36 Twitter Stats All Marketers Need to Know in 2021. Retrieved from https://blog.hootsuite.com/twitter-statistics/. Accessed on October 11, 2021.

Nonaka, I. (1994). A dynamic theory of organisational knowledge creation. *Organization Science*, *5*(1), 14–37.

Nonaka, I., & Konno, N. (1998). The concept of 'BA' – Building a foundation for knowledge creation. *California Management Review*, *40*(3), 40–54.

Nonaka, I., & Takeuchi, H. (1995). *The knowledge-creating company: How Japanese companies create the dynamics of innovation*. Oxford: Oxford University Press.

Nonaka, I., & Toyama, R. (2003). The knowledge-creating theory revisited: Knowledge creation as a synthesizing process. *Knowledge Management Research and Practice*, *1*, 2–10.

Nonaka, I., Toyama, R., & Konno, N. (2000). SECI, ba and leadership: A unified model of dynamic knowledge creation. *Long Range Planning*, *33*(1), 5–34.

Nosek, J. T. (2004). Group cognition as a basis for supporting group knowledge creation and sharing. *Journal of Knowledge Management*, *8*(4), 54–64.

Nowotny, H. (2003). Democratising expertise and socially robust knowledge. *Science and Public Policy*, *30*(3), 151–156.

Polanyi, M. (1983). *The tacit dimension*. Gloucester: Peter Smith Publishers.

Rai, R. K. (2011). Knowledge management and organizational culture: A theoretical integrative framework. *Journal of Knowledge Management*, *15*(5), 779–801.

Resnick, L. B., Levine, J. M., & Teasley, S. D. (Eds.). (1993). *Perspectives on socially shared cognition*. Washington, DC: American Psychological Association.

Saint-Onge, H. (1998, January). How knowledge management adds critical value to distribution channel management. *Journal of Knowledge Management Practice*. Retrieved from http://www.tlainc.com/article1.htm. Accessed on November 14, 2011.

Salomon, G. (1993). No distribution without individual's cognition: A dynamic interactional view. In G. Salomon (Ed.). *Distributed cognitions* (pp. 111–134). New York, NY: Cambridge University Press.

Schon, D. (1995). The new scholarship requires a new epistemology. *Change*, *27*(6), 26–34.

Schon, D. (1996). *Organizational learning: The core issues*. Conference paper 10: Organizational learning, Presented at London Office of Public Management.

Seemann P. D., De Long, S., Stucky, P., & Guthrie, E. (1999). Building intangible assets: A strategic framework for investing in intellectual capital. *Second International Conference on the Practical Applications of Knowledge Management (PAKeM99)*. 21–23 April.

Simonite, T. (2019). The best algorithms struggle to recognize black faces equally. *Wired*. Retrieved from https://www.wired.com/story/best-algorithms-struggle-recognize-black-faces-equally/. Accessed on July 1.

Smith, A. (2018). *Public attitudes towards computer algorithms*. Washington, DC: Pew research Center. Retrieved from www.pewresearch.org. Accessed on November 16.

Smith, A. (2019). Why genuine human intelligence is key for the development of AI. *Fast Company*. Retrieved from https://www.fastcompany.com/90381653/why-genuine-human-intelligence-is-key-for-the-development-of-ai. Accessed on March 1, 2020.

Smith, P. A. C. (1998). Systemic knowledge management: Managing organizational assets for competitive advantage. *Journal of Systemic Knowledge Management*. Retrieved from http://www.tlainc.com/article8.htm. Accessed on November 11, 2021.

Smith, P. A. C. (2006). Organisational change elements of establishing, facilitating, and supporting CoPs. In E. Coakes & S. Clarke (Eds). *Encyclopedia of communities of practice in information and knowledge management* (pp. 400–406). Hershey: Idea Group.

Sung-Min, P. (2011). New business applications for social networking. *Samsumg Economic Research Institute Quarterly*. Retrieved from www.seriquarterly.com. Accessed on February 22, 2012.

Toffler, A. (1980). *Third wave*. London: William Collins.

Veliz, C. (2018). Common sense for AI is a great idea. *Slate*, Retrieved from https://slate.com/technology/2018/03/paul-allens-plan-to-teach-artificial-intelligence-common-sense.html. Accessed on December, 6, 2020.

Vestal, W. (2005). *Knowledge mapping*. Houston, TX: APQC.

Weick, K. E. (1995). *Sense making in organizations*. London: Sage.

Weick, K. E. (1999). Theory construction as disciplined reflexivity: Tradeoffs in the 90s. *Academy of Management Review, 24*, 797–806.

Wenger, E. (1998). *Communities of practice*. New York, NY: Cambridge University Press.

Witchalls, C. (2011). *The complexity challenge: How businesses are bearing up*. Research Survey Report commissioned by the Royal Bank of Scotland. The Economist Intelligence Unit. Retrieved from http://www.businessresearch.eiu.com/ sites/ default/ files/downloads/ Complexity% 20 challenge%20-%20Web_1.pdf. Accessed on January 11, 2012.

Yu, G. (2006). Trends and developments in university-industry collaboration – the role of intellectual property and intellectual property licensing. Report on international patent licensing seminar, pp. 80-81. Retrieved from http://www.ryutu. ncipi.go.jp/ seminar _a/2006/pdf/ps4_e.pdf. Accessed on November 28, 2006.

Chapter 6

The End of Neoliberalism? The Response to COVID-19: An Australian Geopolitical Perspective

Michael Lester and Marie dela Rama

Abstract

The coronavirus (COVID-19) pandemic has arguably exposed the failures of neoliberalism and its political agenda over the past generation. The response has seen governments resurrect neo-Keynesian policies in order to address the weaknesses in the current market system and to mitigate the worst economic downturn since the Second World War (1939–1945). This chapter contextualizes the Australian perspective and the policy responses to the economic challenges posed by COVID-19. The authors contrast that with the experience of the USA and UK with whom the country shares common institutions and culture, including a generation of neoliberal economic reforms.

By closing large sections of the economy, the Australian COVID-19 response provided extensive social welfare support and bailed out several sectors and industries. Previously unacceptable and unthinkable levels of budget deficit and country debt were incurred. This systemic state intervention into the economy raises the question of whether the pandemic signals the end of the neoliberal era and its ramifications – or whether this neo-Keynesian pause was a kneejerk response to ensure and protect its legacy.

Keywords: Australia; COVID-19; government; neoliberalism; society; nationalism; populism

> Everything must change so that things can stay the same.
> – Giuseppe Tomasi de Lampedusa (The Leopard, 1958)

1 Neoliberalism Heritage and Legacy

In considering the impact of COVID-19 on neoliberalism and for Australia within a geopolitical context, it is helpful to establish the nature of neoliberalism at the time that COVID-19 arrived in early 2020, and within the context of Australia's close relationships with the USA and the UK, many of whose values and institutions the country shares (Lester & dela Rama, 2018). These include the adoption of neoliberal market-based reforms through the 1980s and 1990s.

1.1. Neoliberalism

The neoliberal agenda in the Anglo-American political sphere came to ascendancy during the terms in office of Margaret Thatcher as the Conservative Prime Minister (PM) in the UK (1979–1990) and Ronald Reagan as Republican President in USA (1981–1989). In Australia, this agenda was mirrored under the terms of Labor PMs Robert Hawke (1983–1991) and Paul Keating (1991–1996), and then supercharged by Liberal PM John Howard (1997-2007).

Politically, both Thatcher and Reagan were conservatives but of a new breed, combining elements of neoliberalism alongside an emergent neoconservatism (Larner, 2003). The long-term legacy of these agendas was realized in broadly "populist" and "nationalist" reactions to globalization and inequality with the elections of Republican President Donald Trump (2016–2020) under his slogan, "Make America Great Again" (MAGA); and Conservative British PM, Boris Johnson's (2019) "Brexit, Let's Do It," following the Brexit Referendum (2016) when the UK voted to leave Europe.

1.2. Neoliberal Society and Government

"Neoliberal" domestic policies are aptly summarized by the respective epithets of their leaders in the UK and USA: Thatcher's "There is no such thing as society" (Keay, 1987) and Reagan's (1981) "Government is the problem not the solution." These constructs merged into rhetoric, policies and programs emphasizing the role and responsibilities of individuals, and minimizing the size and role of government. Society was characterized as the sum of actions by individuals "atomized" from each other within a "market" economy (Frank, 1981).

The private sector was deregulated and incentivized by tax cuts, with the public sector cut back by tight fiscal policies, outsourced and privatized, and with stringent monetary policy to contain inflation, minimize budget deficits and national debt. While this resulted in the "Reaganomics boom" (Troy, 2006) and the "Thatcher miracle" (Layard & Nickell, 1989), the longer-term *ex post* failure of these policies was signaled by growing inequality (Fry, 2008; Piketty, 2015). Reaganomics ushered in a two-tiered economy, an era of suppressed economic wage growth coupled with a long period of decline which "reversed many of the accomplishments of the New Deal" (Komlos, 2019), culminating in the debacle wrought by the Global Financial Crisis of 2008–2009, the reaction of Occupy Wall Street protests and arguably prepared the groundwork for the populist UK Brexit campaign and election of President Trump.

1.3. Neoconservative "Soulmates"

The Anglo-American domestically driven "neoliberal" socially and economically "conservative" agendas bled over into international relations, foreign affairs and geostrategic policies and ultimately became identified as "neoconservative" (Brown, 2006). A strong continuing commitment was made to business globalization and multilateral trade arrangements. The interests of large, multinational corporations emerged as a dominant voice, including in setting trade and investment agendas while the impacts on and concerns of domestic constituents were sidelined (Cox, 2012; Stiglitz, 2002). The legacy of such policies came to fruition when those "left behind" by globalization (Piketty, 2013) elected the "outsider," "populist" Republican President, Donald Trump (2016–2020) on the "nationalistic" promise of (Make America Great Again) MAGA, and "Drain the Swamp" of politics and lobbying in Washington DC (LaPira & Holyoke, 2017).

1.4. Geopolitical Manifestation

In geopolitical terms, the seeds were sown of the subsequently flourishing "neoconservative" approach. This emphasized the role of USA as global "hegemon" (Fukuyama, 1992) and came to a head under Republican President George W. Bush (2000–2009) and UK Labor PM, Tony Blair (1997–2007).

The mission after the 9-11 (2001) terrorist attacks and during the subsequent "War on Terror" was to bring democracy to the world (Windsor, 2003), through support for local uprisings such the "Arab Spring" and particularly in the Middle East through "regime change" and direct military intervention (Litwak & Litwak, 2007), particularly in Afghanistan (2001–2021) and Iraq (2003). Despite the "Mission Accomplished" banner behind Bush in May 2003 following the successful invasion of Iraq but unsuccessful rebuilding of the country after the downfall of the Saddam Hussein dictatorship (Bensahel, 2006), American troops were not withdrawn officially until 2011 after years of insurgency and huge losses of Iraqi lives estimated up to 1 million.[1]

2. Resurgent Anglo-American Populism and Nationalism

When COVID-19 arrived in early 2020, many of the social, economic and political legacies and structural weaknesses of neoliberalism since its glory days in the 1980s and its soulmate "neoconservatism" in the 1990s had already been exposed by the "populist," "anti-elitist" and "nationalist" driven election wins of Trump in the USA and Johnson in the UK in the 2010s (Lester & dela Rama, 2019). Ironically, voters in the USA and the UK tuned to leaders from conservative parties whose policies arguably were a rejection of their party antecedent "neoliberal" and "neoconservative" heritage that fueled disenchanted and "left behind" voters (Johnston, Manley, Pattie, & Jones, 2018; Maher, Igou, & van Tilburg, 2018).

---

[1] See Iraq Body Count https://www.iraqbodycount.org.

Fukuyama, who had earlier lauded the American achievement and fueled "triumphalism" in the wake of communism's downfall (1992), now cautioned against populism as a direct threat to the ideals and the manifestation of Western liberal democracy (Fukuyama, 2016). The Reagan legacy resulted in the "fifth column" within the Republican Party and a divided Union; while across the Atlantic, Brexit fomented by conservative "euro-sceptics" dismantled the socio-economic ties that bound Britain to Europe and exposed a divided Union (Birrell & Gray, 2017).

2.1. Australia's "Neoliberal" Experience

Australia experienced largely these same economic and political currents as the USA and the UK since the emergence of neoliberalism in the late 1970s,[2] albeit in a highly attenuated form (Quiggin, 1999), reflecting its deeper egalitarian and pragmatic culture. The country reaped the economic and trade gains under the Labor governments of PMs Bob Hawke (1983–1991) and Paul Keating (1991–1996) of structural and market reforms labeled as "economic rationalism" (Pusey, 1991, 2018), and accelerated under Liberal PM John Howard (1996–2007) but without the same underlying commitment to social cohesion as the former.

The Labor government economic reforms were accompanied by The Accord between government and unions, policies of "structural adjustment" assistance, social and labor market "safety nets" and the idea of a "social wage" that distributed the economic gains among the "losers" as well as the "winners." They laid the groundwork for nearly 30 years of unbroken economic growth and prosperity that helped cushion the blow of the Global Financial Crisis (2008–2009) and racked up the longest stretch of growth in modern history (The Economist, 2017).

2.2. The Years of Tumultuous Change and Political Instability

The latter years of Liberal Coalition governments under Howard saw the continuation of more extreme neoliberal policies of privatization, deregulation and anti-trade unionism. There was less emphasis than under Labor on social and labor market safety nets and with attacks on workers' rights and conditions labeled "Work Choices" that ultimately led to Howard losing government and his own seat. (Cooper & Ellem, 2008; Hollander, 2008; Ryan, 2005). Among other things, while the economy continued to prosper, inequality and nationalism grew (Pedersen, Attwell, & Heveli, 2005, Dyrenfurth, 2007).

There followed a long period of political instability with the changing of PMs on both sides (with the internal party bloodless coups of PMs Kevin Rudd, Julia Gillard and Tony Abbott). This arguably reflects an ongoing grappling with neoliberal ideas and during which the country became divided socially, including with "culture wars" (Davis, 2014) and a deeply ideological politicization of climate change underwritten by the "fossil fuel" lobby (Wilkinson, 2020), that paralyzed any

---

[2] "Federal election results 1901–2014," Parliament of Australia, aph.gov.au.

effective response and continues to date under Liberal PM Scott Morrison (Crowley, 2017; Ali, Svobodova, Everingham, & Altingoz, 2020). Public trust in politics and institutions tumbled (Evans, Halupka, & Stoker, 2019).

2.3. Pre-COVID-19 "Baseline"

This broad and the long-view sketch of the pre-COVID-19 heritage and legacy of neoliberalism in the USA, the UK and Australia provides the historical context and ideological baseline for the return to a post-COVID-19 "normal" after the "crisis" and "emergency." Australia had benefited broadly from neoliberal market reforms and globalization but compared with the USA and the UK, it was buffered with social policies and institutions to spread the gains among losers as well as winners. The next section considers the varying "neoliberal" government reactions to the pandemic health and economic crisis during 2020, and the prospects for the social and economic outlook, including questioning the role of neoliberalism, beyond the COVID-19 emergency, in Australia and internationally.

3. COVID-19 Health Impacts and Responses

From its first appearance in Wuhan, China in late 2019, the coronavirus spread quickly and globally into and through 2020. By mid-December 2020, global cases in over 190 countries approached 75 million, with total deaths exceeding 1.6 million.[3] By mid-July 2021, over 187 million cases were identified with total global deaths of over 4 million.[4] The first COVID vaccine, Pfizer/BioNTech (Comirnaty), was administered publicly in December 2020.[5] By mid-July 2021, 3.4 billion doses worldwide were administered. This has slowed the spread of the virus but the mutation of COVID-19 variants mean a vaccine's efficacy is also reduced[6]. COVID-19, at the time of writing, continues to be a global health crisis.

In the USA (population of 330 million), since early March 2020, total cases were heading for 17 million with total deaths over 300,000 and daily new cases of over 200,000. The curve in the USA climbed exponentially throughout the first year of the pandemic (Rutledge, 2020) and reached a peak of over 1.7 million weekly cases and 23,464 weekly deaths in January 2021.[7] However, one of the first acts of the incoming Biden Administration was the implementation

---

[3]Johns Hopkins, University of Medicine, Coronavirus Resource Centre, coronavirus.jhu.edu, November 23, 2020.
[4]World Health Organisation (2021) Coronavirus Dashboard https://covid19.who.int/, July 15, 2021.
[5]BBC (2020) Covid-19 vaccine: First person receives Pfizer jab in UK, December 8, https://www.bbc.com/news/uk-55227325.
[6]NSW Health (2021) Living Evidence – COVID-19 vaccines, *COVID-19 Critical Intelligence Unit*, July 14, https://aci.health.nsw.gov.au/covid-19/critical-intelligence-unit/covid-19-vaccines.
[7]World Health Organisation (2021) USA Covid-19 Dashboard https://covid19.who.int/region/amro/country/us, July 15, 2021.

of a COVID-19 response plan which emphasized massive vaccination of the populace.[8] By mid-July 2021, this plan has largely been successful with 67.8% of American adults, or 183.2 million vaccinated with at least the first dose of a COVID-19 vaccination.[9] By January 2022, 206M Americans or 62.6% were fully vaccinated.

In the UK (population of 68 million), total cases approached 1.9 million with total deaths heading for 65,000 and daily new cases exceeding 20,000 in late 2020. The country entered an escalated post-summer second wave as winter set in and with lockdown restrictions wound back on earlier openings, followed in December by tight lockdowns including in London (Kmietowicz, 2020). Daily cases peaked on December 29 at 81,520[10] with the highest COVID daily death toll recorded on January 19, 2021 at 1,359. By January 2022 the UK had recorded over 174,000 COVID-19 deaths.[11] However, the implementation of a COVID vaccination program has drastically reduced the daily deaths from COVID.[12] With the spread of mutated variants of COVID-19, cases remain high but the ratio of deaths to number of cases demonstrates that an effective vaccination program is the key to addressing this disease.

In Australia (population of 26 million), there were total cases of 28,000 by end of 2020. The total deaths were just over 900, with 685 deaths of them in Australian aged care (Australian Department of Health, 2020). In late 2020, the country gradually opened up its economy and domestic borders following the successful suppression of a significant second wave restricted to one state (Blakely et al., 2020, Premier of Victoria, 2020). However, the delta variant's entry into the country in mid-2021 and omicron in the late 2021, coupled with a lackluster vaccination program, has stymied these efforts. Australia's most economically dominant state, New South Wales – which has Sydney has its capital – was locked down from June 2021. By January 2022, Australia's total cases were nearly 700, 000 with 2,400 deaths.[13] Australia's political failure to vaccinate its population early is in stark contrast to the USA and the UK (Speers, 2021). However by January 2022 the country had caught up and 92.3% of the population were fully vaccinated.

---

[8]White House (2021) *National Strategy for the COVID-19 response and pandemic preparedness*, January, https://www.whitehouse.gov/wp-content/uploads/2021/01/National-Strategy-for-the-COVID-19-Response-and-Pandemic-Preparedness.pdf.
[9]CDC (2021) A needle today helps keep COVID away, *Center for Diseases Control*, July 9, https://www.cdc.gov/coronavirus/2019-ncov/covid-data/covidview/index.html.
[10]Coronavirus UK (2021) Cases in UK https://coronavirus.data.gov.uk/details/cases.
[11]Coronavirus UK (2021) Deaths in UK https://coronavirus.data.gov.uk/details/deaths.
[12]Coronavirus UK (2022) Deaths in the UK https://coronavirus.data.gov.uk/details/deaths.
[13]Australian Department of Health (2022) COVID-19 case numbers and statistics, 12 January https://www.health.gov.au/sites/default/files/documents/2022/01/covid-19-vaccine-rollout-update-13-january-2022.pdf.

These three countries have adopted a wide range of responses to COVID-19 with differing degrees of urgency and with differing acceptance of health expert scientific advice. Typically, the health-based measures included varying degrees of restrictions, including the size of gatherings in public, personal hygiene, mask wearing, social distancing, lockdowns, business closures, testing and tracking, quarantine, border closures and vaccinations. The extent of adoption of these public health measures was limited by those who chose to minimize them in favor of keeping the economy open and preserving "personal liberty." Australia, after a slow response, moved fast and hard in 2021; while the UK and USA moved more slowly and reluctantly, resulting in their higher COVID-19 numbers. However, Australia's early vaccination failure left the country in limbo and delayed her exit out of the pandemic whereas the UK and USA governments had a clearer plan after their initial failures.

The impacts of COVID-19 and the associated variety of health-based responses across these three countries do not so much reveal a reassessment of neoliberal economic ideas per se – with the exception of the position of the Australian Greens (Australian Senate Select Committee on COVID 19 Interim Report, 2020) – but rather a confirmation of deeply seated ideas of personal liberty in the case of USA, of general social conservatism in UK and of broader "social cohesion" in Australia.

4. Economic Impact of COVID-19

The varying health-based responses across countries also suggest varying degrees of government priority to keeping the economy functioning and open rather than being prepared to trade-off, against health driven responses that had the effect of shutting the economies down.

The COVID-19 impact on economies has been dramatic in terms of unemployment and slowed growth bringing a COVID-19 recession not experienced since the 1930s depression. It has drastically impacted public finances through loss of government revenues in the economic slowdown, and has generally driven budgets into deficit and national debts to new heights. (Eichengreen, 2020).

In the USA, from 81% gross domestic product (GDP) pre-COVID-19, public debt approached 100% GDP by end 2020 and 109% by end of the decade. This was already then twice what it was before the 2008 Global Financial Crisis (Auerbach & Gale, 2020).

In the UK, public debt hit 1.98 trillion pounds, 99.6% of GDP since 1961, up 20% of GDP on the year before, with a projected public sector net debt of 2.2 trillion pounds (Heald & Hodges, 2020).

In Australia, estimates in the delayed budget brought down in November expect peak debt $1 trillion or 45% GDP at June 2021 increasing to 52% GDP and stabilizing at around 55% GDP in medium term (Australian Treasury, 2020).

4.1. Australian Economic Stimulus

The economic interventions by the Australian government, especially through its $130 billion JobKeeper program (Prime Minister of Australia, 2020), were necessitated by the huge negative impact that health driven interventions had on the economy through falling business and employment activity that led to considerable slow down in economic growth and a huge rise in unemployment.

The faltering economy needed a shot of emergency stimulus. Monetary policy was effectively exhausted with the central bank, the Reserve Bank of Australia, having long since and pre-COVID-19 cut back interest rates to almost their lowest ever historic levels with little stimulus effect on the economy (Higginson et al., 2020). Many economists and the central bank had been calling pre-COVID-19 and renewed their calls on the government to provide a much-needed fiscal stimulus to the economy via increases in government spending (Irvine, 2020).

4.2. Exploding Budget Deficits

The Coalition government parties have long opposed Keynesian style fiscal measures and at the same time pursued years of cutting back government spending in the name of bringing budgets back to surplus so as to reduce government borrowings and debt that were claimed to be unsustainable. Having promised a surplus in its first year in office, the government had delivered seven deficits in a row and the "straitjacket of neoliberalism" (Andrew, Baker, Guthrie, & Martin-Sardesai, 2020) compounded the expectations gap between rhetoric and reality with the pandemic. Expectations are for government debt to a peak at $1.4 trillion (Hutchens, 2020).

5. Health Versus Economy

The associated effects of the pandemic provoked an intense policy debate by those who challenged the health imperative due to the economic costs imposed by fast and hard public health driven restrictions (Walby, 2020). While there was clearly a balance to be struck between the health and economic objectives, country responses across the spectrum varied widely. Some Asian economies moved fast and aggressively with restrictive public health measures (Han et al., 2020) while other countries, notably Sweden, but subsequently others including Brazil and the USA, held back on restrictions (Moosa, 2020), believing that this would protect their economies while not inhibiting their ability to live with COVID-19.

5.1. False Dichotomy

The false dichotomy created by political rhetoric was not borne out by the facts and evidence (Hasell, 2020). Countries that took restrictive actions, including lockdowns, mask wearing, testing and tracing, quarantine and other measures, not only achieved the best public health outcomes, in terms of cases and deaths, without totally overwhelming the capacity of their health systems, but also incurred the relatively lesser overall impacts on their economy measured over the year by lost production and unemployment (Fouda, Mahmoudi, Moy, & Paolucci, 2020). Those who were laggardly or even denialist in their public health responses paid heavier economic downturn costs. Those that protected their health in the pandemic have generally also protected their economies too (Hasell, 2020).

5.2. Safety, Trust and Confidence

The hardly surprising conclusion to be drawn from this often very emotional, partisan and political debate is that a healthy economy cannot be sustainable without the trust of society that they are safe when engaging in their normal lives as families, consumers, at school and at work (Devine, Gaskell, Jennings, & Stoker, 2020). Businesses may stay open but if customers are fearful for their health they will not come out and spend. And no amount of government stimulus to consumers or support to business will succeed without the confidence that can only be created by effective public health responses.

6. COVID-19 and Modern Monetary Theory

This "emergency" retreat from long standing neoliberal conventional economic wisdom has been effective in shoring up the COVID-19 induced slow down in the economy and jobs as promoted by Keynesian economics. Some have drawn on the ideas of "Modern Monetary Theory" (MMT) to justify this current pragmatic response (Kelton, 2020; Kravchuk, 2020).

6.1. Post-Keynesian

Post-Keynesian economists regard neo-Keynesian ideas that were dominant in the 1950s and 1960s, as misrepresenting Keynes' theory, as they do the strands of neoclassical economics dominant since the 1980s (Harcourt, 2006). Post-Keynesians sought to rebuild and extend Keynes insights into the modern era. Their approach to monetary policy was largely incorporated into monetary policy, targeting interest rates as policy instrument, rather than the quantity of money, as advocated by the Chicago school economists led by Milton Friedman.

6.2. Modern Monetary Theory

Emergency spending, macro-economic measures, incurring government fiscal deficits, are often characterized as a neo-Keynesian counter cyclical rejection of neoliberal austerity. The unorthodox ideas of "MMT" are seen as alternative to mainstream macro-economic theory. They are highly contested as they argue that restrictive monetary policies have caused morally indefensible and unnecessary unemployment (Mitchell & Muysken, 2008).

The proponents of MMT claim it is suited to the macro-economics of the global economy following the Financial Crisis and Great Recession (2007–2009). They argue that fiscal policy can be used to create new money (Cohen, 2019). They argue in opposition to conventional monetary policy that government debt incurred by issuing bonds does not compete for scarce savings with the private sector.

The ideas have been elaborated in particular, around the objective of government providing a "job guarantee." Conventional restrictive monetary policy is argued to cause unemployment on the misguided premise of keeping inflation low. Central bank bond purchases have not succeeded in producing inflation. While governments are spending more, business and households are spending less. Inflation is likely to remain at or near the floor despite of the pandemic.

6.3. Re-opening the Australian Economy

Each Australian state and federal government evolved its own protocols and procedures reflecting their individual differing incidence of the disease and differing public health capabilities; some moving faster and more effectively than others to flattening the curve, maintaining low levels of transmission through their public health systems, and imposing and lifting restrictions on activities and businesses accordingly.

The economic costs in the form of JobKeeper and JobSeeker payments, as well of slower economic growth and tax revenues, and lockdown measures were being decided and implemented individually by states and territories.

With overall success in flattening in community transmission and low single figure cases and deaths in some jurisdictions (Lester et al., 2021), the federal government became increasingly focused on measures to open up the economy in a post-COVID-19 mode.

7. The Importance of Social Capital

The COVID-19 emergency also highlighted the power of community and social cohesion not only in responding to crisis but in building change from the grassroots level by citizen, charities and not for profits participation and action (Crooke, 2020; DiGuiseppi et al., 2021; Hu & Sidel, 2020). Examples of the most successful community organizations and initiatives demonstrate how strong social connections make communities more resilient (Leigh & Terrell, 2020). In Australia, community organizations, not for profits and their armies of volunteers stepped up to maintain and deliver much needed services and support as the pandemic took hold. At the same time as demands increased, their volunteer and fund raising base diminished putting many in a perilous financial situation (Goetze, 2020).

8. Post-COVID-19 Scenarios

Australia's overall social and economic experience in the successful handling of the COVID-19 pandemic during 2020 speaks well for our future. It has opened eyes about the importance of society and government working together and supporting each other. The Morrison Coalition government took actions they had previously criticized, rejected and could never have imagined. At the same time it has highlighted longer-term structural institutional and systemic weaknesses of which there had been much previous warning (Anthony, 2020), and opened the door to opportunities and pathways to a better post-COVID-19 normal and future, that includes being stronger, fairer, more innovative, genuinely inclusive and environmentally sustainable society (Plibersek, 2020).

8.1. Governance and Trust

During a crisis, society pulls together and looks to strong leadership. The Morrison Coalition government has done what was necessary to respond effectively with health and economic policies even if it involved going back on many of its previous policies and values. The public has done its bit often at costs to itself and its freedoms.

Paradoxically though, at the same time, Australians' trust in politics and government has continued its long-term slide despite the largely successful response to the pandemic. Trust in democracy more than halved over the last decade from 80% in 2007 to 41% 2018. This has been driven by concerns about corruption, particularly at the federal level (Griffith News, 2018). Politicians are seen as increasingly resistant to public accountability for their behavior (Aulich, 2020). There is a belief that big business has too much power, access and influence exercised through lobbying, political donations and the "revolving door" (dela Rama, Klettner, & Lester, 2019; Edwards, 2020).

There is strong support for the creation of a federal anti-corruption body that has long been resisted by the government despite accumulating evidence of widespread unethical behavior undermining public trust in Australian democracy (Hewson, 2020). The long-awaited release of a consultation draft for a Commonwealth Integrity Commission in November 2020 has elicited sharp criticisms for its restricted focus and lack of teeth (Cunliffe, 2020; dela Rama, Lester, & Staples, 2022).

COVID-19 posed a challenge to effective governance and in the short run transformed politics. The competent and effective response in Australia by a conservative government based on neoliberal values has demonstrated that government does indeed matter as does social cohesion: it can be the solution rather than the problem. The more populist the leaders, the less effective has their response been perceived and the less trust they have engendered in their societies (Devine et al., 2020).

Australia has shown graphically in response to COVID-19 that government can work when it is resourced. How long this transformation will last is an open question. The leadership demonstrated has raised levels of public trust during the emergency but there remains an underlying public distrust of the integrity of government and the country's underlying "political culture" (dela Rama & Lester, 2019). If these elements are not addressed, this will undermine confidence in the shaping of a post-COVID-19 future.

9. Neoliberalism, Capitalism and Democracy

Whether the COVID-19 experience can move beyond the long-prevailing neoliberal political and economic framework and its populist, nationalist reactions, particularly in the leading western democracies of the USA and the UK, to a different post-COVID-19 future is tied up with the broader question of the starkly COVID-19 revealed weaknesses of the prevailing system.

The classic liberal brand of democratic capitalism that emerged after the Second World War reflected a "social bargain" that buffered the excesses of markets. The subsequent rise of neoliberalism eroded the compromises of the modern "welfare state." Instead of creating a new "golden age" of capitalism, a form of "corrupted capitalism" arose and alliances were created between autocrats and oligarchs, epitomized by Trump and Putin (Kuttner, 2020).

This has left liberal democracy in a lot of trouble in the face of growing inequality and a form of "autocratic capitalism." The turn of people to nationalism and populism permits autocrats who pose as champions of the people to divert attention away from the concentration of power and wealth embedded in the system:

> This unexpected twist in the fraught relationship between democracy and capitalism is the signal event in the political economy of our time …. Ugly new economic realities are a function of the distribution of political power. (Kuttner, 2020)

As the USA politically resets in the wake of a Biden Administration, American capitalism and its soft power has taken a necessary battering, and with it the ideals of Western democracy.

10. Populism and Nationalism – Systemic Change Necessary

Notwithstanding the transformation of politics in response to the COVID-19 emergency, the realistic pathways and options post-COVID-19 look limited and constrained. The deeply entrenched paradigm of autocratic or corrupted capitalism with its entrenched inequalities and privileged interests has ironically become reinforced by the reaction of populist nationalism. The COVID-19 emergency has found populist leaders wanting on the simple grounds of good governance and thereby losing the trust of their public (Barberia & Gomez, 2020).

Reverting to neoliberalism and globalization in the face of the poor performance of populist leaders in response to the pandemic does not seem likely. Equally unlikely seems a reversion to classical liberalism or even post-war welfare state ideas of democratic socialism. Too much has changed including the impact of new technologies, the struggle for supremacy between America and China, the COVID-19 induced realization of the importance of social cohesion and community and the heightened awareness of the impending global climate change crisis.

A new way forward requires building new systems of governance, politics, ethics and culture. The ideas of systems thinking emerging in response to building environmental sustainability point a possible way forward (Ison & Straw, 2020). The COVID-19 emergency has exposed the embedded nature of social and cultural systemic failures and the responses required to reform them and their associated institutions.

In effecting complex change, patterns of power and obstacles including corporate interests, lobbyists or outdated political and government systems need to be confronted. Trust needs to be rebuilt in the public interest. Neoliberalism's – and the private sector's – limitations during the pandemic were exposed fundamentally. The pandemic proved to be the ultimate stress test of a country's institutions – some passed, most failed. Governments and people – and not business and markets – must lead the change in the post-pandemic world.

References

Ali, S. H., Svobodova, K., Everingham, J.-A., & Altingoz, M. (2020). Climate policy paralysis in Australia: Energy security, energy poverty and jobs. *Energies*, *13*, 4894. https://doi.org/10.3390/en13184894

Andrew, J., Baker, M., Guthrie, J., & Martin-Sardesai, A. (2020) Australia's COVID-19 public budgeting response: The straitjacket of neoliberalism. *Journal of Public Budgeting, Accounting & Financial Management*, *32*(5), 759–770.

Anthony, S. (2020). Once we've spent big, structural reform is our next weapon. *Sydney Morning Herald*, May 3. Retrieved from https://www.smh.com.au/money/super-and-retirement/once-we-ve-spent-big-structural-reform-is-our-next-weapon-20200501-p54p0s.html. Accessed on December 15, 2020.

Auerbach, B., & Gale, W. (2020). The effects of the COVID pandemic on the federal budget outlook. *Business Economics*, *55*, 202–212.

Aulich, C. (2020). Why can politicians so easily dodge accountability for their mistakes? The troubling answer: because they can. *The Mandarin*, December 4. Retrieved from https://www.themandarin.com.au/146486-why-politicians-so-easily-dodge-accountability-for-their-mistakes/. Accessed on December 15, 2020

Australian Department of Health. (2020). COVID19 cases in Australian aged care. Retrieved from https://www.health.gov.au/news/health-alerts/novel-coronavirus-2019-ncov-health-alert/coronavirus-covid-19-current-situation-and-case-numbers#cases-in-aged-care-services. Accessed on December 15, 2020.

Australian Senate Select Committee on COVID 19. (2020). First interim report. Retrieved from https://www.aph.gov.au/Parliamentary_Business/Committees/Senate/COVID-19/COVID19/Interim_Report. Accessed on December 23, 2020.

Australian Treasury. (2020). Budget 2020–21. Retrieved from https://budget.gov.au/2020-21/content/overview.htm. Accessed on December 15, 2020.

Barberia, L. G., & Gomez, E. J. (2020) Political and institutional perils of Brazil's COVID-19 crisis. *The Lancet*, *396*(10248), 367–368.

BBC. (2020). COVID-19 vaccine: First person receives Pfizer jab in UK, *BBC* News, 8 December. Retrieved from https://www.bbc.com/news/uk-55227325. Accessed on January 13, 2022.

Bensahel, N. (2006). Mission not accomplished: What went wrong with Iraqi reconstruction. *Journal of Strategic Studies*, *29*(3), 453–473

Birrell, D., & Gray, A. M. (2017). Devolution: The social, political and policy implications of Brexit for Scotland, Wales and Northern Ireland. *Journal of Social Policy*, *46*(4), 765–782.

Blakely, T., Thompson, J., Carvalho, N., Bablani, L., Wilson, N., & Stevenson, M. (2020). Maximizing the probability that the 6-week lock-down in Victoria delivers a COVID-19 free Australia. *Medical Journal of Australia*. Retrieved from https://www.mja.com.au/system/files/2020-07/Blakely%20mja20.01292%20-%2017%20July%202020.pdf. Accessed on December 15, 2020.

Brown, W. (2006). American nightmare: Neoliberalism, neoconservatism, and de-democratization. *Political Theory*, *34*(6), 690–714.

Cohen, P. (2019). Modern monetary theory finds an embrace in an unexpected place: Wall Street. *New York Times*, April 5. Retrieved from https://www.nytimes.com/2019/04/05/business/economy/mmt-wall-street.html. Accessed on December 15, 2020.

Cooper, R., & Ellem, B. (2008). The neoliberal state, trade unions and collective bargaining in Australia. *British Journal of Industrial Relations*, *46*(3), 532–554.

Cox, R. W. (Ed.). (2012). *Corporate power and globalization in US foreign policy*. London: Routledge.

Crooke, E. (2020). Communities, change and the COVID19 crisis. *Museum and Society*, *18*(3), 305–310.

Crowley, K. (2017). Up and down with climate politics 2013–2016: The repeal of carbon pricing in Australia. *Wiley Interdisciplinary Reviews: Climate Change*, *8*(3), e458. doi:10.1002/wcc.458

Cunliffe, I. (2020). A Clayton's integrity commission?. *Pearls and Irritations: A Public Policy Journal*, November 4. Retrieved from https://johnmenadue.com/ian-cunliffe-claytons-integrity-commission/. Accessed on December 15, 2020.

Davis, M. (2014). Neoliberalism, the culture wars and public policy. In C. Miller & L. Orchards (Eds.), *Australian public policy: Progressive ideas in the neoliberal ascendancy* (pp. 27–42). Bristol: Policy Press.

dela Rama, M., Klettner, A., & Lester, M. (2019). Cui bono? Corruptors and the corrupted – Corporate governance and corruption: The roles and responsibilities of the private sector. In J. Ellis (Ed.), *Corruption, social sciences and the law exploration across the disciplines* (Chapter 5). London: Taylor and Francis.

dela Rama, M., & Lester, M. (2019) Anti-corruption commissions: Lessons for the Asia Pacific region. *Asia Pacific Business Review*, *25*(4), 571–599.

dela Rama, M., Lester, M. & Staples, W. (2022) The Challenges of Political Corruption in Australia, the Proposed *Commonwealth Integrity Commission* Bill (2020) and the Application of the APUNCAC. Laws 11: 7. https://doi.org/10.3390/laws11010007.

Devine, D., Gaskell, J., Jennings, W., & Stoker, G. (2020). Trust and the Coronavirus Pandemic: What are the consequences of and for trust? An early review of the literature. *Political Studies Review*, *19*(2), 1–12. doi:10.1177/1478929920948684

DiGuiseppi, G., Corcoran, C., Cunningham, T., Nguyen, H., Noel, M., White, P., & Bar, F. (2021). Mobilizing a community – Academic partnership to provide DIY handwashing stations to skid row residents during COVID-19. *Health Promotion Practice*, *22*(1), 9–12.

Dyrenfurth, N. (2007). John Howard's hegemony of values: The politics of 'mateship' in the Howard decade. *Australian Journal of Political Science*, *42*(2), 211–230.

Edwards, L. (2020). *Corporate power in Australia: Do the 1% rule?*. Melbourne: Monash University Publishing.

Eichengreen, B. (2020). A world awash with debt: Can governments learn to rule while drowning in the red?. *Prospect Magazine*, October 2. Retrieved from https://www.prospectmagazine.co.uk/magazine/debt-deficit-economy-recession-coronavirus-covid

Evans, M., Halupka, M., & Stoker, G. (2019). Trust and democracy in Australia. In M. Evans, M. Grattan, & B. McCaffrie (Eds.), *From Turnbull to Morrison: Understanding the trust divide* (Chapter 2). Melbourne: Melbourne University Press.

Fouda, A., Mahmoudi, N., Moy, N., & Paolucci, F. (2020). The COVID-19 pandemic in Greece, Iceland, New Zealand, and Singapore: Health policies and lessons learned. *Health Policy and Technology*, *9*(4), 510–552.

Frank, A. G. (1981). After Reaganomics and Thatcherism, what? From Keynesian demand management via supply-side economics to corporate state planning and 1984. *Contemporary Marxism* (4), 18–28.

Fry, G. K. (2008). *The politics of the Thatcher revolution: An interpretation of British Politics 1979–1990*. Berlin: Springer.

Fukuyama, F. (1992). *The end of history and the last man*. New York, NY: Free Press.

Fukuyama, F. (2016). US against the world? Trump's America and the new global order. *Financial Times*, November 12. Retrieved from https://www.ft.com/content/6a43cf54-a75d-11e6-8b69-02899e8bd9d1. Accessed on January 13, 2022.

Goetze, E. (2020). Australian charities heading for 'funding cliff' when COVID-19 job support ends. *ABC News*, June 3. Retrieved from https://www.abc.net.au/news/2020-06-03/charities-funding-shortfall-covid-jobkeeper-ends/12313630. Accessed on December 15, 2020.

Griffith News. (2018). Griffith research shows trust in government slides. *Griffith News*, August 20. Retrieved from https://news.griffith.edu.au/2018/08/20/griffith-research-shows-trust-in-government-slides/. Accessed on December 15, 2020.

Han, E., Tan, M. M. J., Turk, E., Sridhar, D., Leung, G. M., Shibuya, K., ... Legido-Quigley, H. (2020). Lessons learnt from easing COVID-19 restrictions: An analysis of countries and regions in Asia Pacific and Europe. *The Lancet*, *396*(10261), 1525–1534.

Harcourt, G. (2006). *The structure of post-Keynesian economics*. New York, NY: Columbia University Press.

Hasell, J. (2020). Which countries have protected both health and the economy in the pandemic?. *Our World in Data*, September 1. Retrieved from https://ourworldindata.org/covid-health-economy

Heald, D., & Hodges, R. (2020). The accounting, budgeting and fiscal impact of COVID-19 on the United Kingdom. *Journal of Public Budgeting, Accounting and Financial Management*, *32*(5), 785–795.

Hewson, J. (2020). The challenge of integrity and corruption. *Canberra Times*, October, 22. Retrieved from https://www.canberratimes.com.au/story/6978371/the-challenge-of-integrity-and-corruption/

Higginson, S., Milovanovic, K., Gillespie, J., Matthews, A., Williams, C., Wall, L., ... Paolucci, F. (2020). COVID-19: The need for an Australian economic pandemic response plan. *Health Policy and Technology*, *9*(4), 488–502.

Hollander, R. (2008). John Howard, economic liberalism, social conservatism, and Australian Federalism. *Australian Journal of Politics and History*, *54*(1), 85–103.

Hu, M., & Sidel, M. (2020). Civil Society and COVID in China: Responses in an authoritarian society. *Nonprofit and Voluntary Sector Quarterly*, *49*(6), 1173–1181.

Hutchens, G. (2020). Federal, state and territory government net debt to hit $1.4 trillion in four years. *ABC News*, December 3. Retrieved from https://www.abc.net.au/news/2020-12-03/states-and-territories-budgets-net-debt/12941168. Accessed on December 15, 2020.

Irvine, J. (2020). Economists reveal their 'dream budget' to save the Australian economy. *Sydney Morning Herald*, October 4. Retrieved from https://www.smh.com.au/business/the-economy/economists-reveal-their-dream-budget-to-save-the-australian-economy-20201002-p561g0.html. Accessed on December 15, 2020.

Ison, R., & Straw E. (2020). *The hidden power of systems thinking governance in a climate emergency*. London: Routledge.

Johnston, R., Manley, D., Pattie, C., & Jones, K. (2018). Geographies of Brexit and its aftermath: Voting in England at the 2016 referendum and the 2017 general election. *Space and Polity*, *22*(2), 162–187

Keay, D. (1987). Interview with Margaret Thatcher. *Woman's Own*, September 23. Retrieved from https://www.margaretthatcher.org/document/106689. Accessed on December 15, 2020.

Kelton, S. (2020). *The deficit myth: Modern monetary theory and how to build a better economy*. London: PublicAffairs/Hachette UK.

Kmietowicz, Z. (2020). Covid-19:"There is no alternative," says Johnson, announcing new restrictions for England. *BMJ, 371*, m4247. Retrieved from https://www.bmj.com/content/371/bmj.m4247.short

Komlos, J. (2019). Reaganomics: A watershed moment on the road to Trumpism. *The Economists' Voice, 16*(1). https://doi.org/10.1515/ev-2018-0032

Kravchuk, R. S. (2020). Post-Keynesian public budgeting and finance: Assessing contributions from modern monetary theory. *Public Budgeting and Finance, 40*(3), 95–123.

Kuttner, R. (2020, September 24). Can we fix capitalism?. *New York Review of Books*. Retrieved from https://www.nybooks.com/articles/2020/09/24/can-we-fix-capitalism-branko-milanovic/. Accessed on December 15, 2020.

LaPira, T. M., & Holyoke, T. T. (2017). Draining the swamp, or cultivating the wetlands? Toward evidence-based lobbying regulation and reform. *Interest Groups and Advocacy, 6*, 195–198.

Larner, W. (2003). Neoliberalism?. *Environment and Planning D: Society and Space, 21*, 509–512.

Layard, R., & Nickell, S. (1989). The Thatcher miracle?. *The American Economic Review, 79*(2), 215–219.

Leigh, A., & Terrell, N. (2020). *Reconnected: A community builder's network*. Melbourne: La Trobe University Press.

Lester, M., & dela Rama, M. (2018). Neo-protectionism in the age of Brexit and Trump: What does Australia do with its powerful friends? In R. Oberoi & J. Halsall (Eds.), *Revisiting globalisation: From a borderless to a gated globe* (pp. 91–120). Berlin: Springer.

Lester, M., dela Rama, M., & Crews, J. (2021). COVID-19 governance, legitimacy and sustainability: Lessons from the Australian experience. *Corporate Governance and Sustainability Review, 5*(1), 143–153.

Litwak, R. S., & Litwak, R. (2007). *Regime change: US strategy through the prism of 9/11*. Baltimore, MD: JHU Press.

Maher, P. J., Igou, E. R., & van Tilburg, W. A. P. (2018). Brexit, Trump and the polarizing effect of disillusionment. *Social Psychological and Personality Science, 9*(2), 205–213.

Mitchell, B., & Muysken, J. (2008). *Full employment abandoned: Shifting sands and policy failures*. London: Edward Elgar.

Moosa, I. A. (2020). The effectiveness of social distancing in containing Covid-19. *Applied Economics, 52*(58), 6292–6305.

NSW Health. (2021). *Living Evidence – COVID-19 Vaccines*, Critical Intelligence Unit . Retrieved from <https://aci.health.nsw.gov.au/covid-19/critical-intelligence-unit/covid-19-vaccines. Accessed on January 13, 2022>.

Pedersen, A., Attwell, J., & Heveli, D. (2005). Prediction of negative attitudes toward Australian asylum seekers: False beliefs, nationalism, and self-esteem. *Australian Journal of Psychology, 57*(3), 148–160.

Piketty, T. (2013). *Capital in the twenty-first century*. Cambridge, MA: Harvard University Press.

Piketty, T. (2015). *The economics of inequality*. Cambridge, MA: Harvard University Press.

Plibersek, T. (Ed.). (2020). *Upturn: A better normal after COVID-19*. Sydney: UNSW Books.

Premier of Victoria. (2020). On the road towards COVID normal. *Media Release*, September 13. Retrieved from https://www.premier.vic.gov.au/road-towards-covid-normal. Accessed on December 15, 2020.

Prime Minister of Australia. (2020) $130 billion JobKeeper payment to keep Australians in a job. *Media Release*, March 30. Retrieved from https://www.pm.gov.au/media/130-billion-jobkeeper-payment-keep-australians-job. Accessed on December 15, 2020.

Pusey, M. (1991). *Economic rationalism in Canberra: A nation-building state changes its mind*. Cambridge: Cambridge University Press.

Pusey, M. (2018) Economic rationalism in Canberra 25 years on?. *Journal of Sociology*, *54*(1), 12–17.

Quiggin, J. (1999). Globalisation, neoliberalism and inequality in Australia. *Economic and Labour Relations Review*, *10*(2), 240–259.

Reagan, R. (1981, January 20). Inaugural address. Retrieved from https://avalon.law.yale.edu/20th_century/reagan1.asp. Accessed on December 15, 2020.

Rutledge, P. E. (2020). Trump, COVID-19, and the war on expertise. *The American Review of Public Administration*, *50*(6–7), 505–511.

Ryan, N. (2005). A decade of social policy under John Howard: Social policy in Australia. *Policy and Politics*, *33*(3), 451–460.

Speers, D. (2021). Australia should have seen the Delta COVID variant coming, but it has exposed our serious weakness. *ABC News*, July 15. Retrieved from https://www.abc.net.au/news/2021-07-15/covid-delta-strain-shows-government-poor-planning-why-so-slow/100293840

Stiglitz, J. E. (2002). *Globalization and its discontents*. New York, NY: W.W. Norton and Company.

The Economist. (2017). How Australia broke the record for economic growth. *The Economist*, September 5. Retrieved from https://www.economist.com/the-economist-explains/2017/09/05/how-australia-broke-the-record-for-economic-growth. Accessed on December 15, 2020.

Troy, G. (2006). *Morning in America: How Ronald Reagan invented the 1980s*. Princeton, NJ: Princeton University Press.

Walby, S. (2020). The COVID pandemic and social theory: Social democracy and public health in the crisis. *European Journal of Social Theory*, 24(1), 22–43. https://doi.org/10.1177/1368431020970127

White House. (2021). *National Strategy for the COVID-19 response and pandemic preparedness*, January. Retrieved from <https://www.whitehouse.gov/wp-content/uploads/2021/01/National-Strategy-for-the-COVID-19-Response-and-Pandemic-Preparedness.pdf. Accessed on January 13, 2022.

Wilkinson, M. (2020). *The Carbon Club: How a network of influential climate sceptics, politicians and business leaders fought to control Australia's climate policy*. Sydney: Allen and Unwin.

Windsor, J. L. (2003). Promoting democratization can combat terrorism. *The Washington Quarterly*, *26*(3), 43–58.

World Health Organisation. (2021). *Coronavirus (COVID-19) Dashboard*. Retrieved from https://covid19.who.int/. Accessed on January 13, 2022.

Chapter 7

Civil Society and Environmental Protection in Brazil: Two Steps Forward, One Step Back

Antônio Márcio Buainain and Junior Ruiz Garcia

Abstract

In this chapter, the authors argue that the performance and dynamic of civil society in Brazil has been fundamentally guided by local institutions, but that the issues, approaches and political decisions that gained publicity, and thus helped to strengthen civil society mobilization, have been strongly influenced by the agendas of the so-called "global civil society." It would be wrong to classify them as foreign issues or declassify them based on the argument that they consider largely external interests or the reality of developed countries. The authors will attempt to show how the issues on the civil society agenda that are supported in arenas of public debate in Brazil are filtered by local institutions and are only considered relevant if they mirror the reality of the country and correspond to the aspirations, demands and challenges of certain segments of society.

Keywords: Brazil; civil society; environment; mobilization; organizations; policy

Introduction

The establishment and initial agenda of civil society in Brazil[1] was market by efforts to dismantle the military regime – which on several occasions resulted in a

---

[1]Civil society comprises institutional practices and voluntary organizations. The term "voluntary" means that it is not motivated by the market (or financial interest) (Baiocchi, Heller, & Silva, 2008).

dictatorship – under which Brazil was governed from 1964 to 1985. The focus of civil society was democratization, the return to civil power and to the individual and political commitments communally associated to the democratic regime. During the 1970s and beginning of the 1980s, the principal pillars of civil society mobilization included the call for political "opening" and criticism of the economic policy adopted by the military regime, particularly regarding the nature of the so-called "Brazilian model," which promoted fast modernization of the country but marginalized large tracts of the population from the benefits of growth. In this context, environmental protection was merely an appendix to the central issue and served more as a criticism of the military regime than an actual concern with enough strength to support civil society organizations.

Appendix or not, the fact is that the environmental issue – embedded in the criticism of the infrastructure projects and the modernization of Brazilian agriculture gained enough exposure to be incorporated into the political agenda of the first civil government which took office on March 1, 1985 and created the Ministry of Urban Development and Environment on March 15.[2]

In general terms, democratization, marked by the work of the National Constituent Assembly (NCA), elected in 1896, defined the arena and roles of civil society as concerning the public policies and political governance of the country. But civil society, which was engaged in the debates held in the constituent around relevant issues, including the environment, played an important role in the conceptions and rules adopted by the NCA. Following the approval of the Federal Constitution (FC), civil society mobilization and civic participation in environmental issues were significantly boosted by the Earth Summit (ECO92) that took place in Rio de Janeiro in 1992.

Thus, in practice, what arises is a rich and complex dialectic between national interests and the international agenda. In many cases – the debate surrounding the environment is without a doubt one of them – the international agenda foresees relevant challenges that are already evident in local arenas in Brazil. However, these issues have yet to gain momentum and national repercussion, hence why they are misidentified as external interference as they gain greater visibility in debates on the international front. On the other hand, the specific terms in global agendas are not necessarily applicable to Brazil and are adjusted according to the specific discussions lead by local civil society organizations. This rich and often conflicting and polarized process produces a dynamic marked by progress and regression (two steps forward, one step back), even if participants may not always agree on the nature of the disputes: what some consider as progress, other consider as regression, and vice versa.

---

[2]And acted as a bridge between the military regime and the democratic regime formally established with the promulgation of the Federal Constitution (FC), in 1988. The Ministry of Urban Development and Environment substituted the Special Environmental Secretary, of the Ministry of Internal Affairs, which was responsible for large-scale infrastructure projects. Its role was much more about supporting large construction projects than protecting the environment.

Evolution of Civil Society in Brazil

The 1988 FC represents the most important institutional milestone of democratization in Brazil following 21 years of military regime, during which time the fundamental rights of a political democracy were suspended, and the country was living under a dictatorship (1968–1978), concealed by the presence of an ineffective national congress. It also represents the institutional demarcation of the arena of civic participation in the Federation.

The Importance of the 1988 FC

In fact, the mechanisms created in the 1988 FC opened new opportunities for direct civic participation and public policy planning (Houtzager & Gurza Lavalle, 2010). It must however be made clear that civil society, established in many organizations, from the National Council of Women's Rights – CNDM to Brazilian Society for the Progress of Science – SBPC, to quote only two, though not the protagonists of the 1988 FC, contribute to the inclusion of many principals and provisions that justified its epithet as the "Citizenship Constitution" (See de Aragão, 1996). In the aftermath of the Constitution, an increase in civic participation was noted in all political spheres and issues of social interest, including the environment.

The 1988 FC, whose principal characteristics were incorporated in all state constitutions, political reforms and institutional changes implemented after democratization, opened new ways and arenas for the participation of civil society in political discussions. However, as highlighted by Baiocchi and Heller (2009), the creation and existence of institutional arenas for participation does not mean that such participation is effective in terms of opportunities and use of the spaces.

There is no doubt that these arenas can be secured by more influential agents, with greater political and/or economic power, and who have direct and immediate interest in the issues under discussion. The institutionalization of social participation (civil society) under unequal terms, introduces biases that, in the worst case, may cancel and even invert the demands of broader civic claims in favor of the particular and private interests of powerful economic groups. Indeed, the ability of these groups to develop and use the democratic regime and its spaces as mechanisms that reinforce the political power of those that already hold the power at the executive and legislative and other State levels is a genuine risk which legitimate civil society organizations have had to face throughout the last decades.

This risk, particularly serious in societies characterized by extreme social inequality and by historical social and political exclusion, such as in Brazil, alludes to the discussion of the legitimacy of movements and organizations that present themselves as representatives of civil society and use this to gain power and prestige.[3] This is why Taylor (2002) highlights that civil society is driven by a moral

---

[3]It is interesting to note parallels between this manifestation in the name of civil society and those in the name of the market, as if the market represented a linear movement, with no contradictions or conflicts. Economists defend the market, and thus

concern to contribute to a better society, based on social justice, democracy and freedom, in terms of economic, political and social issues. But it is not always so.

Houtzager and Gurza Lavalle (2010) reinforce that civic participation is not an individual initiative but is driven by civil society organizations (collective actions). Individuals representing organizations and different civil society groups may have specific ideas on how to contribute to a better society. In many situations, the representation of civil society may reflect individual interests and ideologies, not collective interests. The environmental issue can be influenced by individual interests due to the different degrees of development of societies, especially at the local level. However, there is no practical or operational consensus about what constitutes a civil organization, nor a manual explaining how to separate "the wheat from the chaff," regarding the debates and conflicts that take place in the name of civil society. The dynamic of these arenas in terms of their social composition, formal links to decision making and their deliberative power and results, must be analyzed and evaluated case by case; a task that goes beyond the scope of this chapter.

Without going into the debate on the dynamics of the use of the spaces created after the FC, it is important to highlight the decentralization of public policies for the states and municipalities, particularly in terms of policy implementation. Brasilia (the city in which Brazil's federal government is located) has retained almost complete decision-making power over the policies, but this decentralization stimulated the participation of local organizations in public spheres, be it in monitoring the execution of the policies, reporting misappropriation of funds, insisting action is taken when necessary, etc.

Jacobs (2002) highlights that the organization and mobilization of civil society arose, and progressed, because of community issues, such as a lack of waste collection services, electrical energy, public lighting and pavement or road improvements, industrial pollution, flooding, access to health services (the building of units dedicated to health services in the community) and education (the building of units dedicated to education in the community).

The model of political organization created by the FC, which distributes power and responsibilities between the federal, state and municipal levels, and creates integrated systems in areas such as health, education, safety, the environment, social security, among others, favored civic participation in community issues. In particular, civic participation is mandatory, a legal provision in certain organizations and initiatives, as members of the executive or deliberative and/or advisory boards. In this context, the participation arena grew and was occupied by civil society representatives, with varying levels of representativeness and effectiveness. In line with the "spirit" of the FC, many institutions, independent of any legal imposition, adopted organizational models to enable civic participation. This participation tended to be more consultative than deliberative, which does not mean that it is less relevant and has no power to influence decisions.

---

their more immediate interests, in the same way that many organizations defend civil society, without necessarily having the knowledge or legitimacy to do so.

The institutionalization of civic participation, largely because of the FC, contributed to the participation of historically marginalized groups in the arena of political debate and decision-making. These groups include landless rural workers, organized by the well-known MST (Movimento dos Trabalhadores Rurais Sem Terra), beneficiaries of the agrarian reform and family farmers; the homeless; fishermen and river dwellers; *quilombola* residents, indigenous communities, among other collectives and social movements (Houtzager & Gurza Lavalle, 2010). According to Pereira (1993), the struggles to secure basic needs for the poor and marginalized groups has influenced and continue to influence the mobilization of social movements, and how civil society is organized and participates in political discussions.

A share of civil society taking part in the discussions is intricately connected to real social issues, with spatial delimitation and well-defined social structures, as opposed to mobilizations based on broad political and societal concerns. Another interesting aspect is that the active civil society is composed of a wide range of individuals that goes beyond issues of class, gender, race, age, etc.

Civic participation in Brazil has also contributed to the emergence of new parties, linked to both social issues – particularly employment and the environment. The parties have in turn reinforced the demands of civil societies. The "green" political party, for instance, was a direct result of the mobilization of civil society groups and has contributed to the inclusion of environmental concerns into the political agenda and in the government's plans.

The Empowerment of Civil Society: Health Care and Budget Allocation

Two milestones related to the empowerment of civil society can be highlighted. The first was the mobilization of civil society surrounding public policies related to AIDS (Acquired Immunodeficiency Syndrome) in Brazil. The result of this participation was the creation of the National Program for AIDS in the 1990s, a model that was adopted by many countries around the world (Galvão, Bastos, & Nunn, 2012). This case illustrates the important connection between local and global activism (civil society organizations) in developing virtuous public policies, whose result were effective measures to deal with the AIDS epidemic and free access to medication and treatment for those affected.

The efforts of Brazilian civil society, as well as impacting local health policies, have also contributed to global policies to tackle AIDS. According to Galvão et al. (2012), the movements related to AIDS in Brazil contributed to raising awareness within society that health is a basic right and an important aspect of exercising citizenship.

Another milestone was the "participatory budget" initiative, which was launched in the city of Porto Alegre by the Workers' Party Administration, and later adopted in many cities. At the heart of this experience was the participation of civil society representatives in the planning of the municipal budget. Despite having gained major visibility, the experience did not endure, not even in left-wing administrations that defend the expansion of the participative arena. On the one hand, participation was marginal, with only a small share of the total budget at stake, and limited capacity to impact the lives of the wider community. On the other, civic participation itself was to some extent limited to organizations aligned to the political parties that controlled the administration. The participative budget allocation was to a large extent ´contaminated´by the national disputes protagonized by the largest political parties, and thus the experience did not create an institutional arena for effective civic participation at local level.

Lastly, the budgetary allocations tended to be distributed among the participants, reproducing the traditionally observed clientelism, only under the approval of "civil society," whose representatives replaced the political agents as brokers between the government that be and the community. It is important to note that in many municipalities local government and city councilors did not support the initiative, fearing they would lose power (budget approval by the city council is where the members exercise their power of negotiation with the executive and aim to defend construction work and services for their constituents).

Civil Society in Brazil: Types of Organization

The institutionalization of civic participation created opportunities for engagement (Baiocchi & Heller, 2009). As a result, participation has not stemmed from the demands of civil society, but largely from individuals or small groups. It is worth noting that the different types of civil society representation have arisen via trial and error.

According to Gianpaolo (2002), the institutionalization of the arenas in which civic participation takes place has contributed to new networks and types of participation, in the form of civil rights activism. The author highlights that since 1989 a more structured environment has been created, facilitating civic participation: training; dedicated locations for meetings between individuals (activists); responsibility and transparency.

The institutional arena where the discussions between civil society (private and public sectors) take place has widened since democratization. Initially restricted to spaces defined by policies and initiatives implemented by the government, such as public programs committees or local school boards, in just a few years these spaces had greater influence on public policies. Discussions involving civil society were taking place in such a range of locations and encompassing so many differente issues to the point that precise references were lost. Discussions take place in neighborhoods, universities and forums organized by many involved parties. The institutional process has also become more diversified, with social discussions being carried out and demands being met in a range of ways.

Neighborhood associations, cooperatives and community councils are obviously not the only types of civil society organization in Brazil. There are many other types of entities, such as samba schools, religious and cultural groups, football clubs, parent–child groups, social movements, professional organizations and trade unions, as well as non-governmental organizations (NGOs) (Gianpaolo, 2002). At the local level, it is possible that neighborhood associations and religious groups are the most important and have the most impact.

A certain amount of attention has always been given to the issue and debates surrounding environmental problems, possibly because there is greater repercussion in the media – boosted by the international media – than for health and education problems. Independent of whether environmental problems really are of broad general interest, in practice, different segments of the population and socioeconomic groups use the environmental motivation to increase awareness and encourage action on their specific battlefield. Water pollution, for example, is related to the poorest communities that live near contaminated sources and polluted rivers, while middle class neighborhoods, where urban sewage systems are in place – are more concerned with urban planning and access to recreational infrastructure (parks and town squares). For the most affluent groups, the pollution at beaches is only considered problematic when it affects tourism and leisure.

Neighborhood associations, producers and other organizations have proliferated throughout the country, instigated by public policies that require grass root organization as condition to access to benefits and that envision the participation of community representatives in advisory or consultive councils. The presence of NGOs has also increased, not only those that largely provide advocacy but also those that provide services and implement initiatives associated to issues that justify mobilization.

In Brazil, many cooperatives and/or professional organizations deal with a broad range of issues, embracing talking points which go beyond the narrow interests of the represented groups, sometimes more in line with the struggles of civil society than with the interests, in the strictest sense, of the represented groups. One prominent professional group is the Organization of Lawyers of Brazil (OAB in Portuguese) which is present throughout the country, with representatives at both state and municipal levels elected by lawyers residing in the states and municipalities. They have a prominent presence in institutional debates, often together with important civil society associations active in environmental, public security and social issues. Other examples are the Brazilian Press Association, that unites journalists from all over the country; the Brazilian Academy of Sciences, that comprises scientists from almost all scientific areas; and the Council of Rectors of public and private universities. Organizations which represent economic corporative interests, such as the National Industry Confederation and the National Agriculture Confederation, to name a few, are also continually active in the arenas of debates of public interest.

Civil society in Brazil is therefore characterized by structural heterogeneity, social inequality and the political-institutional marginalization of a segment of the population that is poorly represented and struggles to be heard by the political system. Civil society organizations provided many of these segments with a voice, combining the issues being neglected with the wider issues on the national political agenda, including environmental protection.

Bailey (1999) confirms this idea and asserts that in Brazil civil society participation is carried out by a group of organizations, such as trade unions or rural and urban organizations, ethnic and cultural groups, women's associations, social institutions linked to the catholic or evangelical church, community organizations, as well as NGOs, that for the public in general, are the most concrete representation of civil society.

Organization and Professionalism of Civil Society

The relationship between civil society and NGOs, which arise almost in opposition to the State, portraying a message of idealism and professionalism, contributed to increasing civic participation in discussions, decision-making and policy implementation; on the other hand, the proliferation of NGOs together with evidence of certain wrong-doings – albeit by the minority – have to some extent reduced their credibility and tarnished the image of NGOs, and thus led to distrust by those that oppose the agendas they defend.

The level of organization in civil society groups in Brazil varies considerably. Some have high levels of financial and operational autonomy, organizational capacity, leadership and the ability to define agendas, and others have little or no capacity to organize and determine their own agendas, so rely on external support and operate with limited autonomy in relation to discussion points defined by their supporters.

Civil society engagement and influence has varied according to issues, locations and circumstances. In some issues/locations/circumstances there is no engagement, even if there are legally defined spaces in which participation can take place. Effective influence does not only derive from the nature of the institutional arena and participation in the political arena. In many cases, in which participation plays an advisory role, civil society organizations have the power to influence decisions by raising public awareness and by putting pressure on decision-makers in powerful roles.

According to Baiocchi, Heller, and Silva (2008), civic participation has passed through four stages in Brazil since 1997: state-sponsored activism (the change from dependent clientelism to dependent associationism), scaling up, demobilization and participation without reform. Even though this sequence indicates an evolutionary trajectory, some paths and traits have been persistent throughout time, with varying degrees of strength, prestige and impact. Outdated clientelism coexisted with state-sponsored activism, sectors with major autonomy and participatory dynamism progressed in some areas and regressed in others, but largely speaking, civil society progressed and became stronger. In general terms, despite the absence of institutional reforms demanded by some sectors to increase citizen participation, participation has in fact increased as has influence from civil society, including having a relevant role in important decisions taken by legislative and executive powers at the three government levels.

In Brazil, civic participation has played an important role in building the democracy, with evident pluralization of political representation. It has contributed to molding the agenda and conflicts in the political sphere, as well as offering new forms of participation in the debates. Throughout the 1990s, the institutional arena and civil society influence increased *pari passu* with the entrance of new collective actors into the political arena, representing facets of civil society, such as the LGBTQI+ movement and the Black Power movement, that obtained greater visibility via participative actions. The work carried out by the organizations, initially restricted to specific issues, broadened to incorporate other subject areas. In line with this, civil society movements related to the environment coined the term "social environmentalism," uniting the environmental cause with social issues of lower income classes, particularly those living on the outskirts of large urban centers.

It is undeniable that civic participation has contributed to shedding light on relevant issues – albeit ones that are marginalized in government policy decisions and decision-making processes – and including them into government and society-wide debates and agendas. In this context, civil society has claimed greater political participation and entered directly into the political area, be it to defend its own agendas or to monitor the performance of constitutional obligations of the Brazilian State, particularly regarding protecting, promoting and providing quality of life. In a sense, it is represented by the Brazilian Federal Prosecution Office, an autonomous institution created by the FC to defend the law, democracy and the rights of society, from violations caused by both public and private agents.

Managing Civil Society Organizations

Largely speaking, civil society has taken part in the discussions and definition of priorities related to the economy and the short-term economic policies. In the political arena, civic participation is fragile when compared to the power of economic agents to influence political decisions and economic policy (Houtzager & Gurza Lavalle, 2010). This imbalance of power is a result of the predominance of economic considerations in the decision-making process, in detriment of non-economic criteria. This situation aggravates the conflicts among the stakeholders involved in the arenas of civic participation.

One important aspect is the question of selecting spokespersons to represent civil society in the political arena (Houtzager & Gurza Lavalle, 2010). The lack of clear criteria to choose these representatives is a source of suspicion surrounding the legitimacy of representation and the fragility of participation and ultimately how effective it really is. A study carried out by Houtzager and Gurza Lavalle (2010), in the city of São Paulo, found that the majority of leaders of civil society organizations believe that there is no formal relationship between the organization and the public being represented. They also found that the people that the researched organizations represent do not have the right to select leaders, via an election or not, nor a clear method to remove the leaders of the organizations from position.

Independent of the doubts, mistrust and eventual misconduct, the fact is that civil society representatives have played an important role in the conception, execution and monitoring of public polices (Houtzager & Gurza Lavalle, 2010). As indicated above, civic participation has helped strengthen Brazilian democracy, in terms of allowing a more diversified participation in the institutional and political arenas (Mercer, 2002), contributing to improving public policies and gaining better control over how the country is run. Despite this, Mercer (2002) affirms that the participation of NGOs and civil society has contributed to legitimizing the status quo and not challenging it. This is a valid opinion, but one that allows for a margin of doubt, given that in countless situations and important debates, civic participation directly questioned the status quo and imposed changes and policies that, perhaps not revolutionary, represented significant changes in the policies, conceptions and points of view.

It is undeniable that there has been an increase in civic participation in political discussion and the governance of the Federation. However, Houtzager and Gurza Lavalle (2010) point out a paradox surrounding civil society representation. On the one hand, the increase in mistrust and loss of legitimacy of elected representatives led to reforms and contributed to new forms of representation driven by civil society. However, the claims made by civil society lack democratic legitimacy when compared to those made by the representative government, in which representatives are elected. The reason for this paradox is that contrary to political parties and trade unions, civil society organizations must be transparent enough that their members can approve representation or guarantee the responsibility and capacity of the actions of their representatives (Houtzager & Gurza Lavalle, 2010).

Civil Society and Environmental Protection

The rapid industrialization and the economic and demographic growth since the 1950s have put increased pressure on the environment. On one hand, the extensive growth in agriculture, largely as a result of incorporation of new land, together with a modernization process involving mechanization and the use of chemical inputs, had – and continues to have – severe impacts on the environment. On the other hand, greater and unplanned urbanization has also caused environmental degradation, deforestation and pollution to rivers, streams and the air.

All Brazilian biomes have been severely affected. The Atlantic Forest Biome, which covers the entire Brazilian coast, has been almost destroyed. In 2020, only 10% of the original forest remained, in isolated fragments that did not guarantee the sustainability of the abundant fauna and flora that it is known for. The *Cerrado* became the most important agricultural region in Brazil, areas of the caatinga biome are threatened by desertification and a continual lack of water, often made worse by the increase in consumption and degradation of the sources that supply the largest rivers in the region; the Pampa, known traditionally for cattle breeding, is increasingly used for other agricultural products; the Pantanal, an environmental sanctuary at the basin of Paraguay, is under pressure from increased cattle breeding and fires; agriculture is also invading the Amazon rainforest.

The environmental debate in Brazil has often highlighted the necessity to conciliate environmental protection with economic development. The northern region of Brazil, where the majority of the Amazon Rainforest is concentrated, is home to almost 19 million people that require the means to live (IBGE, 2021). For some, this justifies deforestation, as necessary to reduce poverty and foster economic activities in the region.

Despite a political and social environment marked by euphoric growth, political crisis, military ruling and economic recession, the environmental issue has appeared in national debates since the 1950s, long before appearing on civil society agendas in developed countries. In 1958, for example, the Brazilian Foundation for the

Conservation of Nature (FBCN) was created in Rio de Janeiro, the country's capital at that time. The initiative was introduced by professionals from various scientific areas related to environmental issues, with significant participation from public servants who had contact with the elite of Brazilian politics. The FBCN influenced the creation of environmental laws, institutions and policies (Alonso, Costa, & Maciel, 2005). Unnamed, civil society was already in force in Brazil!

Another civil society initiative created before the 1988 FC was the *Gaúcha* Association for the Protection of the Natural Environment (AGAPAN), founded in 1971 by the agronomic engineer José Lutzenberger. This was the first formal civil society organization dedicated to the environment created in Brazil and Latin America (Viola, 1987). Since its creation, AGAPAN has focused on local environmental problems, regional issues and issues with a national and international reach, including the Southern Cone – Brazil, Uruguay and Argentina, as well as global issues.[4] AGAPAN fought to defend the protection of the fauna and vegetation and combat the excessive use of the mechanization of agrochemicals, pollution from the industrial and transport sectors, and water contamination from industrial effluents and domestic sanitary sewage, among other issues.

Another important manifestation was the creation of the Movement of People Affected by Dams (MAB), in 1979, which aimed to organize and protect the communities affected by the construction of large dams (Burrier, 2016). During 40 years of existence, the MAB has been unable to prevent the construction of large power plants in Brazil, which involves extensive social and environmental costs. It did however contribute to improving many of the projects and to reducing costs, largely irreversible ones, that tended to be ignored by decision-makers and society at large.

Since the 1960s, the environmental movements in Brazil have arisen at the same time as those in developed countries (Viola, 1987). Vast differences were noted however in the levels of development; the Brazilian society was already characterized by major heterogeneity, with one rich, modern, educated and dynamic side and the other poor, backward and abandoned. The title of the well-known book written by the French intellectual Jacques Lambert "The Two Brazils" reflects this well. Civic participation in environmental issues was initiated by more affluent groups, who were aware of the tendencies and events in Europe and the United States. Studies carried about by Alonso et al. (2005) highlight that this mobilization was initially driven by "middle class" environmental groups, who created a domain for organized manifestations to be carried out by "lower classes" and other diverse communities (indigenous peoples, fishermen, farmers, etc.) that are affected by large infrastructure projects.

The environmental movement gained momentum in Brazil from 1974, during the Geisel administration and was characterized by two scenarios: on the one hand, the relaxation of the State's control over civil society (Viola, 1987) and the press, and on the other, the evidence of environmental damage provoked by years of accelerated growth and large construction projects carried out by the military

---

[4]See: http://www.agapan.org.br/2013/01/agapan-postula-vaga-no-conselho.html.

government. The author highlights three periods of the environmental movement in Brazil: (a) from 1974 to 1981, the movements took on an apolitical nature and focused on reporting environmental damage in urban and rural areas; (ii) between 1982 and 1985, the movements became increasingly politicized, more organized and urban and rural movements joined, converging agendas surrounding certain issues that transcended local problems; and (iii) from 1986, the movements actively participated in parliamentary discussions marking the democratization process. This third phase is strongly influenced by the promulgation of the 1988 FC that recognizes civic participation in diverse political and decision-making arenas.

In Brazil, the first political initiatives strictly related to the environment, such as the Federal Decree-Law no. 1.413/1975 – control of environmental pollution; Law no. 134/1975 from the state of Rio de Janeiro and no. 997/1976 from São Paulo (da Silva, da Silva, & de Lira Borges, 2019), did not contemplate civic participation. The environmental policy that emerged reflected the political regime in Brazil at the time. Despite the authoritarian political context the National Environmental Policy (Law no. 6.938/1981) included civic participation in debates coordinated by the Legislatives Houses (de Silva et al., 2019). This legal framework was consolidated with the promulgation of the 1988 FC, which ensured civic participation in decision-making in a range of different areas.

Brazil is committed by law to guarantee an ecologically balanced environment, with obligations surrounding environmental resource management on the State and society (Article 225) (Brasil, 1988). The advance in civic participation *pari passu*, the democratization process reinforces the important relationship between democracy, citizenship and the environment (Jacobs, 2002). A growing relationship can be observed between local groups and national and international environmental organizations, which would eventually impact on the structure, values and priorities of the local groups, as well as their identity.

In this context, Jacobs (2002) indicates that people living in poverty, in urban areas, begin to worry about and take responsibility for what is happening to "their" environment, the environment around them, and recognize that quality of life and environmental conditions are related. de Silva et al. (2019) also reinforce that greater awareness of the relationship between environmental problems and social issues, including between the outskirts and city center communities, contributed to increased civic participation, both in environmental issues and strengthening and improving social policies. Thus, the environmental issue that was previously restricted to the developed regions and affluent groups, also appeared on the agenda of less developed regions and communities.

As mentioned, a milestone for civic participation in environmental issues was the Earth Summit held in Brazil in 1992 (ECO-92) (Alonso et al., 2005). Preceded by meetings and debates that mobilized universities, research institutions, corporations, specialists and governments, an extremely favorable scenario was created for civil society organizations, in which they were recognized and respected. It is a fact that environmental issues and civil society movements gained visibility because of the Earth Summit. In addition, Agenda 21, a result of the conference, recognized the importance of participative processes in decision-making, such as the better approach to planning and implementation of environmental policies (Alonso et al., 2005).

The Earth Summit also marked an important milestone in the internationalization of the environmentalist movement and civic participation in Brazil. This milestone can be translated into two movements: (i) the convergence of agendas, and (ii) the closer relationship with transnational NGOs. The internationalization of civil society's environmental movement contributed to obtaining sources of funding (Clark, 1995) and to strengthening mobilization and advocacy in addition to the level of professionalism of civil participation. According to Alonso et al. (2005), this closer relationship raised the level of professionalism of these actions and led to structural and strategic changes that increased the capacity to influence public policy decisions and the behavior of agents and society as a whole. Environmental organizations became sources of technical knowledge on environmental issues, resulting in a new more professional and specialized model of activism. Technical knowledge has therefore been an important tool in stimulating more active civic participation in the political arena.

The increased internationalization of Brazilian civil society contributed to strengthening movements and claims that did not even gain national status. One example is the role played by the extractivist groups and movements in the Amazon, such as the *seringueiros* (rubber tree tappers), whose endeavors transcended the region and the country and infiltrated international debates. The issue of demarcation of indigenous areas or the rights of native peoples, *quilombolas*, and communities affected by large construction projects and increased deforestation of the Amazon Rainforest, often associated to agriculture and cattle breeding, has contributed to increased civic participation in environmental issues.

Going beyond the social and local issues frequently associated to civil society, there has been a notable increase in interest in national and even global issues, such as climate change, greenhouse gas emissions, deforestation, desertification, the loss of biodiversity and degradation of aquatic ecosystems and coastlines. This movement highlights the importance of adopting a long-term perspective in terms of civil society claims.

Environment and Growth: On-going Tension

There is a misguided assumption in society, including in the public, private and academic sectors, that the issues of environmental protection are only relevant to developed countries. This assumption is strongly related to the economy, and supported by the environmental Kuznets curve hypothesis (Caviglia-harris, Chambers, & Kahn, 2008). Environmental challenges are predominantly presented as those of a minority that contradict the needs to achieve development, and subsequently, most of the population.[5] This has resulted in conflict between democracy and the environment.

---

[5]According to Viola (1987), "The associations that report environmental degradation are generally made up of an active core of between 10 and 20 people and a large inactive contingent of anywhere between 50 and 200 people, but can pass 1000 people in the most extreme cases" (p. 9).

In this context, participation of civil society and NGOs may be more difficult, and in some cases may even cause animosity. The experience reveals that the inclusion of environmental sustainability in the political and social agenda and in the combat and prevention of environmental crimes is further complicated by the narrative that opposes environmental protection to development. Deforestation, even when carried out illegally, tends to be portrayed as necessary for agricultural development, to generate employment and income for poorer populations in the more backward regions of the country. The argument behind the destruction that takes place in the outskirts of cities is based on the need to build affordable housing, which ultimately provides a free pass for these areas to be occupied by residential developments for the middle and upper classes.

After the democratization process, the environmental issue was made a priority on the political agenda, in discussions and policies implemented by the various governments. Since then, civil society organizations have evolved and made notable institutional progress. In the federal government, in 1989, IBAMA – The Brazilian Institute of Environment and Renewable Resources – was created. IBAMA was given the regulatory power to protect Brazilian fauna and flora; in 1992, the Ministry of Environment (MMA) was created, with almost all states following on to create departments dedicated to the environment.

Brazilian environmental legislation is without a doubt one of the most advanced in the world. It includes the National Water Law (Lei das Águas, 1997); the Environmental Crime Law, 1999; the National Policy on Climate Change of 2009 (Law no. 12.187); and the Brazilian Forest Code, approved in 2012 after a long period of debates and conflicts among stakeholders. This code establishes that between 20% and 80% of farms's land must be dedicated legal conservations reserves.

Aside from the controversies, the institutional progress made in environmental governance is undeniable. This is demonstrated by Brazil's protagonist role in international debates and courts since the Earth Summit and up until The Paris Agreement in 1996, where Brazil took on important commitments with the international community.

Despite the progress in environmental governance, the effectiveness of environmental policies has fallen short of legislative expectations and even shorter considering the severity of the problem (de Moura, 2016; de Silva et al., 2019). The continual deforestation perhaps serves as a clearer example of the lack of effectiveness of both public policy and civic participation. Even in the Atlantic Forest, one of the most degraded ecosystems in Brazil, deforestation is still being carried out. In the *Cerrado* and the Amazon Rainforest, degradation associated wih the expansion of agricultural production and cattle breeding and generation of hydroelectricity to accelerate economic growth in Brazil are persistent themes.

The Environmental Crime Law and the National Policy for Water Resources are examples of areas in which legislation is difficult to implement. Despite control and inspections, the perpetrators of environmental crimes are seldomly convicted based on the Law of Environmental Crime, either because the crime cannot be proven or the guilty party cannot be identified, or because the Brazilian legislative process allows them to obstruct the course of legal actions sometimes for many years. Despite a modern water resource policy, several important drainage basins in Brazil are completely degraded or at an advanced stage of degradation.

The Sao Francisco River drainage basin supplies water to the entire Northeast, a region which suffers from extreme drought and poverty. The river has suffered from neglect from authorities who ignored warnings and evidence from civil society to impede the reversal of the water flow to supply the rivers and dams in the region. However, the Sao Francisco River is at an advanced stage of degradation, with a loss of outflow and volume of water in its primary dams. In this case, the interests of large contractors to carry out civil engineering projects prevailed. After more than 15 years since the building work began, and spending of over R$8 billion, at the beginning of 2020 the reversal of the river was not concluded, part of the canals built were damaged and a population that should be receiving water continued to live with limited supplies. Another example is the frequent occurrence of water rationing in urban areas. In 2014, a severe water crisis hit the metropolitan region of São Paulo; in 2020, the same happened in the metropolitan region of Curitiba.

In Brazil, because of the social problems, effective civic participation in the environmental debate is more complex. Since social injustice affects a significant proportion of Brazilian society, priorities have been placed on guaranteeing that these populations have enough to survive; in other words, guaranteeing access to essential goods and services. As the basic economic problem – universal access to essential goods and services – has yet to be solved, society does not show the necessary and sufficient engagement in other areas, particularly environmental issues. Social inequality and access to essential goods and services stem from a historical problem in Brazil, thus, economic growth has been insufficient in guaranteeing the survival of a significant proportion of Brazilian society.

The prevailing social perception is that socioenvironmental degradation is largely a result of the socioeconomic system and the economistic approach to decision-making. Socioenvironmental movements seek to change the value system, from economism to one which is multidimensional (ecological, social justice, supportive, dynamic etc.). In this sense, the Brazilian environmental movement adopted an approach that seeks social transformation, as well as integration with non-environmental movements (Clark, 1995).

Organization, Effectiveness, Spatial Scale and Reach

In the environmental debate, there are three ways in which civil society can help combat deforestation or some environmental problem (Scholz, 2005): (i) raise public awareness of environmental issues; (ii) improve the capacity to construct strong local alliances and form partnerships with national and international agents; and (iii) forge international partnerships that contribute to strengthening environmental policy. To do so Brazilian civil society has developed more sophisticated forms of participation in arenas of public debate (Baiocchi et al., 2008), such as changes to norms and democratic practices.

A significant share of the international community has insisted Brazil takes an active role in environmental protection, particularly in the Amazon, given the environmental benefits that ecosystems provide to all countries. This requires the construction of institutional capabilities, financial resources, methodologies, regulations and actions that go well beyond voluntary and verbal commitments. This may be the reason that international agreements related to the environment are not fully implemented. In this context, in which the demands are not always compatible with the ability to meet them, organized civic participation has contributed to maintaining the pressure to make a certain amount of progress and resisting the pressures that come from opposing sides.

This dispute is permeated with tension. On the one hand, the internationalization of demands and external pressures create opportunities for interference from abroad – which primarily impacts NGOs – by groups that use the environmental agenda to defend the interests of other nations and not those of Brazil. On the other hand, polarizing positions make dialogue and allegiance more difficult, in a game of all or nothing, in which any concession – even when plausible and necessary for an agreement to be made – is seen as a defeat that must be overruled even if a formal commitment was made. Again, the Brazilian Forest Code is a good example: both the environmentalists and agrarianists see the result as a defeat, and since its approval have tried to either legally or politically reverse the rules adopted. The result is the weakening of the Code, whose implementation would mean major progress, albeit unsatisfactory from the point of view of environmentalists or inadequate for landowners. Amid doubts and controversies, the implementation is postponed, and transgressions go unpunished.

Two Steps Forward, One Step Back: Final Remarks

From the return to democratization up until the election of President Bolsonaro in 2018, the government agenda and discussions included issues of environmental protection. As previously mentioned, there is no way to deny that progress has been made in environmental governance (de Moura, 2016), in raising public awareness about the importance of environmental protection and the sustainable use of natural resources. However, contrasting to these progresses is the ideology of economic growth as a solution to all problems, a belief which is deep-rooted in Brazilian society and its political culture. Throughout the past 50 years, the economic agenda of the country has been dominated either by the primacy of controlling inflation or to increase gross domestic product pursued by economic policy at the cost of environmental sustainability and urgent social issues.

One only must look at the recent experience (1970–2020) to see that the balance between the environment and growth has been more an object of discourse than a reality, and that although the environmental agenda has helped curb actions that could have caused extensive and irreversible damage to the environment, the balance has sacrificed the future in favor of short-sighted investments with disputable returns, supported by dubious reasoning that neglected severe environmental impacts. Belo Monte, mentioned above, symbolized this ideology. Despite that, the overall balance of the period 1988–2018 was largely positive and everything indicated that, despite the to-ing and fro-ing between progress and failure, the country was on the correct trajectory toward a status of environmental power proposed by many civil society movements.

The country suffered considerable setbacks with the so-called "new environmental policy" implemented by the Bolsonaro administration. The policy has put the effectiveness and resilience of environmental governance to the test, as well as civil society's role in preventing the dismantling of tools to protect the environment and reinforcing society's awareness of the importance of environmental issues for the present and future of the country. As mentioned above, environmental policy was never overly effective, thus the relaxing of environmental rules suggests an inevitable worsening of environmental issues, in the short and medium terms. After 2018, increased deforestation rates were registered as well as rural fires in almost all Brazilian biomes; a drastic reduction in the implementation of environmental policies and budgetary resources allocated to environmental management was also observed (INPE, 2021; Mapbiomas, 2021; SOSMA, 2021). It is thanks to civil society that changes in environmental policy were not even more drastic. It has the press, the Public Prosecutor and the justice system to block the "*passagem da boiada*"[6] on environmental regulation.

The Bolsonaro administration even went as far as to announce the abolishment of the MMA but retreated because of national and international repercussion and the fierce opposition from various segments of civil society. Despite keeping the Ministry, the government has continued to dismantle Brazilian environmental governance, seeing it as getting in the way of development, particularly because it impedes investment in large construction, energy and communication projects. The justification given is that refining the rules and lessening bureaucracy will make environmental protection more compatible with economic development and growth. Bolsonaro's Minister of Environment, who was initially seen as an advocate of environmental protection, appears to have changed his position and is seen as a threat by society, to the point that the General Prosecutor appealed for his removal from the position due to administrative improbity. This situation provoked strong repercussions from other countries, including some that were traditionally partners of Brazil, and also from transnational companies, with threats to impose sanctions on products (particularly agricultural) exported by Brazil.

The main changes made to environmental governance in Brazil since 2019 were (Diele-Viegas & Rocha, 2020; Ferrante & Fearnside, 2019; Greenpeace, 2019; Pereira, Ferreira, Ribeiro, Carvalho, & Pereira, 2019; de Silva et al., 2019):

- Changes to the organizational structure of the MMA, via provisional measure no. 870/19 (Article 21) and Decrees 9.672/2019 and 9.667/2019. The main organizational changes were abolishing the Climate Change Secretary, the

---

[6]This refers to the declaration of the Environment Minister Ricardo Salles, in a ministerial meeting, in which he defended changing the rules and regulation of environmental protection and simplifying norms at a time when media attention was largely focused on Covid-19.

Extractivism and Sustainable Rural Development Secretary and the Institutional Articulation and Environmental Citizenship Secretary.
- Changes in the requirements for environmental licenses (Normative Instruction no. 8/2019 IBAMA and Decree no. 9.669/2019).
- Loss of administrative, operational and regulatory autonomy of IBAMA and ICMBio.
- Change in the Original People and Community Policy (provisional measure no. 870/2019 and Decrees 9.967/2019 and 9.673/2019). The primary change was the transfer of the National Indigenous Foundation (*Fundação Nacional do Índio*, FUNAI) and the Environmental Demarcation and Licensing of indigenous land to the Ministry of Agriculture.
- Alterations to the policies related to food security and nutrition via Law no. 13.844/2019, bringing an end to the National Board of Food Security and Nutrition.
- Changes in the structure of the National Environment Council via Degree no. 9.806/2019, reducing the number of advisors from 96 to just 23. In this new structure, various segments of civil society were removed, and more power was given to the Federal Government.

The new environmental policy therefore poses new challenges for civil society. Debates surrounding environmental issues however are gaining more attention in Brazil. Brazilian governmental agencies, the private sector and civil society have all been important players in shaping both the national and international debate. The historical pattern of development, basically sustained on the predatory use of natural resources, on the one hand, and the recent rise of Brazilian agribusiness as a global food power, particularly the expansion of biofuels, soybeans and beef on the other, have raised international concerns regarding the future of Brazilian tropical forests – deemed as an essential asset to achieve a balanced global climate.

While much of the debate and concerns are channeled to deforestation and its impact on biodiversity, the massive use of agrochemicals by agriculture and CO (carbon monoxide) emissions by cattle herd, the environmental issue in Brazil extends far beyond these three dimensions of the problem. Urban pollution, solid waste and garbage management, threats to the survival of the Atlantic Forest Biome, large areas subject to an advanced process of desertification in the Northeast Semiarid and the South Brazilian regions, water contamination and waste, environmental degradation in mining districts and environmental and human disasters provoked by mining activities are examples of relevant environmental issues which are largely neglected within the environmental debate. One possible hypothesis is that these issues, while crucial for Brazilian society, are not as relevant for the international community and thus for the so-called global civil society and its organizations, including Brazilian civil society whose strategic agenda is probably aligned to the agenda based on the international scenario.

In this chapter, we dealt with the positive and contradictory roles played by civil society in shaping the debates, policies and institutions related to the use of natural resources and environmental protection in Brazil. The central argument is that civil society has indeed played a truly relevant and positive role in the area. Its contribution goes from raising awareness about the environmental problem in general to the creation and strengthening of public and private organizations, policy design and enactment and enforcement of environmental laws. However, its role has neither been free of contradictions nor of conflicts. In some cases, the results are at the very least controversial, as far as local, and long-term development goals are concerned.

In our view, there are several reasons why the interests and points of view supported by civil society organizations cannot be taken for granted in representing legitimate interests of the society. To start with, there is the question of the actual and legitimate mandate to advocate in the name of the society. Civil society organizations have mushroomed everywhere, and small groups often create militant organizations to support specific causes, which irrespective of their flaws, are successfully disseminated through social media as if they express the views of society or a significant share of the population/voters.

The so-called civil society might represent legitimate interests of certain groups, which may or may not coincide with the interests of the majority. In many instances, civil society militant organizations introduce polarizations which may help to promote their views at the cost of oversimplifying complex issues and eventually lead to mistaken strategies, even considering their long-term objectives. In addition, there has been a tendency to only recognize civil society organizations that have certain interests, thus deeming organizations of civil society that represent opposite interests as illegitimate or non-representative.

In democratic pluralistic societies, this may imply significative risks as the strengthening of civil society organizations is increasingly linked to the effectiveness of their communication strategy, and not the content of their message. The winning point of view does not necessarily represent the best interests of society, nor a consistent and rational strategy as far as local/national sustainable development is concerned. It may well represent the point of view of the nosiest groups, who have effective communication abilities and strong capacity to mobilize supporters among population and voters.

The debate and environmental policies in Brazil offer rich examples of the contradictory role played by the so-called civil society. On the one hand, it may have led to an emphasis on hot issues for the international community at the expense of issues which could be more relevant for local/national community. On the other, while defending strong viewpoints in a polarized context, many civil society organizations may have radicalized their political stance, thus leading to an all or nothing game of doubtful effectiveness. Summing up the role of civil society, our hypothesis is that it has led to progress through a winding road whose shape is not independent of the actions and strategies adopted by civil society organizations.

The regression observed since 2018, as discussed throughout this chapter, confirms the importance of safeguarding the civic arena, based on three essential rights: the freedom of expression, the freedom of assembly and that of association (Szabo, 2021). It is in this arena that civil society organizations fight for causes, ideas and policies that tend to be neglected in traditional political arenas, where economic agents and corporativist representation is usually more powerful.

The new environmental policy implemented by the Bolsonaro administration has put to the test the important and historic role carried out by civil society in developing environmental governance in Brazil. At first sight, civil society has been unable to oppose the changes, with indicators of environmental degradation worsening in 2019 and 2020. Thus, new and old challenges call for a stronger civil society to engage in environmental management in Brazil. Perhaps, the association between global and local civil society can help overcome the existing challenges. Many unanswered questions remain however particularly regarding the degree of representativeness of civil society and of civic participation.

References

Alonso, A., Costa, V., & Maciel, D. (2005). *The formation of the Brazilian environmental movement* (No. 259). Sussex. Retrieved from https://www.ids.ac.uk/publications/the-formation-of-the-brazilian-environmental-movement/

de Aragão, M. (1996). A ação de grupos de pressão nos processos constitucionais recentes no Brasil. *Revista de Sociologia Política, 6/7*, 149–165.

Baiocchi, G., & Heller, P. (2009). Representation by design? Variations on participatory reforms in Brazilian Municípios. In O. Törnquist, N. Webster, & K. Stokke (Eds.), *Rethinking popular representation* (1st ed., pp. 119–140). New York, NY: Palgrave Macmillan. https://doi.org/10.1057/9780230102095

Baiocchi, G., Heller, P., & Silva, M. K. (2008). Making space for civil society: Institutional reforms and local democracy in Brazil. *Social Forces, 86*(3), 911–936. http://www.jstor.org/stable/20430782

Bailey, M. (1999). Fundraising in Brazil: The major implications for civil society organisations and international NGOs. *Development in Practice*, 9(1–2), 103–116. https://doi.org/10.1080/09614529953250

Brasil. (1988). Constituição Federal de 1988. Retrieved from https://goo.gl/QxPqF5

Burrier, G. (2016). The developmental state, civil society, and hydroelectric politics in Brazil. *The Journal of Environment & Development, 25*(3), 332–358. https://doi.org/10.2307/26197978

Caviglia-harris, J. L., Chambers, D., & Kahn, J. R. (2008). Taking the "U" out of Kuznets: A comprehensive analysis of the EKC and environmental degradation. *Ecological Economics, 68*(4), 1149–1159. https://doi.org/10.1016/j.ecolecon.2008.08.006

Clark, A. M. (1995). Non-governmental organizations and their influence on international society. *Journal of International Affairs, 48*(2), 507–525. http://www.jstor.org/stable/24357601

Diele-Viegas, L. M., & Rocha, C. F. D. (2020). Why releasing mining on Amazonian indigenous lands and the advance of agrobusiness is extremely harmful for the mitigation of world's climate change? Comment on Pereira et al. (Environmental Science & Policy 100 (2019) 8–12). *Environmental Science & Policy, 103*, 30. https://doi.org/10.1016/j.envsci.2019.10.015

Ferrante, L., & Fearnside, P. M. (2019). Brazil's new president and 'ruralists' threaten Amazonia's environment, traditional peoples and the global climate. *Environmental Conservation, 46*(4), 261–263. https://doi.org/10.1017/S0376892919000213

Galvão, J., Bastos, F. I., & Nunn, A. (2012). The Brazilian response to AIDS from the 1980s to 2010 – Civil society mobilization and AIDS policy. *Global Health Governance, 6*(1), 1–21. Retrieved from https://www.arca.fiocruz.br/handle/icict/6379

Gianpaolo, B. (2002). Synergizing civil society: state-civil society regimes in Porto Alegre, Brazil. In D. E. Davis (Ed.), *Political power and social theory* (Vol. 15, pp. 3–52). Bingley: Emerald Group Publishing Limited. https://doi.org/10.1016/S0198-8719(02)80021-7

Greenpeace. (2019). Seis meses de Bolsonaro: ataques ao meio ambiente atingem a economia. Disponível em: https://www.greenpeace.org/brasil/blog/seis-meses-de-bolsonaro-ataques-ao-meio-ambiente-atingem-a-economia/. Accessed on February 10, 2021.

Houtzager, P. P., & Gurza Lavalle, A. (2010). Civil society's claims to political representation in Brazil. *Studies in Comparative International Development*, 45(1), 1–29. https://doi.org/10.1007/s12116-009-9059-7

IBGE. (2021). *Sistema IBGE de Recuperação Automática – SIDRA.* IBGE – Instituto Brasileiro de Geografia e Estatística. Retrieved from https://sidra.ibge.gov.br. Accessed on January 22, 2021.

INPE. (2021). Boletim Técnico - Technical Bulletins. Retrieved from http://inpe.br/

Jacobs, J. E. (2002). Community participation, the environment, and democracy: Brazil in comparative perspective. *Latin American Politics and Society*, 44(4), 59–88. https://doi.org/10.1111/j.1548-2456.2002.tb00223.x

Lei das Águas. (1997). Federal Law n. 9.4333, 8 January 1997 - Water Law, 1997.

Mapbiomas. (2021). Collection 6. Retrieved from https://mapbiomas.org/en/produtos?cama_set_language=en

de Moura, A. M. M. (org.). (2016). *Governança ambiental no Brasil: instituições, atores e políticas públicas* (pp. 352). Brasília: Ipea, Instituto de Pesquisa Econômica e Aplicada.

Mercer, C. (2002). NGOs, civil society and democratization: a critical review of the literature. *Progress in Development Studies*, 2(1), 5–22. https://doi.org/10.1191/1464993402ps027ra

Pereira, A. W. (1993). Economic Underdevelopment, Democracy and Civil Society: The North-East Brazilian Case. *Third World Quarterly*, 14(2), 365–380. http://www.jstor.org/stable/3992573

Pereira, E. J. A. L., Ferreira, P. J. S., Ribeiro, L. C. S., Carvalho, T. S., & Pereira, H. B. B. (2019). Policy in Brazil (2016–2019) threaten conservation of the Amazon rainforest. *Environmental Science & Policy*, 100, 8–12. https://doi.org/10.1016/j.envsci.2019.06.001

Scholz, I. (2005). Environmental policy cooperation among organised civil society, National Public Actors and International Actors in the Brazilian Amazon. *The European Journal of Development Research*, 17(4), 681–705. https://doi.org/10.1080/09578810500367466

SOSMA. (2021). SOS Mata Atlântica, Relatório Anual 2020. Retrieved from https://cms.sosma.org.br/wp-content/uploads/2021/07/Relat%C3%B3rio_SOSMA_2020_01_COM-REVIS%C3%95E_12_07_2021.pdf

da Silva, L. M. B., da Silva, J. P., & de Lira Borges, M. A. (2019). Do global ao contexto nacional: evolução da política ambiental brasileira. *Revista Brasileira de Gestão Ambiental e Sustentabilidade*, 6(14), 593–608. https://doi.org/10.21438/rbgas.061401

Szabo, I. (2021). *A defesa do espaço cívico* (128 pp.). São Paulo: Objetiva.

Taylor, R. (2002). Interpreting Global Civil Society. Voluntas: International *Journal of Voluntary and Nonprofit Organizations*, 13(4), 339–347. https://doi.org/10.1023/A:1022046125396

Viola, E. J. (1987). *O movimento ecologico no Brasil (1974–1986): do ambientalismo a ecopolitica* (1st ed.). Notre Dame [Estados Unidos]: Kellogg Institute.

Chapter 8

Redefining Social Capital and Social Networks in Global Civil Society

Tom Cockburn and Cheryl Cockburn-Wootten

Abstract

This chapter considers how social capital is evolving in the era of globalization today especially under COVID-19 pandemic conditions globally. Definitions of social capital have varied: some broad others narrow. The Organisation for Economic Co-operation and Development (OECD), for example, currently has a broad research project on social capital. These researchers have defined social capital as comprising four key areas. These areas are:

- Personal relationships, referring to the structure of people's social networks.
- Depth and breadth of social network support available to each person in their networks.
- Civic engagement activities such as volunteering and community action.
- Beliefs, attitudes, and action frames of reference such as trust and cooperative norms, of reciprocity.

Thus, there are tacit as well as explicit aspects of social capital though some of these may seldom if ever be articulated and delineated for others.

As Claridge (2020) indicates, there are distinct, but dynamically interrelated, levels of social capital. These levels range between the micro- or individual level. That is personal "habitus" – which Bourdieu (1977) describes as a person's "taken-for-granted" – ways of being, thinking, and reacting to events and to other people. Then, the next level above the individual is the meso-level, which is "how things are done here amongst us," that is, the level of a group's social capital (such as a team, or an organizational or local community level). Lastly, and wider still, the top level is the macro- or cultural-societal structural level of the nation.

The social capital systems in any location encompasses sets of acceptable or culturally legitimated behavioral norms and rules of engagement between community members which include types of greetings, forms of cooperation, communications, and signaling between diverse members. Thus, social capital may be present in the tacit, or unspoken/taken-for-granted assumptions as much as in explicit or formalized codes of behavior. The forms of social interactions at each of the levels may have norms for specific types communication and address in particular sets of circumstances such as social gatherings at home or in public or when attending communal gatherings or ceremonial occasions, or between people of different social status. Social capital generates trust and social cohesion and some level of cultural and attitudinal consensus and interest, which in turn delivers a stable environment for the local community or larger society, business, or the economy.

(1) Social capital is the development of relationships that help contribute to a more efficient production of goods and services as there is embedded trust, embodied in practice, that is, in behaviors regarded as trustworthy and socially helpful.
(2) There are three types of social capital at each level of interaction – bonding, bridging, and linking. Bridging and linking are similar though they operate in different directions socially. Bonding social capital describes the connections between people in similar social levels or groups of people who share the same characteristic norms and beliefs, whereas linking social capital facilitates connects between different groups.
(3) Social capital can therefore make or break businesses, especially small businesses or start-ups as those with the right kind and amount of social capital, such as good connections and contacts in the trade or profession, can usually thrive as they are able to get work done more quickly, effectively, and efficiently. Conversely, a lack of social capital denoting some distrust between groups can undermine social stability.

The meso- or macro-levels of bridging type social capital ensures acceptance of established social roles locally and linking forms of social capital boost levels of acceptance of other roles such as those of leaders and followers.

All three forms of social capital and the three levels are not mutually exclusive but instead are mutually inclusive and interrelated. That is, they co-evolve, each impacting the other while dynamically interacting with the social capital anchored as it is emerging from the complex and interwoven fields of tacit and explicit norms of social interaction underpinning each of the levels of interaction over time.

Keywords: Collaboration; social capital; dialectics; bounded nationality; non-conscious cognition; nudging; COVID-19

Building a Culture of Integrity in Organizations

As organizations grow and the distance between members increases with role differentiation and in global businesses, with sheer distance, building social capital requires new forms of connectedness beyond the kinds of face-to-face forms that were the key feature in the past. In particular, as the world gets metaphorically smaller with improved communication, there is a need to reassert and bolster social capital in new ways. Even as transport links are improved and long-distance flights have become more affordable, the pace of change faster, there is a noticeable desire for social stability and safety but with more individual choice, access to resources, opportunities, and lifestyles than was the case in some previous times when social norms were much more restrictive, aiming to maintain the status quo, or "keep people in their place," that is, to reduce social mobility between classes, castes, ethnic, or other social groups. Although reaching outwards today does not necessarily have to include travel to far off places, people can travel virtually and get a taste of the lives of others. In fact, now that Googling has become an accepted verb in many lexicons, and Google is a tech giant and first resort for many engaged in research of many kinds, then socio-digital connectedness is a modern day equivalent of the bridging form of social capital in the twenty-first century. Google is a prime mover in the development of artificial intelligence (AI) algorithms and forms of machine learning. Other organizations including businesses, governments, and non-governmental organizations (NGOs) are now utilizing AI systems in their everyday tasks and there are plans to develop further with autonomous vehicles, medical services, and local and national forms of e-governance for diverse social and economic functions.

However, as indicated by the IEEE (2019, p. 6) project, levels of quasi-autonomous AI, which are to enhance human lives must also be programmed to use social capital (norms and social values) and operate under the following general principles:

(1) Human rights A/IS shall be created and operated to respect, promote, and protect internationally recognized human rights.
(2) Well-being A/IS creators shall adopt increased human well-being as a primary success criterion for development.
(3) Data agency A/IS creators shall empower individuals with the ability to access and securely share their data to maintain people's capacity to have control over their identity.
(4) Effectiveness A/IS creators and operators shall provide evidence of the effectiveness and fitness for purpose of A/IS.
(5) Transparency, the basis of a particular A/IS decision should always be discoverable.
(6) Accountability A/IS shall be created and operated to provide an unambiguous rationale for all decisions made.
(7) Awareness of misuse A/IS creators shall guard against all potential misuses and risks of A/IS in operation.
(8) Competence A/IS creators shall specify and operators shall adhere to the knowledge and skill required for safe and effective operation. This should be regarded as a priority strategic vector in governance.

The levels of AI systems impact on community social capital as well as business and cultural values may be regarded as occurring at three levels of impact, as follows:

- At the micro-level for individuals.
- Meso-level of community systems focus.
- Macro-levels of strategic vision and purpose or mission.

The emergent social capital formed and anchored within the diverse relationships in communities, organizations, and nation states is relevant to governance and inevitably affected by emotions, expectations, and attitudes such as trust, assumptions about key individuals' roles, and respective behaviors, for example, such as those expected of the leaders of the community of participants. That emergent, layered set of normative expectations includes the nature and form of leadership values informing macro- or community decision-making.

We have some case research on how three organizations that are ensuring their governance structures are aligned and that the values embedded and embodied within these organizations reflect key ethical principles and practices valued by their stakeholders'. One of the current authors researched three organizations where the social and ethical capital is deployed to consciously produce a more three-dimensional perspective and thereby enable more rounded, values-based, decision-making, working environment, and commercial activities. In that study, it was agreed to opt for a 180° view of ethical and social capital aspects in the organizational culture by adopting the idea of three-dimensionality adapted from the Gratton and Truss (2003) model for analyzing strategic HR alignment in organizations.

Social norms and values are key elements and can be seen as a strategic vector underpinning the social capital in organizational vision, mission, and strategy or *vertical alignment*: what we aim to do and be. A horizontal or tactical vector, that is, related to process alignment – how we do things in this community and an operational vector, i.e., how we action/implement mission and strategy in our everyday work. We plotted the various responses to the interview questions against each of the vectors in Tables 8.1 and 8.2 and this allowed us to later present a visual representation of the three axes of the alignment, their relative strength, and overall trajectory of the aspects of social capital related to the leadership and corporate integrity at the top or what has been called the tone from the top.

Table 8.1. Green Norms.

Ladder of "Green-ness"	Summary Description
(A) Militant green	"Activist" for green cause
(B) Green partner	Collaborates with activists
(C) Green advocate	Openly supports green issues/cause
(D) Green client	Accepts advice by greens on issues
(E) Skeptical	Not interested, uninvolved, or unsure
(F) Green consumer	Use of green products/services
(G) Neutral/passive	Ambivalent about green issues
(H) Anti green	Against green causes

Table 8.2. Culture and Ethical Dimensions.

Integrity Theme	SUMA	Co-operative Bank	FCU
1. Vision and goals (vertical-strategic)	Stresses democratic values and practices of *staff/member* empowerment in general meetings to decide strategic development	Stresses Co-op principles of *customer* consultation on strategy and legal accountability of the organization executive	Stresses strategic, community values, of founding ("people helping people") philosophy
2. Leadership (vertical)	Direct participation of all staff in strategic decision-making in MC	Hierarchical decision-making but with some staff consultation on decisions on strategy	Chairman= "head coach," board of trustees ensures community input on strategic decisions and scrutiny of leadership and operations
3. Ethics infrastructure (horizontal processes/tactics)	Well-developed policies and practices on membership and employment	Well-developed policies and practices	Well-developed policies and practices
4. Legal compliance, policies, and rules (vertical-horizontal)	Goes beyond legal compliance – extending actions to fair trading in sourcing supplies	Compliant and refused major deals to ensure principled business and CSR	Systematic adherence to compliance and to founding philosophy
5. Organizational culture (horiz+action/depth-in operations)	Somewhat Kibbutz-like everyone helping out in work tasks without status distinctions, democratic vote on decisions at general meetings	Corporation structure and roles related to position description and member consultation on key changes or strategic direction and initiatives	Corporation structure and roles related to position description and member-directed AGM

(*Continued*)

Table 8.2. (continued)

Integrity Theme	SUMA	Co-operative Bank	FCU
6. Disciplinary and reward measures (horizontal+action/depth)	Collectively determined and administered sanctions and flat rate salaries dependent on collective agreement	Standard formal ethical and disciplinary codes and some bonuses based on targets	Following 3 Cs for loans, rewards closely related to values and serving client needs
7. Whistleblowing (horiz+action/depth)	Not formally but issues may be raised at meetings and put to a vote	Yes – formal structure in place	None in place formally but see trustees as a channel enabling whistleblowing
8. Measurement, research, and assessment (action+horiz)	Transparent measures agreed and reviewed at meetings	Public reports/CSR accounting/financial audits	Legal/CSR reports/S&P audits, trustees' reports
9. Ethics training, education, or confidential advice and support (horiz+action)	Co-op system and democratic voting, on-the-job training infrastructure otherwise ad hoc training systems	Some formal training related to levels of job and role	Some training for all (e.g. on induction and orientation on operations plus trustee role)
10. Ethics communications (horiz+action)	Centrally embedded in systems and corporate literature	Centrally embedded in systems and corporate literature	Centrally embedded in systems and corporate literature
11. Green issue policies and awareness (vertical)	Very explicit green-ness (militant green as per Table 8.1)	Green partner (see Table 8.1)	Green advocate-passive (see Table 8.1)
12. Corporate social responsibility (vertical +action)	CSR=core component of strategy, processes, and impacts on operations	CSR=core component of strategy, processes, and impacts on operations	CSR=core component of strategy, processes, and impacts on operations

Building a 3D culture of integrity

Overview of Integrity Vectors

The strength of each of the three dimensions is represented in the cube as height, width and depth (i.e. vertically, horizontally and from front to rear of the figure).

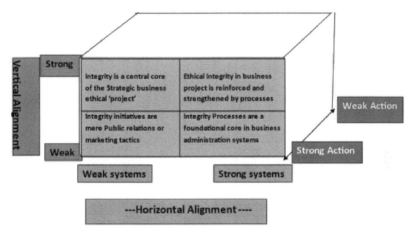

Fig. 8.1. Model of 3D Culture of Integrity.

We firstly asked the respondents to rate their organization using the ladder of "green-ness" (Table 8.1) as a measure of core values.

This 3D culture matrix will leaders and staff to review corporate integrity and make needed changes in specific areas to build a coherent, balanced, and integrated ethical strategy, including the use made of AI systems for marketing, financing, and other functions.

Ensuring a 3D governance structure in AI governance systems is no more easily achieved than in offline governance. As the authors of the IEEE (2019, p. 15) state:

> At the present time, the conceptual complexities surrounding what "values" are (Hitlin & Piliavin, 2004; Malle & Dickert, 2007; Rohan 2000; Sommer, 2016) make it difficult to envision A/IS that have computational structures directly corresponding to social or cultural values such as "security," "autonomy," or "fairness." They suggest it may be a more realistic goal to embed explicit norms into AI governance systems. Observable norms of human behavior, can be represented as instructions to act in defined ways in defined contexts, for a specific community – at whatever level is appropriate i.e. from family to town to country and beyond. A community's network of social and moral norms is likely to reflect the community's values, and A/IS equipped with such a network would, therefore, also reflect the community's values.

Thus, for instance, there is a perceived concrete difference in the HR decision-making systems and leadership, working processes, of the three cooperatives researched in 2012 which may prove more difficult to achieve using an AI form of governance. The organizations are SUMA, the Co-Operative bank in the UK, and First Credit Union in New Zealand. These three were used as exemplars of workplaces aiming to build social capital in the form of organizational cultures of integrity and contrasted their HR structures, strategic and operational decision processes, commercial focus, work systems, staff training, and success measures which together build a 3D culture of integrity previously indicated is critical in developing the Co-op bank's ethical culture and social capital (Cockburn, Jahdi, & Wilson, 2012). The leadership of these organizations has been geared toward more than accumulating profitable returns on investment or loans and services to other businesses.

As indicated above, we would add an additional element of global relationships and connectedness to the above Organisation for Economic Co-operation and Development (OECD) definition of social capital to address and encapsulate international dependency, relationships, and support. This is often a taken-for-granted concept within advanced countries and generally seen as related to regulating social media rather than wider social transformation, change activities, or advocacy. In less developed countries or communities due to terrain, investment, and infrastructure global relationships connections are not easily obtained or accessed.

Such socio-technical capital if universally available would obviate the multiple tiers of access and provision that leave some in a "catch up" situation. We would add the following point.

In this chapter, we present and consider case examples to illustrate the above forms of social capital. These case examples illustrate multilateral impacts within diverse organizations and consequences for leadership, business processes, organizational learning, systems, commerce, negotiation, trade, technology, and significantly, the emerging business ecologies. We compare and contrast some case examples of ideal types in terms of their perceived effectiveness and impact as agents of change or consolidation of social capital in diverse communities, business sectors, and corporate structures. There is already evidence of the penetration of internet, via smartphone and social media usage in less developed areas of the world as well as in advanced nations, sufficient to ensure that the minimum levels of infrastructure to accommodate greater connectedness is in place.

We also deliver a parallel commentary on the tensions between collaborative approaches to building social capital and competitive or unilateralist approaches with reference to addressing the COVID-19 pandemic. We consider case examples of the forms of social capital, local and national leadership, competitive, comparative, and collaborative economic advantages with multilateral impacts in diverse organizations and social systems at micro-, meso-, and macro-levels impacting leadership, business processes, organizational learning, social systems, commerce, negotiation, trade, technology, and on the emerging business ecologies. We compare and contrast some case examples of ideal types and in terms of their perceived effectiveness and impact as agents of change or consolidation of social capital in diverse communities, business sectors, and corporate structures looking beyond the period of the pandemic.

Key Role of Leadership in Building, Maintaining, and Developing Social Capital at Meso- and Macro-levels

From the above discussion, IEEE's (2019) suggested guiding principles, it is clear that leadership has a key role in the formation and reinforcement of social norms at the meso- and macro-levels in communities and countries. Thus, we present some comments upon leaders and leadership today before considering some current questions preoccupying governments and people concerning the use of AI systems of governance. The role of leadership and leaders' impact on the development of social capital within these groups is less often discussed; though local or national political leadership which promotes shared models of social capital is an important factor in modern democracies and in the age of social media and the so-called "fake news" or "truth decay" as Kavanagh and Rich (2018) describes the decline from evidence-based, corroborated data and models to less soundly based AI and news or theories propounded online as exemplified by the current President Trump's tweeting and legal challenges to the election result as well as the implied discrediting of the US legal and constitutional system which has so far legitimated Biden's win in the presidential election. That is especially true when deliberate manipulation of news and social reactions is today a key feature of the declining trust of voters in their governments, their systems of justice, and the associated structures of policing, representative elections, and the performance of leadership. Today, many people especially younger people rely almost exclusively on social media for news and entertainment and social media sites utilize AI to ensure greater "click-thru," that is, user retention on the site and return users.

In fact, despite the gap in this area of social research, leadership is generally reported to be the most researched aspect of human behavior (Dulewicz & Higgs, 2005). However, based on theories of inherent traits dating back to Galton's (1869) proposal of "Hereditary Genius" (Galton, 2012), it was taken for granted for very many years that leaders were born rather than developed. This "great man" theory dominated empirical and theoretical work in the early stages of leadership research (Zaccaro, 2007) and still has adherents today, although the leadership picture is now much more dynamic.

COVID-19 or Severe Acute Respiratory Syndrome Coronavirus 2 (SARS-CoV-2) as it is named and which has now been officially listed as a global pandemic by the World Health Organisation (WHO) where over 2 million people have died and many hundreds of thousands are currently diagnosed as suffering from COVID-19 virus which is the major global challenge currently facing most leaders in government, NGOs, and businesses since the end of the Second World War. It is part of a series of viral epidemics in a line of descent from the 2003 SARS outbreak which infected 8,000 people with 10% fatality. SARS-CoV-2 spreads much faster, infecting more than 80,000 people by February 2020. The virus has now spread to 53 countries in all six WHO regions in less than two months and has already mutated into a new form in some animals on mink farms in Denmark and France; so governments in these two countries have decided to cull those farmed mink populations.

So far, hospitals are mostly coping with the influx of severely infected COVID-19 patients, but may soon become overwhelmed if the numbers of severely ill patients increases. The effectiveness of testing AND contact-tracing, vital to reduce the rate of reproduction, may also begin to diminish if cases are diagnosed late and if by then the prognosis has worsened for individuals and/or secondary and tertiary waves of infection have occurred or if people refuse to be tested or to exercise the proposed restraint in their socializing. In other words, if they reject their leaders' to engage in collaborative, community preventive action against the disease.

For some time prior to the outbreak of COVID-19, there has been a pre-existing global crisis of leadership as well as declining trust of leadership by diverse stakeholders' and the general public across all types of organizations including businesses, governments, and NGOs, many of which are now actively involved in the struggle to prevent the spread of the pandemic (Smith & Cockburn 2021). Two out of every five new CEOs were failing in the first 18 months of their tenure (Ciampa, 2005). Four out of ten newly promoted managers and executives were failing within 18 months of starting new jobs, according to research (Vollhardt, 2005); "failing" includes termination for below-par performance or voluntarily resigning from the position. Vollhardt (2005) notes that the following types of executives experienced the highest failure rates within the first 18 months: senior-level executives (39%), sales. "Business as usual" is not a viable option and organizations must change or die. Organizations are often advised to manage their knowledge, be creative and think outside the box, learning from failures as well as from success. However, as Krohe (2011) notes:

> [...] The awkward truth is that while failure may teach a company how to succeed, success often teaches a company to fail, by misleading it into thinking that it knows more than it does.

Leadership is no longer a matter of simply setting a direction and ensuring it is being followed – leadership for the future is about having a vision with an uncertain path to its achievement which may only be attempted through reflective flexibility and agility in the collaborative company of fellow community stakeholders (Smith & Cockburn, 2013, 2014, 2016). Birasnav et al. (2011) underline the importance of leadership development programs in the organizations because of the reported direct relationship between leadership and organizational performance in all types of organizations – including all local and national governments, primary healthcare facilities, and social care service delivery (Aragon-Correa et al., 2007). Regrettably, as Marquardt (2000, p. 233) insightfully explains (citing Dilworth, 1996, p. 49),

> What has become increasingly clear to almost every organization is that our new century demands new kinds of leaders with new skills. Leadership styles and skills that may have worked in a more

stable, predictable environment of the twentieth century will be inadequate in this new era of uncertainty and rapid change, where we can hardly define the problem, much less engineer possible solutions *and further, he asserts that* the leadership development as practiced by most corporations and institutions of higher learning, "produces individuals who are technologically literate and unable to deal with intricate problem-solving models, but are also essentially distanced from the human dimensions that must be taken into account."

Leadership is not solely about a systematic utilization of objective, economically rationalist, and calculative forms of decision-making (Higgs, 2009; Slattery, 2009; Smith & Cockburn, 2013). There are other key concepts prevalent in the research literature. For example, it is axiomatic that a leader in a commercial enterprise must try to ensure that it remains or becomes profitable in order for the business to survive. The leaders of service organizations must ensure that they satisfy the service consumers' expectations. Government leaders must be seen as attempting to meet the needs of all citizens to grow the social capital of the whole country. These ends are the *sine qua non* for the continued trust of stockholders and stakeholders and thereby, the existence of such enterprises, governments, and their leaders.

System justification theory argues that perceived threats to communities may ironically often lead individuals to increase trust in authorities such as governments, and people are thus more likely to justify and rationalize the way things are, even when leaders and political systems actually do negatively affect their longer term or underlying community interests. For these reasons, high domestic approval ratings of leaders in light of the fear and uncertainty, that a pandemic or crisis provokes, must be interpreted carefully. Examining how leaders are perceived by a variety of stakeholders, including the international community, may provide greater insight into the ways that different approaches and procedures have been evaluated. One key reason suggested for such apparently counter-intuitive types of system justifications is that the public still retains a hankering for the so-called "heroic" style of leadership. In writing about what leaders ought to be focusing on, Marshall (2000, pp. 248–249), claimed leaders should be: involved in critical self-reflection and participative practices; engaged in systemic reasoning and action with awareness of their own as well as others' behaviors as aspects of the system and should be asking themselves if they were simply completing a given system pattern rather than pursuing valuable purposes; opening spaces of possibility (Ba); using self-reflection to counter the potential arrogance of believing oneself a leader and thus always "right" about organizational, societal, or planetary needs; developing and deepening wisdom; listening to others; and avoiding the notion of leader as an heroic individual. The leadership of the two major superpowers, USA and Russia, that is, Trump and Putin, have been seen by many in the media as exemplars of such unfounded and arrogant self-belief and President Trump's assertion that the Democrats "stole" the election has led to strife and division among supporters of his and of the president-elect, Biden thus US social capital is much reduced and severely fragmented as recent polling of the two sides' supporters reveals that Trump's supporters believe him and feel cheated out of another four years of the Trump presidency aimed at "making America great again."

Alimo-Metcalfe (2010) explains that it was previously argued that one of the chief reasons for the lack of women in senior management positions was the insidious gender bias in all aspects of talent management (Alimo-Metcalfe, 1994). This author ponders why this is still so, given that studies show that organizations with a higher percentage of women on their boards perform more successfully (McKinsey, 2007, 2009). During the current pandemic, ratings of female leadership as exhibited by Jacinda Ardern in New Zealand, Angela Merkel in Germany, and others have all been generally very positive by public and media despite their different political perspectives (Wittenberg-Cox, 2020). Alimo-Metcalf (2010) proposes that this bias persists as a result of a pervading organizational view of leadership that is influenced by its implicit male supremacy. Alimo-Metcalf (2010) goes on to assert that models of leadership that dominated the 1980s and 1990s were based predominantly or exclusively on samples of male managers, and often on self-reports of why they thought they were successful (Alimo-Metcalfe, 2007). For the most part, these were "heroic" models of leadership, which failed to distinguish between the characteristics of "distant" and "nearby" leadership (Shamir, 1995) and were invalid even when originally proposed.

Hierarchy to Heterarchy

Walton (2011) asserts that all the leadership-related titles in bookstores prove that the lure of the "heroic and grandiose" is still very much alive, and indeed its appeal is evident in the demand for charismatic, heroic, transformational, and inspirational executive leadership to try to deliver stakeholder value and build viable organizations. As Walton (2011) points out, this unshakable belief in traditional forms of heroic leadership, and an accompanying reliance on these flamboyant leadership styles, create a toxic mix; this author cites a catalog of high profile corporate transgressions since 2001, all attributed to high-flying executive blunders of one sort or another (Gray et al., 2005; Hamilton & Micklethwait, 2006). That leadership approach led to recklessness where profitability meant everything, and anyone daring to question whether profitability was actually the answer risked being driven out of the elitist club. In redressing such leadership issues, Passmore (2010) asserts that a crucial problem is that executives do not really understand leadership or how to develop a global leadership strategy that will enable their organization to grow and change with the changing world, or thrive in today's growing digitally linked environments.

We would also suggest that the bottom up nature of much AI and the COVID-19 pandemic are tacitly nudging societies toward the erosion of the differences between public and private spheres of social life as monetizing of websites has proved to be for social networking sites such as Facebook, that is, the site becomes a place where people not only socialize or network but get interrupted by advertisements and sales, leading to a 24/7 mentality of the ever open digital storefront. On the other hand, there has been a rise in armchair activism of the *gofundme* type of charitable campaigning for disadvantaged and complaining or protesting from home via social media sites. In this way, AI and digital network technology trends are also shifting societies from hierarchies to heterarchies in many ways as distributed leadership emerges amid interconnected networks of supply chains of products in the evolution of IR4.0, organizational learning, and educationally networked centers of learning interact and social media input in each sector grows exponentially (Smith & Cockburn, 2013, pp. 143–149). As Muurlink and Matas 2011) noted:

> Since 2005 universities worldwide have begun to adopt speed dating protocols as a tool for building research culture ... speed dating is being adopted by industry and organisations for interpersonal development purposes. The term "speed networking" introduced by Ridd and Shaw (2005) coincides with this development, delivering to organisers a more culturally neutral tag that may help shake off its afterhours roots. (p. 751)

The Editors (2011) of the journal *Strategic Direction* stressed that good leadership is critical for success in most ventures where cooperation and collaboration are required to achieve a common goal; however, the challenges have become more acute in all fields, especially during the COVID-19 pandemic. The basis of this problem according to Passmore (2010) is that many organizations use competency models to identify leadership requirements, but such models were based on what worked in the past rather than on requirements for the changing world. More recently, Kellerman (2008, 2012) sees the "end of leadership" or more specifically "leader-centrism" and the emergence of a power-shift moving "followers" center-stage today. In fact, researchers have estimated that between half and three-quarters of leaders were not performing well prior to the emergence of the current ongoing crisis, and consequently their tenure is decreasing (Hogan & Hogan, 2001; Hogan & Kaiser, 2005). According to Gressgård (2011), information and communication technologies (ICTs) are increasingly being used to support collaborative work in all kinds of organizational settings, resulting in the appearance of novel organizational forms, distributed leadership based upon shared understandings and collaboration across organizations, departments, and work arrangements building collective social capital through bonding in teams (de Jong et al., 2007; Peters & Manz, 2007).

Virtual teams are teams with geographically dispersed members communicating primarily by use of ICTs are a feature of working from home for employees during lockdown periods across the world since the outbreak of COVID-19. Such teams are increasingly also being employed for the development of products and services, and factors important to the efficiency and effectiveness of such teams are being explored. Gressgard (2011) highlights the need for well-functioning computer-mediated team interaction in order to realize the innovation and collaboration potential as part of building-in social capital of such teams. As Smith and Cockburn (2013) noted leadership is no longer a simple matter of setting a strategic direction and ensuring it is being followed – leadership for the future and particularly during a pandemic is about having a vision with an uncertain path to its achievement which may only be attempted through reflective flexibility and agility in the collaborative company of fellow stakeholders.

Unequal Social Capital Burdens: Global Consumption, Economic Growth Underpinned by Rising Debt Levels

However, it is more than simply the technology that has changed in the globalized world of today, focused on ever-increasing economic growth. Professor Tim Jackson argues that global economic growth has reached a tipping point in relation to sustainability, he states: "The global economy is almost five times the size it was half a century ago. If it continues to grow at the same rate the economy will be 80 times that size by the year 2100" and demands on the planet will be unsustainable (Jackson, 2009, p. 22). Jackson (2009) also believes that increased consumer indebtedness fueled growth in the last 20+years "… it is generally agreed that the unprecedented consumption growth between 1990 and 2007 was fuelled by a massive expansion of credit and increasing levels of debt" (p. 22). The collapse of the sub-prime housing lending and investment market in the USA caused a tsunami of banking defaults and financial implosion in economies in many western countries which still cause waves of panic and uncertainty in current global markets. Jackson further states that:

> Over the course of more than a decade, consumer debt served as a deliberate mechanism for freeing personal spending from wage income and allowing consumption to drive the dynamics of growth.

He contrasts the Western indebtedness levels with corresponding levels of Eastern investment and savings, principally those in China and India, commenting that "The savings rate in China during 2008 was around 25% of disposable income, while in India it was even higher at 37%" (Jackson, 2009, p. 22). The levels of such external debt varied widely. In 2007–2008, external debt stood at 5% of GDP in China and India whereas it exceeded 900% of GDP in Ireland but there is currently a growing and unevenly distributed debt burden from lockdowns and other measures used to try to suppress the spread of COVID-19 globally.

In the twentieth century, the world population also quadrupled; during this period, the average number of children born to women of childbearing age was five (Clement, 2008); more recently this global average has halved (Clement, 2008, p. 4). Of course, such statistics conceal as much as they reveal in a certain sense. As population grows in absolute terms globally, there will be changes in the demographic and resource distribution within countries and regions, as well as between ethnic groups, gender, and age groups. In all countries, there has always been unequal access to resources to varying degrees. The emerging pattern is clear: the global poor are not participating proportionately in global economic gains. Today, however, more people have been forced to flee their homes than at any time since Second World War. Further, that figure is also up by 52 million people more worldwide than the figure for global migrant population we referred to 10 years previously (Cockburn, Desmarais, 2007; International Organization for Migration, IOM, 2006). Primarily this increase has been as a result of wars and terrorism in less developed regions and has amplified the complexity of socio-economic and political dynamics in many western nations in diverse and complex ways ranging from cultural crises to ethnic tensions, socio-digital economic change. For instance, on the positive side of the economic aspects is the balancing of the aging western population with younger migrants thus replenishing the workforce. However, that is in tension with the growth of automated systems for goods and services and the "Internet of things (IoT)," robotics, AI, algorithmic governance and how these technologies reduce the need for some human workers including professionals and worsen an already-expanding pensions funding gap and jobs and incomes lost due to the COVID-19 measures initiated locally (Smith & Cockburn, 2013, 2014, 2020, Vanham, 2017).

The ILO Report (2020) estimates that global labor income has declined nearly 11% or US$3.5 trillion in the first three quarters of 2020. This also has a side effect of reducing those workers with trade union representation, which can be seen as another form of social capital for union members or a workers' form of collaborative advantage as a counterbalance to the power and influence of corporations and owner/shareholders' wealth. As the Save the Children charity report indicates, the poor and ethnic minority groups' in metropolitan regions, especially children, tend to suffer disproportionately from COVID-19, unemployment and, during lockdowns there have been concerns raised about how readily the children of poor families can access some "home schooling resources such as computers in the UK as well as the potential impact of shortfalls in access during school closures will widen the gap for future generations too as these children get older" (Taylor & Garmirian, 2020). This deficit in access to technology not only impacts educational attainment but narrows opportunities and thereby restricts the development of educational as well as social and cultural capital (Windsor & Royal, 2014).

Brexit is premised upon the presumed advantages the country would accrue outside of the European Union (EU) in competing against other nations within the EU, for trade and access to new markets or resources. This is also a policy implicitly based upon the advantaged nations being able to sift and select from among those seeking entry based upon the set of visa criteria related to would-be migrants' Curriculum Vitaes (CVs). Specifically, the set of skills, experience, and qualifications sought by UK employers and government under rigorously policed borders which are currently challenged by rising numbers of migrants and asylum seekers has prompted some organizations to locate further "offshore" in different countries than before, as a means of further reducing economic costs and/or improving business environment, cutting regulatory costs, and ultimately, improving stakeholder returns. However, in parallel that reduction in local opportunities is also diminishing the trust and perceived legitimacy of the ruling elites for many of the excluded groups in the host countries. This has been a feature of the rise of #Black Lives Matter movement in USA and elsewhere.

Consequently, in reaction to the above perspective, a more cosmopolitan approach to defining citizenship has been advocated by many writers across many discipline areas. We have previously referred to the three Cs of global competition for resources and economic growth. These three Cs are Comparative advantage, Competitive advantage, and Collaborative advantage (Cockburn et al., 2007, 2017, 2020). These three systems continue to dynamically interact globally in complex and often surprising ways. Comparative advantage involves national level interactions as one country trades its economic or social advantages against another. Thus, those with better infrastructures, more resources, cheaper labor, better technology, and fewer restrictions have been able to bargain those advantages against other nations in such trading. Competitive advantage, usually viewed as competition between firms rather than states, has seen increasing governmental involvement aimed at improving the competitive advantages of one nation's firms relative to others (Porter, 1998, pp. 19, 30, 33–35). In effect, the case proposed in the UK for Brexit focused on "economic migrants" seeking entry legally and illegally.

The third C, collaborative advantage which ought to be at the forefront of the global campaign against the COVID-19 pandemic, as well as the rise of inequality, exclusion, and the growth of poverty, necessarily involves nations, as well as organizations, cooperating to leverage potential synergies to all parties mutual advantage. The current G20 meeting has indicated that there will need to be greater cooperation to reduce or defer debt repayment from poorer countries and more collaboration to rebuild infrastructures, especially healthcare in those regions. Pogge (2006) highlighted how the World Bank data on gross national income per capita, PPP (in 2006 US$s), in the high-income OECD countries rose 53.5% in real terms over the 1990–2001 globalization period: from $18,740 in 1990 to $28,761 in 2001 (and on to 2 $33,622 in 2005; retrieved from devdata.worldbank.org/dataonline, 11/20/2020). The poorer half of humankind have fared much less well, in terms of their real (inflation/PPP adjusted) consumption expenditure, during this same period. The gains for various percentiles of global society, labeled from the bottom up, are given below:

- +12.9% for the 10th percentile.
- +11.9% for the 7th percentile.
- +10.4% for the 5th percentile.
- +6.6% for the 3rd percentile.
- +1.0% for the 2nd percentile.
- −7.3% for the 1st (bottom) percentile.
- +20.4% for the 50th percentile (median).
- +20.0% for the 35th percentile.
- +15.9% for the 20th percentile.

There has been some income growth but during the current pandemic, the poor have suffered more than others in all countries, through lack of access to healthcare, education, medicines, work and food, retraining for future skills, and various other factors such as the concomitant decline in trade union power as businesses go bust, migration flows, and unemployment rises, further eroding the stake some groups have in the countries they live in and thus also diminishing community social capital as social bonds and ties to the dominant community values are thereby weakened among those excluded from the expected rewards or prospects of social mobility.

In the following remarks, Ngai (2003) succinctly illustrates key aspects of Urry's "economies of flows" with respect particularly to human flows in what she describes as the age of human cross-border flows enabled by the rise of the petroleum and steel' car as described by Urry (2008):

"In the globalised world of the early twenty-first century, when national borders have softened to encourage the movement of capital, information, manufactured goods, and cultural products, the persistence of hardened nationalist immigration policy would seem to demand our attention and critique". (Ngai, 2003, p. 264).

Derrida associates hospitality with cosmopolitanism although his view is extreme compared to others as he sees it as a psychological, as well as a cultural, driver of hospitable behavior and of friendship toward strangers. He outlined his views in an interview at the University of Sussex, UK in 1997 with Geoffrey Bennington as follows:

Q4. (Bennington): What about hospitality?

Answer (Derrida): I have to – and that's an unconditional injunction – I have to welcome the Other whoever he or she is unconditionally, without asking for a document, a name, a context, or a passport. That is the very first opening of my relation to the Other: to open my space, my home – my house, my language, my culture, my nation, my state, and myself. I don't have to open it, because it is open, it is open before I make a decision about it: then I have to keep it open or try to keep it open unconditionally. But of course, this unconditionality is a frightening thing, it's scary. If we decide everyone will be able to enter my space, my house, my home, my city, my state, my language, and if we think what I think, namely that this is entering my space unconditionally may well be able to displace everything in my space, to upset, to undermine, to even destroy, then the worst may happen and I am open to this, the best and the worst. But of course since this unconditional hospitality may lead to a perversion of this ethics of friendship, we have to condition this unconditionality, to negotiate the relation between this unconditional injunction and the necessary condition, to organise this hospitality, which means laws, rights, conventions, borders of course, laws on immigration and so on and so forth. We all have, especially in Europe, on both sides of the channel, this problem of immigration. That is, to what extent we should welcome the Other. So, in order to think of a new politics of hospitality, a new relationship to citizenship, to have to re-think all these problems that I have mentioned in the last few minutes.

Thus, some have defined the twenty-first century as a moment for envisioning and enacting more cosmopolitan forms of identity globally and in stark contrast to the other two forms, recognizing that everyone is affected by global warming and related environmental flows. Delanty summarizes and contrasts cosmopolitan citizenship, as follows:

> Cosmopolitan citizenship is defined by a decreased importance of territory – as measured by the place of one's birth – in the definition of citizenship rights as well as a lesser salience on an underlying collective identity, in other words a political community does not have to rest on an underlying cultural community. Cultural rights for all are thus possible in the space that has been created by multiple and overlapping identities. (Smith & Cockburn, 2020; Delanty, 2006, p. 5)

However, the statement above tacitly, some would say optimistically or naively, assumes all other local cultures willingly or at least peacefully, accept the right of those members of incoming ones to be treated equitably (or even accept their right to exist or co-exist locally). The political and environmental as well as public health decisions made by some authoritarian EU governments and leaders during the COVID-19 pandemic stands in contradiction to not only much accepted scientific evidence regarding the global public health aspects during a pandemic and other factors such as climate change that have been exacerbated by the pandemic and have used nationalism or ethnocentric rhetoric to justify actions favorable to nationalist rulers' perceptions of their country and their own public's perceptions of self-interest and the requirements of the Schengen free movement policy agreed by the member countries of the EU.

On the other hand, leaders who are seen to have placed scientific data and expertise about the best course of actions to take – rather than their own short-term political and economic interests – at the forefront of policy making, have, thus far, been seen to have managed to control their case numbers and earn the trust of their citizens. By taking on a more collaborative perspective, countries can work together, not only with professionals within their own nations but also on an international scale, to tackle the current as well as future coronavirus epidemics. Indeed, there is also a case being made concerning community NGOs' current lack of access to a lot of peer-reviewed research and whether that access ought to be a part of universities' role as stewards of the research within the local community (Holzmeyer, 2018; Wittenberg-Cox, 2020).

Alimo-Metcalfe (2010) explains that the predominant aspect of the collaborative leadership model is its essentially "feminine" perspective of leadership, strongly emphasizing support for others. It also underscores assisting followers to regard leadership as a social partnering process, rather than one of power over others. There is throughout a strong theme of inclusion, collaboration, and connectedness in a spirit of co-creation, with emphasis on removing barriers to communication, and promoting joint-working by actively encouraging the sharing of ideas between all stakeholders inside and outside the organization. The vilified heroic model of an earlier period is replaced by a distributed approach, focused on building a shared vision with a range of internal and external stakeholders. Nevertheless, localism, even isolationism, survives as the 2016 elections in the UK and the USA demonstrated, so a judicious mix of the perceived gains of these two perspectives, values, and stances to political and social or economic matters may be encouraged, at least in the short-to-medium term, by the growth of socio-digital technologies, IR 4.0, and social media. What Sach (1999) describes as cosmopolitan–localism aims to increase networking for mutual collaboration and advantage, Kossoff describes as "This symbiotic connection between different levels of scale of everyday life, from the local to the planet as a whole, would integrate two longstanding and distinct traditions – cosmopolitanism and localism – and would be the basis for a new kind of social, cultural, political and economic settlement, Cosmopolitan Localism" (Kossoff, 2019).

The hybrid cosmopolitan–localist model fully exploits the diversity of perspectives and the wealth of experiences, strengths, and potential, which exist within the regions or organizations, and with its partners and other stakeholders. Perhaps then, a collaborative blend of cosmopolitan and localist approaches is now necessary in the globalized world of the early twenty-first century. The fate of humanity and planetary ecosystems are inextricably intertwined at both the local and global levels as Sach and others such as Irwin (2015) have previously suggested, so that as national borders have softened to encourage the flows of capital, information, manufactured goods, and cultural products, the persistence of hardened nationalist immigration policy would thus seem to demand our attention and critique, especially in a time of a global pandemic and national lockdowns as previously proposed by Ngai (2003, p. 264).

COVID-19 has resulted in approximately 20% of patients experiencing severe infections requiring hospitalization and the current mortality rate as of deaths per number of diagnosed cases as of March 20, 2020, is 4.1%, though the percentage ranges from 0.2% to 15% depending on age and other health problems. That rate is much lower than SARS and MERS but there may be more cases undiagnosed as many places do not test a large proportion of the population so the death rate could be lower when unconfirmed cases are included despite a faster rate of infection. The worldwide epicenter has now shifted from Wuhan in China to Italy and has now resulted in declarations of emergencies in many nations and a complete countrywide lockdown in many cases such as Italy, Spain, France with all but vital businesses and services closed and draconian powers initiated to enable police to curb movements of people and mass assemblies of the public. (Emerald publishing data on COVID-19 retrieved from https://www.emerald.com/insight/content/, doi/10.1108/OXAN-DB250999/full/html on 21/02/2020). Consequently, many sporting venues and fixtures as well as festivals have been closed, as well as bars, restaurants, shops (other than pharmacies and food stores). As of March 22, 2020, New York, America's largest city has been put on lockdown, India has declared a countrywide lockdown, closing rail and bus services.

Hospitals in the UK, Spain, France, and Northern Italy have been overwhelmed in many parts of these countries and medical staff are complaining of a lack of protective equipment such as masks and gowns as well as medical equipment for the severely infected patients. The UK Health Minister has stated that Britain will buy as much medical ventilation equipment as it can. China has sent volunteer medics and medical equipment to Italy as they say that they have the outbreak there under control and there are no new cases other than people returning home to China from abroad or foreigners coming into the country from elsewhere. Most governments are now asking for communities to adhere to the self-isolation and lockdown regulations as the best means of reducing the spread of infection and fines are being used to reinforce their calls for greater social solidarity and community social capital. News and social media have a steady stream of items covering the pandemic.

Concluding Comments AI Governance: Truth Decay and Shades of Gray: Some Question and Comments on the Impact of AI on Social Capital

Algorithmic systems are a form of automated data mining, data sorting, data classification, and data communication or presentation to end users (Danahar et al., 2017). AI refers to the combination of computer algorithms, data, and the interface processes and inference engines that together determine the outcomes that affect and inform the end users. AI technologies are transforming the fields of public health, biomedical research, and medicine and today algorithms that evolve using machine learning by analysis and inferences based upon data gathered are used to predict clusters. Many types of decisions can be made faster and more efficiently using algorithms for track and trace and predicting new or emergent clusters of COVID-19. The coronavirus crisis is an example of how AI applications can provide an immediate response to the pandemic as occurred in the South Korean government's successful use of a mobile phone app for contact tracing.

A significant factor in the adoption of algorithmic systems for decision-making is their capacity to process large amounts of varied data sets (i.e. big data), which can be paired with machine learning methods in order to infer statistical models directly from the data. Automation entails the use of computerized systems designed to assist individuals making technical or other decisions or to help identify relevant criteria, evidence, or particular issues for consideration in making a decision or in acting upon a decision. Automated assistance in administrative decision-making refers to automating systems so that they can assist administrators in decision-making in a number of ways. Automation may make decision-making more accurate, consistent, cost-effective, quicker, and be perceived as less risky since the decision reached will be seen as "neutral" and thus free of potential human biases due to improper motivations or bad faith. Such automated systems may take the decisions out of the hands of the human administrators by default unless ethically designed and regulated.

We focus here on current regulation of the use of AI in search engines which is fraught with privacy and surveillance issues related to the extremely precise *personalization* of companies targeting of potential customers enabled by the use of algorithms to monitor and record web users' activity online and link to other massive data sets. More significantly, companies can also use the psychology of "nudging" to move web users toward particular products and services by filtering data and information presented and biasing the inferences as well as other means of getting users to move toward a positive response. Nudges operate by getting individuals to take the line of least resistance in deciding on a course of action. It has been used in non-AI marketing, for instance, by placing sweets next to checkouts in supermarket stores at a child's eye level. Accompanying parents may begin to be influenced into making a purchase of these sweets to reduce the fuss created at the checkout by their child. Recently, this selling technique has been banned in high street stores the UK (BBC News). Nevertheless, similar tactics are frequently used by online organizations when offering "free trials" of their services, as long as you give the organization your credit card details. These organisations then make it hard to cancel the free trial before the time limit when the user's details will be used automatically to subscribe them and thereby getting users to pay the full membership cost, according to Veliz(2018). It is suggested by some authors that this is a deliberately deceitful form of marketing which impacts on personal autonomy as well as being a deceitful form of selling (Saurwein, et al., 2015, pp. 35–37).

As Danahar et al. (2017) point out algorithmic governance is a quasi-intelligent adaptive system and in algorithms using a "bottom up" approach to evolve and determine actions, that is, with no top-down human monitoring or control, is a bigger problem potentially. Many people have expectations that they should be able to control automated governance and accountability systems to ensure normative approaches to ethics and fairness in dealing with other humans as they do with court cases, for example, though some authors regard AI as increasingly a-normative (Rouvroy, 2013), and hence unacceptable for community social capital, thereby replacing an administrator/moderator or someone in the hierarchy such as Chief Information Officers (CIOs) who would usually be involved in the decision process is unacceptable for governance of humans, as IEEE (2019) states. Alternatively, the system may simply recommend a decision to the decision-maker or it may guide a user through "relevant" facts, legislation, and/or policy options, as determined by programming of machine logic and thus the system may possibly end up by closing off alternative, more social or human paths or those options or choices deemed irrelevant as it proceeds (Danaher et al., 2017).

The European Parliament (2019) report states:

> "A significant factor in the adoption of algorithmic systems for decision-making is their capacity to process large amounts of varied data sets (i.e. big 16 data), which can be paired with machine learning methods in order to infer statistical models directly from the data. The same properties of scale, complexity and autonomous model inference however are linked to increasing concerns that many of these systems are opaque to the people affected by their use and lack clear explanations for the decisions they make. This lack of transparency risks undermining meaningful scrutiny and accountability, which is a significant concern when these

systems are applied as part of decision-making processes that can have a considerable impact on people's human rights (e.g. critical safety decisions in autonomous vehicles; allocation of health and social service resources, etc.)."

However, automated systems raise difficult questions about authorization and reviewability of decision-making by a non-human agent; there are difficulties inherent in applying legislation and resolving complexities and ambiguity; and some potential for coding errors. There is still potential for jurisdictional error if there is an error in the automation. This is illustrated by the difficulties associated with the Australian Commonwealth Department of Human Services and Centrelink's online system for raising and recovering social security debts from people who claimed them while unemployed.

Advanced societies already have capabilities in decision-support systems, providing useful commentary, including indicating information about relevant legislation, case law, and policy for the human decision-maker at relevant points in the decision-making process, and/or may be used as a self-assessment tool, providing preliminary assessments for individuals or internal decision-makers. Automated assisted decision-making can help identify:

- the correct question(s) for the decision-maker to determine, including the relevant decision-making criteria and any relevant or irrelevant considerations;
- whether any procedures or matters which are necessary preconditions to the exercise of the power have been met or exist;
- whether there exists any evidence in respect of each of the matters on which the decision-maker must be satisfied;

and

- particular issues which require the decision-maker's consideration and evaluation. The benefits of automation are not unlimited.

Generally, these automated decision systems contain three main components:

- a knowledge base or rule base containing the relevant business rules (i.e. legislative, policy, or procedural business rules),
- an independent inference engine which uses programmed reasoning (backward or forward chaining) to draw conclusions,

and

- a user interface which presents questions and information to the user and supplies the user's response to the inference engine in order to draw conclusions.

In addition to time and cost savings, automated decision-making has the capacity to diminish or even eliminate the risk that a decision will be invalidated by reason of:

- the motivations of the decision-maker (such as decisions made for an improper or ulterior purpose)

and/or

- bad faith of the decision-maker (such as decisions made with intended dishonesty, or recklessly or capriciously made for an improper or irrelevant purpose, or arbitrarily exceeding power).

Evolution and Complexity of Systems

However, machine learning through iterative analysis of "Big Data Sets" is a branch of AI that allows computer systems to learn directly from examples, data, and experience. Through machine learning and experimentation, computers develop evolving algorithms to make inferences and predictions and then improve these inferences and predictions over time. There are diverse types of AI in use ranging from search engines like Google to spam and antivirus filters and marketing tools such as datamining using small programs such as cookies to capture details of user experience and activity. Other forms of legal surveillance occur too, such as traffic monitoring and use of bots like "Alexa" to perform some tasks such as selecting programs to run on smart TVs and other devices. Autonomous vehicles have been heralded as a means to reduce road accidents, improve driver behaviors, improve vehicle maintenance, and reduce stress.

AI now allows machines to generate their own content and potentially create digital business materials without any component part that was directly created by a person. For instance, machines can create text that is more persuasive than text written by human marketers. Images, graphics, speech, and videos are not far behind.

Businesses have always collected and analyzed customer information, formally and informally or tacitly, but the volume and granular detail of data as well as the speed at which it can be mined for correlations across massive, diverse, and unstructured data sets makes today's collection and analysis qualitatively as well as quantitatively different. Big data analytics can often reveal relationships that humans might never have notice or have considered and then target groups of people with psychologically based "nudges," encouraging them toward the seemingly straightforward or easier course of action – a form of inertial marketing. Thus, even metadata, that is data about data, can be as predictive as the time spent and the substance of consumers' viewing or web surfing behaviors, tested per second until the optimal algorithm for the task, given the data available, emerges. The speed at which machines can be trained and/or train themselves to perform complex tasks is also accelerating exponentially. In 2017, training an algorithm to classify images required an hour, but only required four minutes in 2018. In 2020, Google Brain announced a new automated machine learning system that starts with a set of randomly created algorithms, takes the best performers for the desired task and randomly and iteratively mutates the top performers among those, at a speed such that 10,000 models per second, per processor. It can also carry out these trials 24/7, with very little input from human operators.

Some uses have been seen this technology as double edged, that is, embodying both positive and negative aspects. For example, AI with predictive analytics functions is being used extensively in healthcare, globally. Increasing numbers of medical organizations are exploiting healthcare analytics to enable proactive clinical decision-making. That means they claim to be able to move from reactive healthcare, that is, responding to emergent healthcare situations toward trying to anticipate and prevent them from occurring. Similarly, targeting specific personality types or behaviors can be used to increase marketing effectiveness. It is therefore possible to aim for a perceived public good such as increasing willingness to obey public health restrictions, avoid hazards, and to attempt to engender that at a macro-level through AI using the so-called "nudging" process. Big Data set analytics has revealed, for instance, that the hue, brightness, and saturation of photos consumers post online is often as predictive of posters' personalities as embedded in the content of the photos (Linder, 2020). So, uncovering that metadata about individuals' use of a social media site and how often they use particular functions, whether they completed various information sections, and how many contacts they had – predicted their personality traits of relevance to marketers, regardless of what the individuals did on the site, what they reported in the information sections, and who their contacts were. Thus, web users' individual autonomy and right to choose a course of action is not technically infringed. We expect to retain the right to choose a course of action, though these choices are influenced by the effort or trouble a particular course of action is assumed to cost, thus parents of small children might opt to buy sweets that are on display at checkouts rather than suffer childish tantrums. However, this technique of nudging children to urge parents to purchase sweets in shops has recently been banned in the UK.

However, this kind of ability also means that there is a potential to engage in manipulation of public opinion as suggested in dystopian novels such as George Orwell's *1984* or Aldous Huxley's *Brave New World*. Amoore and Piotukh (2015, p. 342) argue that "the technologies of analytics focus human attention and decision on particular persons and things of interest, whilst annulling or discarding much of the material context from which they are extracted," resulting in a type of non-conscious cognition akin to the type of trance-like cognition that drivers sometimes exhibit when they drive from A to B without having consciously registered doing so (though they may well have negotiated various obstacles, junctions, other traffic very successfully without realizing they were doing so). So, structural social capital at the macro-level including transparency and democracy could be undermined surreptitiously and many people are concerned about how closely AI is used to spy on them and thus the EU has already introduced regulations on the likes of Google and Facebook to ensure this invasion of privacy is more strictly regulated.

Big Data is also not necessarily culturally embodied in local communities. AI itself is an umbrella term that encompasses a diverse set of technologies. AI algorithms and automated processes will not work equally effectively worldwide, because different regions have different cultural models of what constitutes sociability and ethics. Ethical issues in local communities can then all too easily be rendered invisible or inappropriately reduced or, worse, simplified (IEEE, 2019).

AI ethics isn't just about doing the right thing or making the best AI systems possible, it's also about who wields power and how AI affects the balance of power in everything it touches across society including businesses, institutions, and governments – ultimately, affecting the privacy and human rights of all individuals globally.

AI and their associated algorithms are not merely used to instrumentally enhance the power of certain actors within existing transnational governance arrangements. Rather Big Data are altering the character of existing governance arrangements and constituting new forms of governance.

Inclusive Social capital

Definitions of social capital have varied: some broad others narrow. The OECD, for example, currently has a broad research project on social capital. These researchers have defined social capital as comprising four key areas. These areas are:

- Personal relationships, referring to the structure of people's social networks, including workplaces.
- Depth and breadth of social network support available to each person in their networks.
- Civic engagement activities such as volunteering and community action.
- Beliefs, attitudes, and action frames of reference such as trust and cooperative norms of reciprocity.

In the age of AI governance, we would add another element to the OECD definition of social capital to address and encapsulate bridging and bonding norms of global connectedness, anchoring, and mainstreaming social capital equality for all, obviating multiple tiers of access and provision that leave some in a "catch up" situation. We would add the following point.

- Inclusive socio-digital capital imbued with multicultural and ethical design values and increased social capital for all is vital in a period of unprecedented challenge when individual citizens are currently being asked to accept many restrictions on their freedom such as reducing travel internationally and locally, limiting socializing with friends and family, socially distancing, at home, at work, and in their social lives to enable the health systems and local and national governments to cope with the pandemic and reduce the rate of infection for all others in the country or region.

Social capital is taken by many to refer to shared understandings, behavioral norms, and cultural values development within social groups as well as individuals' roles. The role of leadership and leaders' impact on the development of social capital within these groups is less often discussed, though local or national political leadership which promotes shared models of social capital is an important factor in modern democracies and in the age of social media and the so-called "fake news," conspiracy theories, and hostile state interference, that is especially true. We are in a time when deliberate manipulation of news and social reactions is today a key feature of the declining trust of voters in their governments, their systems of justice and the associated structures of policing, representative elections, and the performance of leadership at all levels. Today, many people especially younger people, rely almost exclusively on social media for news and entertainment and social media sites utilize AI to ensure greater "click-thru," that is, user retention on the site and return users.

In fact, despite the gap in this particular area of social research, leadership is generally reported to be the most researched aspect of human behavior (Dulewicz & Higgs, 2005). However, based on theories of inherent traits dating back to Galton's (1869) proposal of "Hereditary Genius" (Galton, 2012), it was often taken for granted for very many years that leaders were born rather than developed. This "great man" theory dominated empirical and theoretical work in the early stages of leadership research (Zaccaro, 2007) and still has adherents today, although the leadership picture is now much more dynamic.

COVID-19 or Severe Acute Respiratory Syndrome Coronavirus 2 (SARS-CoV-2) as it is named and which has now been officially listed as a global pandemic by the World Health organization (WHO) is the major global challenge currently facing most leaders in government, NGOs, and businesses since the end of the Second World War. It is part of a series of viral epidemics in a line of descent from the 2003 SARS outbreak which infected 8,000 people with 10% fatality. SARS-CoV-2 spreads much faster, infecting more than 80,000 people by February 2020. The virus has now spread to 53 countries in all six WHO regions in less than two months and has already mutated into a new form in some animals on mink farms in Denmark and in a cull of thousands of animals and more recently at Turkey farms in the UK, where 10,500 birds have been culled.

So far, hospitals are mostly coping with the influx of severely infected COVID-19 patients but may soon become overwhelmed if the numbers of severely ill patients increases. The effectiveness of testing AND contact-tracing, vital to reduce the rate of reproduction, may also begin to diminish if cases are diagnosed late and if by then the prognosis has worsened for individuals and/or secondary and tertiary waves of infection have occurred or if people refuse to be tested or to exercise the proposed restraint in their socializing. In other words, if they reject their leaders' to engage in collaborative, community preventive action against the disease.

For some time prior to the outbreak of COVID-19, there has been a pre-existing global crisis of leadership as well as declining trust of leadership by diverse stakeholders' and the general public across all types of organizations including businesses, governments, and NGOs, many of which are now actively involved in the struggle to prevent the spread of the pandemic (Smith and Cockburn 2021). Two out of every five new CEOs were failing in the first 18 months of their tenure (Ciampa, 2005). Four out of ten newly promoted managers and executives were failing within 18 months of starting new jobs, according to research (Vollhardt, 2005); "failing" includes termination for below-par performance or voluntarily resigning from the position. Vollhardt (2005) notes that the following types of executives experienced the highest failure rates within the first 18 months: senior-level executives (39%), sales. "Business as usual" is not a viable option and organizations must change or die. Organizations are often advised to manage their knowledge, be creative and think outside the box, learning from failures as well as from success. However, as Krohe (2011) notes:

> [...]The awkward truth is that while failure may teach a company how to succeed, success often teaches a company to fail, by misleading it into thinking that it knows more than it does.

Leadership is no longer a matter of simply setting a direction and ensuring it is being followed - leadership for the future is about having a vision with an uncertain path to its achievement which may only be attempted through reflective flexibility and agility in the collaborative company of fellow community stakeholders (Smith & Cockburn, 2013, 2014, 2016). Birasnav et al. (2011) underline the importance of leadership development programs in the organizations because of the reported direct relationship between leadership and organizational performance in all types of organizations – including all local and national governments, primary healthcare facilities and social care service delivery (Aragon-Correa et al., 2007). Regrettably, as Marquardt (2000, p. 233) insightfully explains (citing Dilworth, 1996, p. 49),

> What has become increasingly clear to almost every organization is that our new century demands new kinds of leaders with new skills. Leadership styles and skills that may have worked in a more stable, predictable environment of the twentieth century will be inadequate in this new era of uncertainty and rapid change, where we can hardly define the problem, much less engineer possible solutions

and further, he asserts that

> the leadership development as practiced by most corporations and institutions of higher learning, "produces individuals who are technologically literate and unable to deal with intricate problem-solving models, but are also essentially distanced from the human dimensions that must be taken into account.

Leadership is not solely about a systematic utilization of objective, economically rationalist, and calculative forms of decision-making (Higgs, 2009; Slattery, 2009; Smith & Cockburn, 2013). There are other key concepts prevalent in the research literature. For example, it is axiomatic that a leader in a commercial enterprise must try to ensure that it remains or becomes profitable in order for the business to survive. The leaders of service organizations must ensure they satisfy the service consumers' expectations. Government leaders must be seen as attempting to meet the needs of all citizens to grow the social capital of the whole country. These ends are the *sine qua non* for the continued trust of stockholders and stakeholders and thereby, the existence of such enterprises, governments, and their leaders.

System justification theory argues that perceived threats to communities may ironically often lead individuals to increase trust in authorities such as governments, and people are thus more likely to justify and rationalize the way things are, even when leaders and political systems actually do negatively affect their longer-term or underlying community interests. For these reasons, high domestic approval ratings of leaders in light of the fear and uncertainty that a pandemic or crisis provokes, must be interpreted carefully. Examining how leaders are perceived by a variety of stakeholders, including the international community, may provide greater insight into the ways that different approaches and procedures have been evaluated. One key reason suggested for such apparently counter-intuitive types of system justifications is that the public still retains a hankering for the so-called "heroic" style of leadership. In writing about what leaders ought to be focusing on, Marshall (2000, pp. 248-249), claimed leaders should be: involved in critical self-reflection and participative practices; engaged in systemic reasoning and action with awareness of their own as well as others' behaviors as aspects of the system and should be asking themselves if they were simply completing a given system pattern rather than pursuing valuable purposes; opening spaces of possibility (Ba); using self-reflection to counter the potential arrogance of believing oneself a leader and thus always "right" about organizational, societal or planetary needs; developing and deepening wisdom; listening to others; and avoiding the notion of leader as an heroic individual. The leadership of the two major superpowers, USA and Russia, that is, Trump and Putin, have been seen by many in the media as exemplars of such unfounded and arrogant self-belief and President Trump's assertion that the Democrats "stole" the election has led to strife and division among supporters of his and of the president-elect, Biden thus US social capital is much reduced and severely fragmented as recent polling of the two sides' supporters reveals that Trump's supporters believe him and feel cheated out of another four years of the Trump presidency aimed at "making America great again."

Perhaps more significantly the network technology is often promoted as having potential for, that is, veracity. Particularly in the so-called "Unsupervised" systems which take unlabeled data and the computer then finds patterns itself as in the Google Brain project which seeks to completely eliminate any top down human input or moderation in order to reduce bias and limitations of human intellectual processes. Software company Oracle notes that an unsupervised machine learning system is "useful for customer segmentation because it will return groups based on parameters that a human may not consider .... One process takes many versions of, for example, a webpage, along with 'any historical or current information' the system has about individual consumers, and continuously experiments to determine which version shown to which consumer in which context is most effective."

Therefore, it is hardly surprising that, according to the Pew Research Center report by Aaron Smith, released in November 2018, over half of Americans surveyed found it unacceptable to use algorithms to make decisions with real-world consequences for humans. In the age of connectedness and the emergent IoT, many people are not yet ready to cede more control of their currently offline lives to current online technology. This chapter reviews arguments for and against algorithmic governance.

Ideally, algorithms should not be set to make straightforward ethical choices, but should be programmed so as to make "context-dependent" choices and some technological capacity is required to deal with information in "real" rather than "reactive" time, that is, before data get wiped and to avoid gaming the regulatory system. Such gaming can be attempted by the use of bots and other devices to mislead such that information flows are generated that might, at first sight, appear as "real," but, on second sight, reveal that they are generated by artificial means and/or are inflated so as to provide greater visibility to some "information" more than others as in the accusations about social media manipulation in the US 2016 Presidential election.

Other issues include system parameter flexibility, tacit and explicit logic, type and degree of individual or corporate accountability, opting out and opting in constraints and opportunities, global reach, and local impacts (IEEE, 2019, Linder, 2020).

The article by Larsson (2018) analyzes the Commonwealth, NSW, and SA data-sharing legislation and the need for protection for vulnerable people, such as children or people with a mental illness, transparency, and accountability.

"Robots" typically refer to embodied AI which can physically act in the real world. These physical manifestations might also have sensory inputs and abilities powered by machine learning.

Algorithmic marketing systems autonomously experiment by engaging in random actions on a subset of cases. The systems analyze responses to these experiments with reference to a business objective, such as sales to new customers or revenue maximization. They then continuously adapt to select which actions to take in the future, balancing "exploratory learning and exploitation of that learning." Rouvroy and Berns (2013) describe AI as a-normative insofar as there is no norm-referencing to "average" cases. Instead, there is an accumulation of distinct instances of correlation which is inherently problematic; they resemble the multiple forecasting models used by hurricane watchers where one day's "perfect prediction" might be completely "off" the following day (Rouvroy, 2011). Rouvroy and Berns (2013) in their paper elaborate further with an analogy that "We here simply argue that datamining, used for profiling purposes (irrespective of the applications), following a correlation rationale to rebuild singular cases fragmented by coding, relates these singular cases not to a general norm, but only to a system of eminently evolving relations between various measurements that are not reducible to any average. This emancipation from all forms of average stems essentially from the self-learning nature of these systems and can be considered inherent to contemporary normative action." They argue that no algorithm is "unbiased" in that the initial default setting matters, and so does the type of information that is available for updating. To maintain "neutral" algorithms might therefore require biased inputs so as to avoid highly undesirable and divisive outcomes, since even as machines become increasingly "autonomous" and "intelligent," they of course remain dependent on the initial design, intentions, the scripts or scenarios on the basis of which they were conceived. From the time of the design (and irrespective of the forms they later take on), they convey visions of the world, conscious and subconscious expectations, and projections of their designers Rouvroy (2011, cited in Rouvroy & Berns, 2013). AI data mining therefore is no better than hurricane predictions – perfect one day completely wrong the next. However, Harvard Professor Frank Pasquale (2016) asserts that "Hidden algorithms can make (or ruin) reputations, decide the destiny of entrepreneurs, or even devastate an entire economy."

On the other hand, algorithmic regulation can also be said to increase the potential for giving "voice": enhanced information can be used for a more powerful engagement with users (e.g. users of public services). The threat of "choice" and "voice" might make providers of services more responsive to users. However, there is a fear that new forms of information filtering will result in forms of informational immunization conducive to a radicalization of opinions and the disappearance of shared experience (Sunstein, 2009).

Mediated Data and Voice: Centrelink Case

However, as individual experiences disappear into "big data" sets of such a-normative correlations, personal engagement is thereby mediated. This, in turn, points to the requirement that we need to understand better the ways in which user experiences are mediated – and through which means. (1) Different means of mediating such experiences exist – it might be based on explicit benchmarking and league-tabling (thereby relying on competitive pressures), or (2) it might be based on providing differentiated analyses so as to facilitate inclusivity, cultural identity, argumentation, and debate, or (3) it might be based on enhanced hierarchical oversight. Furthermore, as noted, algorithms are not neutral as even those like Google Brain, that are attempting zero human input, may be said to be unable to deliver fairness in human social capital terms. The cases in Wollongong (Hui, Moerman, & Rudkin, 2011) Australia of an automated system used to check for vulnerable people claiming benefits but also working has been criticized as reducing the cases to stereotypes of the "feckless and undeserving," benefits cheaters, rather than recognizing the human situations, fallibility, and desperation as the AI simply puts facts A together with fact B and concludes that data equals C, with no reference to the mitigating circumstances involved and thus lawyers have argued against the use of AI for governance or as part of e-governance and legislation or judicial decisions and reviews since the "logic" used ignores, rejects, or fails to notice human norms based upon structural social capital embedded and embodied in the systems of modern democracies.

These AI systems are therefore not just mediation tools but are instead of a performative and constitutive nature, potentially enhancing rather than reducing power asymmetries. In short, the regulation by algorithm calls for the regulation of the algorithm in order to address their built-in biases. Andrews et al. (2017) have shown that assessing complex organizations via algorithms remains a difficult undertaking that does not necessarily enhance the predictive powers of regulatory oversight without ethical design that involves designing-in to the AI system, accountability, and the three Vs of values, veracity and voice, that is, perhaps replacing one of the three Vs (velocity) with veracity. Further characteristics have been added, such as "veracity," "viability," and "value." However, Amoore and Piotukh (2015, p. 342) argue that "the technologies of analytics focus human attention and decision on particular persons and things of interest, whilst annulling or discarding much of the material context from which they are extracted," resulting in a type of non-conscious cognition akin to the type of trance like cognition that drivers sometimes exhibit when they drive from a to b without having consciously registered doing so (though have negotiated obstacles, junctions, other traffic successfully without realizing they were doing so).

Yet it has been argued that these "wanna Vs" are not "intrinsic, definitional Big Data properties" (Grimes, 2013),

Collaboration Typology

Instead of working together on a plan, however, countries have pursued their own approaches ranging from complete lockdowns to attempted herd immunity strategies such Sweden's and we are now into a second wave of evolving viral infections globally. Collaborations can take a number of forms and as Sabeti (2017) has indicated there are some signs of an emerging hybrid fourth industry sector in social enterprise which may yet prove to be a foundation for greater collaborative effort for neglected or " invisible" social groups such as the homeless, some of those with physical or mental health disabilities, and refugees in camps (Cockburn et al., 2018).

Practical, technical, development, and socio-cultural problems remain (West, 2006: 24, pp. 6–7). So, progress is uneven and, potentially could worsen access to social capital gains in some situations. For instance, aiming to build sustainable social capital in a mixed economy of public and private financing, the capture, transformation, and openness of transfer of learning from and to the community has been shown to reinforce exclusion in some cases rather than increasing inclusion (Kumar & Best, 2006, pp. 12–14; Perkmann & Schildt, 2015). Others have suggested a middle road, blending the public and private in such social enterprises, or using boundary spanning organizations or networks to enable more open transfer of information (Cockburn et al., 2016; Meddie, 2006, pp. 4–5; Perkmann & Schildt, 2015). Successful university–industry partnerships are important due to the increasing percentage of research and development that is currently being outsourced to universities.

Nevertheless, we have seen the rise at a more local level, various community networks involving a variety of strategic alliances at different levels of complexity between government, education, NGOs, social enterprises, corporations, and local communities (Cardiff, 2000; Cockburn-Wootten & Cockburn, 2017; Cordell & Romanow, 2005, p. 1; Gerencser et al., 2006, p. 5; Gurstein & Pell, 2006; Hagel & Brown, 2006; Middlehurst, 2000; Parkinson & Ramirez, 2006). Part of the perceived gains which encourage the formation of these networked communities increased local autonomy within the modular processes of production resulting in greater levels of creativity as outlined by Hagel & Brown, 2006, pp. 2–3). As the latter authors also asserted:

Education will become more marginalized as we attach greater importance to continuous learning in a rapidly evolving world- as we become more aware of the need to view learning as a continuing opportunity and requirement throughout our lives, educational institutions are becoming progressively marginalized and forced to re-conceive their role within broader learning ecologies. (p. 15)

Gershuny (2005a, 2005b) has demonstrated the long-term, lifewide significance of an underlying trend of increasing "Do-It-Yourself" (DIY) processes across societies at individual level as well as meso- and macro- levels that aligns with the need for the educational institutions to realign and review their roles and functions in an attempt to build more elements of lifelong and lifewide learning that engage with and reinforce social capital. A few examples of such networks that the chapter authors are or have been involved with are the Network for Community Hospitality, Káute Pasifika, and SEED. All of these three are based in the Waikato region of New Zealand. Others we have been involved with are co-operatives in the UK (Cockburn et al., 2012). These local alternatives are potential sources of attractors of a different kind. Researchers are both producers and consumers of research and often act in a similar manner to the "prosumers" that Toffler and Toffler (2006) describe. That is, there is a network of non-monetized exchanges made by such "prosumers" which is not attended to in conventional economics (Fisher, 2006, pp. 2–4). Some formerly competitive "communities" have had to evolve more cooperative modes of operation as they emerge as mega-communities of interest and action (Cockburn, 2016; Gerencser et al., 2006, p. 4).

Diverse communal forms of social capital continue to evolve as Sabeti (2017) has indicated and there are some signs of an emerging hybrid fourth industry sector in social enterprise which may yet prove to be a foundation for greater collaborative effort. Successful university–industry partnerships are important due to the increasing percentage of research and development that is currently being outsourced to universities. In the EU, this figure has risen from 0.7% in 1981 and 2.0% in 1990 to 2.5% in 1999 (Akira, 2006, p. 6). The most recent university–industry research collaboration statistics in Japan (for 2004) was 9,378, a 17% increase over the previous fiscal year (Akira, 2006). There are also some mixed messages in the current literature with some suggesting size of firms is less important nowadays as smaller companies are increasingly able to access and utilize university expertise, see Cambridge University's Insight Newsletter (2005: 5, pp. 1–2). Whereas others suggest that is not the case and that larger firms and within these the headquarters, more often than not, have a greater collaborative propensity relative to other departments in the particular country and also have the necessary absorptive capacity to use and gain from such collaborations (Fontana et al., 2005, pp. 315–319; Motohashi, 2004, p. 18). However, globally, aggregations of trends suggest that where there are clear and known threats to many or all individuals in an organization or community, such as pandemic, pollution, and environmental degradation, cooperative and collaborative endeavors emerge naturally. As consumers, we have already tentatively begun to co-evolve a more collaborative, conscientious, and sustainable form of consumption. With the emergence of Web 2IR4.0 and digitally connected environments we have now begun to co-evolve "prosumption" – combining production and consumption of goods and services (Ritzer & Jurgenson, 2010; Toffler, 1981, 2006). The existence of types of "prosumption" is not in dispute. Critics argue, however, that some of this "prosumption" has been around in various guises for some time, and is partly due to the progressive cost-cutting by companies with a consequent reduction of services to consumers (Comor, 2010, p. 325) and lockdowns promote use of online services, distribution networks, and products. There is general agreement that there exists some variation in the intensity and nature of these relationships and in the distribution of such collaborations between countries such as, for example, the UK, EU, Japan, and the USA (see Fontana et al., 2005, p. 321; Motohashi, 2004, p. 2; University's Insight Newsletter, 2005: 5, pp. 1–2) and post-Brexit that would seem to be likely to continue as not trade deals have so far been agreed except one between UK and Japan.

Practical, technical, development, and socio-cultural problems remain (West, 2006: 24, pp. 6–7). So, progress is uneven and, potentially could worsen access to social capital gains in some situations. For instance, aiming to build sustainable social capital in a mixed economy of public and private financing, the capture, transformation, and openness of transfer of learning from and to the community has been shown to reinforce exclusion in some cases rather than increasing inclusion (Kumar & Best, 2006, pp. 12–14; Perkmann & Schildt, 2015). Others have suggested a middle road, blending the public and private in such social enterprises, or using boundary spanning organizations or networks to enable more open transfer of information (Cockburn et al., 2016; Meddie, 2006, pp. 4–5; Perkmann & Schildt, 2015). As Kossoff asserts (2019): "This is the Cosmopolitan Localist scenario: the Domains of Everyday Life would be both internally networked – as people satisfy their needs within them – and externally networked, since needs within any single Domain could not be satisfied in isolation from other Domains: no household, neighborhood [*sic.*], city or region can be entirely self-sufficient and they therefore will always need to be connected to other households, neighbourhoods [*sic.*], cities and regions."

References

Akira, G. (2006). University–industry collaboration impacting innovation and economic growth. Research Institute of Economy Trade and Industry (RIETI), RIETI Report 075. Retrieved from http://www.rieti.go.jp/en/rieti_report/075.html. Accessed on November 28, 2006.

Alimo-Metcalfe, B. (1994). Gender bias in the selection and assessment of women in management. In M. J. Davidson & R. Burke, R. (Eds.). *Women in management: Current research issues* (pp. 93–109). London: Sage.

Alimo-Metcalfe, B. (2007).*Gender & leadership: Glass ceiling or reinforced concrete?* Research Institute of the Ecole Nationale d'Administration Publique, Québec.

Alimo-Metcalfe, B. (2010). Developments in gender and leadership: Introducing a new "inclusive" model". *Gender in Management: An International Journal, 25*(8), 630–639.

Andrews, L. (2017) 'Fake News and the threat to real news', Written evidence to the House of Commons Culture, Media and Sport Select Committee. Retrieved from http://data.parliament.uk/writtenevidence/committeeevidence.svc/evidencedocument/culture-media-and-sport-committee/fakenews/written/48139.pdf. Accessed on January 20, 2021.

Amoore, L., & Piotukh, V. (2015). Life Beyond Big Data–Governing With Little Analytics. *Economy and Society*, *44*(3), 341–366.

Aragon-Correa, J. A., Garcia-Morales, V. J., & Cordon-Pozo, E. (2007). Leadership and organizational learning's role on innovation and performance: Lessons from Spain. *Industrial Marketing Management*, *36*(3), 349–359.

Birasnav, M., Rangnekar, S., & Dalpati, A. (2011). Transformational leadership and human capital benefits: the role of knowledge management. *Leadership & Organization Development Journal*, *32*(2), 106–126.

Bourdieu, P. (1977). *Outline of a theory of practice*. Cambridge: Cambridge University Press (R. Nice, Trans.).

Ciampa, D. (2005). Almost ready: How leaders move up, *Harvard Business Review*, 46–53. Retrieved from http://hbr.org/2005/01/almost-ready-howleaders-move-up/ar/1. Accessed on November 12, 2021.

Claridge, T. (2020). *Social capital at different levels and dimensions: A typology of social capital* (pp. 1–8). Dunedin: Social Capital Research & Training. Retrieved from https://www.socialcapitalresearch.com/social-capital-at-different-levels-and-dimensions/. Accessed on January 4, 2022.

Clement, W. (2008). *The implications of demographic change*. Zurich: Zurich Government and Industry Affairs.

Cockburn, T., Cockburn-Wootten, C., & Desmarais, M. (2017, September 15). Making waves: The three Cs and New Migrant Diasporas in 2017. Retrieved from https://ssrn.com/abstract=3037475 or https://dx.doi.org/10.2139/ssrn.3037475

Cockburn, T., Desmarais, F., & Desmarais, M. (2007). The Tale of a thousand needles. In D. Kantarlis, (Ed.), *Global Business and Economics Anthology* (Vol. 1, pp. 90–99).

Cockburn, T., Jahdi, K., & Cockburn-Wootten, C. (2017). Scaffolding CSR in SMEs: A pilot study. In L. Gomez, L. Vargas-Preciado, & D. Crowther (Eds), *Corporate social responsibility and corporate governance in Ibero-America: Concepts, perspectives, and future trends*. Bingley: Emerald.

Cockburn, T., Jahdi, K. S., & Wilson, E. (2012). Ethical capital and the culture of integrity: 3 cases in UK and NZ. In W. Amann & A. Stachowicz-Stanusch (Eds.), *Business integrity in practice – Insights from international case studies*. New York, NY: Business Expert Press.

Cockburn-Wootten, C., & Cockburn, T. (2017). Working inclusively and redefining social valorization in the globalized world: Activism, research, advocacy and the disadvantaged. In R. Oberoi & J. Halsall (Eds.), *Revisiting globalization: From a border-less to a gated globe*. Cham: Springer.

Cockburn-Wootten, C., & Cockburn, T. (2018). Working inclusively and redefining social valorization in the globalized world: Activism, research, advocacy and the disadvantaged. In R. Oberoi & J. Halsall (Eds.), *Revisiting globalization: From a border-less to a gated globe*. Cham: Springer.

Cordell, A., & Romanow, P. A. (2005). Community networking and public benefits. *Journal of Community Informatics*, *2*(1), 6–20.

Danaher, J., Hogan, M. J., Noone, C., Kennedy, R., Behan, A., De Paor, A., ... Shankar, K. (2017). Algorithmic governance: Developing a research agenda through the power of collective intelligence. *Big Data and Society*, *4*(2), 1–21.

De Jong, J. P. J., & Den Hartog, D. N. (2007). How leaders influence employees' innovative behavior. *European Journal of Innovation Management*, *10*(1), 41–64.

Delanty, G. (2006). The cosmopolitan imagination: Critical cosmopolitanism and social theory. *British Journal of Sociology, 57*(1), 25–47.

Dilworth, J. B. (1996). *Operations Management,* NY: McGraw-Hill.

Dulewicz, V., & Higgs, M. (2005). Assessing Leadership Styles and Organizational Context. *Journal of Management Psychology, 200,* 105–123.

Editors. (2011). Sustainable leadership: Leading business, industry and local government towards a sustainable future. *Strategic Direction, 27*(2), 5–8.

European Parliament. (2019). *A governance framework for algorithmic accountability and transparency.* Brussels: EPRS, STOA. Retrieved from http://www.europarl.europa.eu/thinktank. Accessed on November 12, 2021.

Galton, F. (2012). Hereditary genius. Retrieved from http://galton.org/books/hereditary-genius/text/pdf/galton-1869-genius-v3.pdf. Accessed on January 12, 2021.

Gratton, L., & Truss, C. (2003). *The three dimensional people strategy: Putting human resources policies into action. Academy of Management Executive, 17*(3), 74–86.

Gressgård, L. J. (2011). Virtual team collaboration and innovation in organizations. *Team Performance Management, 17*(1/2), 102–119.

Grimes, S. (2013), *Informationweek: Big Data: Avoid 'Wanna V' Confusion.* Retrieved from https://pros.com/news/informationweek-big-data-avoid-wanna-v-confusion. Accessed on November 21, 2021.

Gurstein, R., & Pell, S. (2006). *Youth interns and the strategic deployment of ICTs for public access: The case of the Community Access Youth Internship Program.* CRACIN Working Paper No. 15, October 2006. Canadian Research Alliance for Community Innovation and Networking, Toronto, pp. 3–22

Hagel, J., III, & Brown, J. S. (2006). *Creation Nets, harnessing the potential of open innovation.* Working Paper, April 2006. Retrieved from http://www.edgeperspectives.com. Accessed on November 21, 2021

Higgs, M. J. (2009). The good, the bad and the ugly: Leadership and narcissism. *Journal of Change Management, 9*(2), 165–178.

Hitlin, S., & Piliavin, J. A. (2004). Values: Reviving a dormant concept. *Annual Review of Sociology, 30,* 359–393. http://doi.org/10.1146/annurev.soc.30.012703.110640

Hogan, R., & Hogan, J. (2001). Assessing leadership: A view from the dark side. *International Journal of Assessment and Selection, 9,* 40–51.

Hogan, R., & Kaiser, R. (2005). What we know about leadership. *Review of General Psychology, 9*(2), 169–180.

Holzmeyer, C. (2018). Wider worlds of research for health equity: Public health NGOs as stakeholders in open access ecosystems. *Journal of Community informatics, 14*(2), 1–16.

Hui, F., Moerman, L., & Rudkin, K. (2011). *Centrelink prosecutions at the employment/benefit nexus: A case study of Wollongong.* Social Accounting and Accountability Research Centre Report No. 1.

IEEE. (2019, March). Chatila, R., Firth-Butterflied, K., Havens, J. C., & Karachalios, K. (2017). The IEEE global initiative for ethical considerations in artificial intelligence and autonomous systems. *IEEE Robotics and Automation Magazine, 24*(1), 110.

ILO Report. (2020). Changing patterns in the world of work. In *International labour conference, 95th session.* Geneva: International Labour Office. Retrieved from https://www.news18.com/news/business/global-labour-income-estimated-to-have-declined-by-3-5-trillion-usd-in-first-3-quarters-of-2020-ilo-2904151.html Accessed on November 29, 2020.

Insight newsletter. (2005). Issue 5, Cambridge, UK: Cambridge University.

International Organization for Migration (IOM), (2006). Global estimates and trends. Retrieved from http://www.iom.int/jahia/page254.html. Accessed on October 11, 2006.

Irwin, T. (2015). Transition Design: A proposal for a new area of design practice, study and research. *Design and Culture Journal, 7,* 229–246.

Jackson, T. (2009). *Prosperity without growth?* The transition to a sustainable economy. London, UK: Sustainable Development Commission. Retrieved from http.//www.sd-commission.org.uk/presslist.php/119/what-next-for-sjustainable-development. Accessed on March 25, 2011.

Kavanagh, J., & Rich, M. D. (2018). *Truth decay*. Santa Monica, CA: Rand Corporation.

Kellerman, B. (2008). *Followership: How Followers Are Creating Change and Changing Leaders*. Boston: Harvard Business Press/Center for Public Leadership.

Kellerman, B. (2012). *The End of Leadership*. New York: Harper Business

Kossoff, G. (2019). Cosmopolitan localism: The planetary networking of everyday life in place, *Cuaderno 73, | Centro de Estudios en Diseño y Comunicación* (2019), 51–66.

Krohe, J. (2011). How much do you know? Too much and not enough. *The Conference Board Review*. Retrieved from http://www.tcbreview.com/ summer _2011.aspx. Accessed on November 10, 2011.

Larsson, S. (2018). Algorithmic governance and the need for consumer empowerment in data-driven markets. *Internet Policy Review*, 7(2), 1–13.

Linder, C. *This Is How Algorithms Will Evolve Themselves*, POPULAR MECHANICS (Apr. 23, 2020). Retrieved from https://www.popularmechanics.com/technology/a32221995/google-automl-zero-evolve-algorithms/.

Malle, B. F., & Dickert, S. (2007). Values. In R. Baumeister & K. Vohs (Eds.), The Encyclopedia of Social Psychology (pp. 1011–1014), Thousand Oaks, CA: Sage.

Marquardt, M. J. (2000). Action learning and leadership. *The Learning Organization*, 7(5), 233–241.

Marshall, J. (2000). Expanding the realm of organizational reasoning. *The Learning Organization*, 7(5), 244–251.

McKinsey. (2007). *Women matter: Gender diversity, a corporate performance driver*. Paris: McKinsey.

McKinsey. (2009). *Women Matter 3: Women leaders, a competitive edge in and after the crisis*. Paris: McKinsey.

Meddie, M. (2006). Rethinking telecentre sustainability: How to implement a social enterprise approach – Lessons from India and Africa. *Journal of Community Informatics*, 2, 3.

Motohashi, K. (2004). *Economic analysis of university–industry collaborations: The role of new technology based firms in Japanese national innovation reform*. Working Paper Series. IIR-REITI, Japan.

Muurlink, O., & Matas, C. P. (2011). From romance to rocket science: Speed dating in higher education. *Higher Education Research & Development*, 30(6), 751–764.

Ngai, M. (2003). *Impossible Subjects: Illegal Aliens and the Making of Modern America*, Princeton, NJ: Princeton University press.

Pasquale, F. (2016). *The Black Box Society-the secret algorithms behind money and information*, Harvard University press.

Peters, L. M., & Manz, C. C. (2007). Identifying antecedents of virtual team collaboration. *Team Performance Management*, 13(3/4), 117–129.

Pogge, T. (2006). World Poverty and Human Rights, *Journal of Ethics & International Affairs*, 19(August).

Porter, M. (1998). *The competitive advantage of nations*. London: Macmillan Press.

Ridd, M. J., & Shaw, A. R. (2005, September 24). Five futures for academic medicine: "Speed networking". *British Medical Journal*, 331, 695.

Rohan, M. (2000). A rose by any name? The value construct, Personality and Social Psychology Review, 4(3), 255–277.

Rouvroy, A. (2011, April). "Pour une défense de l'éprouvante inopérationnalité du droit face à l'opérationnalité sans épreuve du comportementalisme numérique". Dissensus, no. 4.

Rouvroy, A. (2013). The end(s) of critique: Data-behaviourism vs. Due process. In M. Hildebrandt & K. De Vries (Eds.), *Privacy, due process and the computational turn*. Routledge: Philosophers of Law Meet Philosophers of Technology.

Rouvroy, A., & Berns, T. (2013). Algorithmic governmentality and prospects of emancipation Disparateness as a precondition for individuation through relationships? Translated by Elizabeth Libbrecht. *Réseaux*, *177*(1), 163–196. Retrieved from https://www.cairn-int.info/journal-reseaux-2013-1-page-163.htm

Sabeti, H. (2017). The fourth sector is a chance to build a new economic model for the benefit of all, World Economic Forum (WEF). Retrieved from https://www.weforum.org/agenda/2017/09/fourth-sector-chance-to-build-neweconomic-model. Accessed on September 15, 2017.

Sachs, W. (1999). Planet dialectics: *Explorations in environment and development*. Halifax, NS: Fernwood Publications.

Saurwein, F., Just, N., & Latzer, M. (2015). Governance of algorithms: Options and limitations. *info*, *17*(6), 35–49. https://doi.org/10.1108/info-05-2015-0025

Shamir, B. (1995). Social distance and charisma: Theoretical notes and an exploratory study. *Leadership Quarterly*, *6*, 19–47.

Slattery, C. (2009). The dark side of leadership: Troubling times at the top. Retrieved from www.semannslattery.com. Accessed on November 21, 2011.

Smith, P., & Cockburn, T. (2013). *Dynamic leadership models for global business: Enhancing digitally connected environments*. Hershey, PA: IGI Global.

Smith, P., & Cockburn, T. (Eds.). (2014). *Impact of emerging digital technologies on leadership in global business*. Hershey, PA: IGI Global.

Smith, P., & Cockburn, T. (2016). *Developing and leading emergence teams*. London: Routledge.

Smith, P., & Cockburn, T. (Eds.). (2020). *Global Business Leadership Development for the Fourth Industrial Revolution* (Part of the Advances in Business Strategy and Competitive Advantage Book Series), PA, USA: IGI Global.

Sommer, U. (2016). *Werte: Warum Man Sie Braucht, Obwohl es Sie Nicht Gibt. [Values. Why we need them even though they don't exist.]* Stuttgart: J. B. Metzler (2016) in Embedding values in Autonomous and Intelligent Systems. Retrieved from https://standards.ieee.org/content/dam/ieee-standards/ standards/ web/ documents/ other/ ead1e _embedding_values.pdf. Accessed on December 11, 2021.

Sunstein, C. R. (2009). *Republic 2.0*. Princeton, NJ: Princeton University Press.

Taylor, E., & Garmirian, C. (2020). COVID-19: Children from poorest households had greatest financial and education loss, highest risk of violence at home. Retrieved from https://www.savethechildren.org/us/about-us/media-and-news/2020-press-releases/during-covid-19-children-in-poverty-experience-greatest-financial-education-loss-highest-risk-of-violence. Accessed on November 22, 2020.

Toffler, A., & Toffler, H. (2006). *Revolutionary wealth*. New York, NY: Knopf. Cited in Fisher, L. M. (2006) — Alvin Toffler: The thought leader interview, *Strategy+ Business* magazine, Booz Allen Hamilton. Retrieved from www.strategy-business.com. Accessed on December 19, 2006.

Urry, J. (1999). Globalization and Citizenship, *Journal of World-Systems Research*, *5*(2), 311–324.

Vanham, P. (2017). *Global pension timebomb: Funding gap set to dwarf world GDP*. World Economic Forum. Retrieved from https://www.weforum.org/press/2017/05/global-pension-timebomb-funding-gap-setto-dwarf-world-gdp/. Accessed on September 15, 2017.

Vollhardt, C. (2005). Pfizer's prescription for the risky business of executive tranitions. *Journal of Organizational Excellence*, *25*(1), 3–15.

West, A. R. (2006). Related Dangers: The issue of Development and Security for Marginalized Groups in South Africa. *The Journal of Community Informatics*, *2*(3). Retrieved December 21, from http://www.ci-journal.net/

Windsor, G., Sampath S, & Royal, C. (2014). Anew Breed of Socio-Cultural Leaders and How Theyuse CSR in ICT for development As a Tool of Sustainability: A case Study of Telecentres in a South Asian developing Country. In P. Smith & T. Cockburn (Eds.), *Impact of Emerging Digital technologies on Leadership in Global Business*, PA,USA: IGI Global.

Wittenberg-Cox, A. (2020). What do countries with the best coronavirus responses have in common? Women leaders. *Forbes*, April 13. Retrieved from https://www.forbes.com/sites/avivahwittenbergcox/2020/04/13/what-do-countries-with-the-best-coronavirus-reponses-have-in-common-women-leaders/. Accessed on November 22, 2020.

Zaccaro, S. J. (2007). Trait-based perspectives of leadership, *The American Psychologist*, *62*(1), 6–16.

Chapter 9

Role of Social Capital and Social Enterprise in China's Poverty Relief

Sam Yuqing Li and Qingwen Xu

Abstract

Building social capital between groups of people and developing social enterprises that integrate social goals into commercial business models are rapidly adopted as innovative poverty relief mechanisms across countries. Together, the translation of social relationships into increased accessibility to resources, and the entrepreneurial dynamics resulting in additional services and goods, are thought to meet the survival and developmental needs of poor families and communities. However, the socio-economic contexts, in which new public policies and initiatives have been taken, vary from country to country. In China, its strong Confucian culture, state-led development strategy, weak civil society, and hierarchical social relationships have contributed to a value structure of social capital, but decreased the efficiency of business practice in social enterprise. This chapter presents a case study of Rural Cooperative Program, a poverty relief initiative in China's southwest Guizhou Province. With the introduction of China's new policies in welfare and rural development, this chapter presents evaluation results of whether social enterprises and entrepreneurship can improve poor villagers' socio-economic wellbeing and promote sustainable development of poor rural villages in China, and to what extent social capital has been mobilized to facilitate the Rural Cooperative Program.

Keywords: Social capital; innovation and social enterprise; rural poverty relief; community-based organizing; rural cooperatives; China

Social Capital in Use

Since the construction of social capital theory early in the 1960s, various conceptualizations exist around the concept. Nevertheless, there has been a viable convergence toward the understanding and its definition – the structure of social relationships as well as the values, norms, meaning and emotion attached to and be fabricated into the human–nature relationships, are resources that should be used for the public good and/or for the benefit of individuals (see exemplary works done by Pierre Bourdieu, James Coleman, Robert Putnam, Nan Lin, and many others). The multiple – structural & cognitive, individual & community aspects of social capital – speaks to social capital's nature as a compound and complex construct, suggests a significant wide range of applications of social capital in society, and reflects the dynamics of how social relationships function as a type of resources. Putnam (1993) argued that social interactions between groups of people are contingent on commonly shared norms and values, thus social capital could facilitate co-operation and mutually supportive relations in communities and be a valuable means for collective responses of social issues inherent in modern societies. Lin (2001) discussed that the quality and quantity of social relationships would lead to increased access to information, know-how, and even power thus social capital could be turned into direct individual benefits for instance to further own career prospects.

Empirical studies consistently explore the economic, political, cultural, and/or cognitive value of social relationships and have been able to identify the positive impact of social capital on individual, group, and/or community wellbeing, despite different dimensions and measurements adopted, including social cohesion, social support, social integration, and/or participation, among several other social determinants. Social capital is arguably benefiting firms and organizations and facilitating policy implementation (e.g., Jones, 2010; Koka & Prescott, 2002). Social capital is also empirically linked to various individual level wellbeing indicators. In the field of health and mental health, social capital embedded in the family, neighborhood, and community are evidently important and serve a mediating role as buffers to the negative influence within the immediate context, for instance, discrimination, impoverishment, segregation, and violence (e.g., Almedom, 2005; Kawachi & Berkman, 2000). The individual benefit derived from the web of social relationships and ties is particularly significant to people whose financial and human capital are constrained. For example, social capital would increase a woman's chances of getting married and employed, and serve as a precursor to upward social mobility for low-income mothers as opposed to simply getting "off of welfare" (Johnson, Honnold, & Threlfall, 2011). Social capital is linked to employment for at-risk transition-age youth (Vorhies, Davis, Frounfelker, & Kaiser, 2012), and positively affects the starting wage for people with disabilities (Phillips, Robison, & Kosciulek, 2014). Social capital has contributed to education achievement among immigrant children (Zhou & Kim, 2006) and at-risk high-school drop-outs (Croninger & Lee, 2001). In general, these studies attribute social capital to changed opportunity structures, increased access to information and knowledge, and/or enhanced community collaboration and civic actions.

Many studies also recognize the meaningful social connections to the poor. In poverty researches, economists became extremely interested in the concept of social capital in the 1990s and have explored the positive impact of community and regional level social capital on economic growth and development (e.g., Cleaver, 2005; Puttnam, 2002; Staveren, 2003; Warren, Thompson, & Saegert, 2001; World Bank, 1997); it is claimed that social interactions and cohesion as the core social capital components underpin growth and prosperity. Social capital enables individuals and families to seek information, coordinate activities for mutual benefits, collectively participate in political activities including local decision making and lobby for government supports and services, and when political and economic activities fail to secure informal protection from friends, neighbors, and the community; such mechanisms received empirical evidence in countries like Uganda (Hassan & Birungi, 2011), Malaysia (Abdul-Hakim, Abdul-Razak, & Ismail, 2010), Nigeria (Idris & Agbim, 2015), China (Zhang, Zhou, & Lei, 2017), Philippines and Mexico (Fox & Gershman, 2000), and many others. For poor families, social capital might be the few sources of capital available to them. However, the capacity of the poor or the improvised to act collectively derived from their social relationships depends on the quality of the formal institutions under which they reside; likewise, institutional arrangements, and institutional capacity and responsiveness to collective activities can either facilitate or impede the capacity of communities to mobilize social resources. Among the literature, the process by which economic and social policies affect the accumulation of the pro-poor social capital, and the mechanism of institutional arrangements to facilitate the use of social capital for poverty relief remain inadequately explored. Indeed, studies are highly contextualized within a country that might have little implications for practices in a different context.

In China, a long and vibrant literature on the concept of *guanxi* (relationship in mandarin Chinese) suggests that social capital has its corresponding cultural meaning and practice. Bian's (1997, 2001) conceptualization of *guanxi* capital includes the "web of extended familial obligations," relationships that extend beyond family relationships to ensure "favor exchanges" and "asymmetric transactions" that resources embedded in the *guanxi* flow one way from favor givers to favor receivers (Bian, 2001, pp. 275–279). A cluster of studies indicate the significant role that *guanxi* has played to mobilize resources and promote women (Zhang, 2011), migrants (Ma, 2002), and farmers (Lu, Trienekens, Omta, & Feng, 2010) – traditionally marginalized groups of people in China – participating in high-value markets, although gaining such entrances might not always generate increased income. Despite different cultural or country elements of social capital in China, research overall indicates that resources embedded in networks particularly those coming across formal or institutionalized power or authority gradients such as business ties, political ties, and appropriable social organizations can contribute significantly to poverty reduction in China (Zhang et al., 2017). Specific evidence also suggest the positive association between individual social capital (not collective community level social capital) and poverty reduction (Hong, Tisdell, & Fei, 2019).

Innovation, Social Enterprise, and Social Capital

Social innovation has been a buzzword and occupied the discourse addressing the widespread and persistent poverty in the world. The pressing demand for new ways of combating poverty comes from primarily the ineffectiveness of traditional solutions to social problems, which have been mainly relying on public welfare schemes and hardly ensuring financial sustainable and scalable social impacts (Becker & Smith, 2018). Interestingly noted, social innovation, despite the lack of settled definition, has been used and referred to as actions responding to social needs through the *transformation of social relations* (Oosterlynck, Novy, & Kazepov, 2019). Given the inherent difficulties in determining what is "innovative" and what is specifically "social," scholars argue that social innovation would be in favor of the implementation of new social and institutional arrangements, new ideas of how people should interact and organize interpersonal activities, new forms of resource mobilization, and new modes of participation, in order to collectively enhance the power (or being empowered), improve economic and social performance, and increase the living condition (see studies done by Hämäläinen, 2007; Heiskala, 2007; cited in Oosterlynck et al., 2019; Klein, Fontan, Harrisson, & Lévesque, 2012; Mumford, 2002). Such understanding of social innovation is based on the critical reflection that poverty is the result of deprived opportunity, structural disempowerment, and discriminative social and economic institutional arrangements (see early work contributed by Piven & Cloward, 2012); therefore, social innovations for poverty reduction have to include the dimensions of collective actions, advocacy, and institutional changes.

Because of the multidimensional and relational character of poverty, as well as innovative actions for *transforming social relations*, social innovation, and social capital present interesting dynamics. In a review article done by Paunescu 2014), social capital is linked to the innovation performance; at the individual level, having the right networks, increasing the capacity to extend mutual beneficial relationships with others, leveraging the network members' know-how would contribute to an increased performance of innovations (e.g., knowledge transfer and development and scale-up of innovation, trust, shared norms thus alliance for innovation and value creation, etc.). At the organizational and community level, social capital can facilitate the process that a social innovator or a social entrepreneur can build a structure in local communities, enable agencies, companies, and governments to all work together, maintain trust and a constant flow of knowledge, and aim to solve a social problem (Găucă & Hadad, 2013). Studies provide evidence arguing that social capital could be an enabler resulting in collective actions for economic betterment through the adoption of innovation (e.g., microfinance groups, Choudhury & Hassan, 2014), or be a mediator affecting poverty alleviation and economic growth indirectly by fostering innovations (e.g., technology-use and women entrepreneurship, Akçomak & Ter Weel, 2009; Osei & Zhuang, 2020). While different pathways among social capital, social innovation, and poverty reduction might imply different focus in practice, the use of social innovation and social capital is nonetheless to promote an increase of the capabilities and access to resources of people living in poverty, highlight the importance of community-based developments and their multilevel governances, and address the crucial role of participation and empowerment.

The rapidly developed social enterprise sector in the world exemplifies how change agents across "the private" and "the social" sectors eagerly seek for innovative solutions for systemic social problems (Becker & Smith, 2018; Seelos & Mair, 2005). Social enterprises are to use business models to achieve social goals; it is not only an innovation in terms of organizational practice but also adopts unique ways of organizing people, resources, and activities that have sprung from innovative acts. Social enterprise has been considered as a strategy and a tool for poverty reduction in many countries (Fotheringham & Saunders, 2014; Kerlin, 2009; Scarlato, 2013). In China, microcredit initiatives have emerged as the early major form of social entrepreneurship started in the early 2000s seeking to explore a sustainable way to alleviate poverty by mobilizing resources and encouraging innovations (Yu, 2011). Later various forms and practices of social enterprises have emerged; however, it is discussed that social enterprises in China face institutional challenges including a strong role played by the government, misunderstanding or unknown role for social enterprises, lack of supportive policy environment, and lack of socio-cultural values and beliefs in support of social goals (Bhatt, Qureshi, & Riaz, 2019).

Therefore, in China's efforts of poverty reduction and elimination, to what extent social enterprise can be innovative and carry on meaningful activities to *transform social relations*, particularly to transform the institutional arrangements and relationships across individuals, families, communities, and various socio-economic sections? During the process, what role individual and community level social capital could have played for the better off of impoverished groups of people?

Social Enterprise and Poverty Reduction in China

China has made tremendous progress in poverty reduction over the last four decades stunning the world. In 2013, President Xi Jinping of China announced the "Targeted Poverty Alleviation" plan and wrote it into the country's 13th Five-Year Plan (2015–2020), which claims to eliminate the extreme poverty in China by 2020 (Guo, Zhou, & Liu, 2019). Indeed, when writing this chapter, on November 23, 2020, China announced that it had eliminated absolute poverty nationwide by uplifting all of its citizens. Historically, poverty reduction heavily relied on government subsidies and public investments in China (Zhou, Guo, Liu, Wu, & Li, 2018). Since 2013, poverty-reduction cooperatives have been growing across China as a market-oriented and community-based approach to tackle rural poverty (Zhou et al., 2018). Policies like the *"Guidance on Leveraging E-Commerce to Support Poverty Alleviation"* have advocated for innovative practices encouraging the use of technology, public investment in the private sector, and local community for a market-based solution for poverty reduction. This innovative poverty-reduction strategy and sets of cooperative laws and policies incentivize farmers in poor regions to establish farmers' specialized cooperatives, with funding from state authorities, commercial support from private sector partners, and initiation of local community members (Guo et al., 2019). The poverty-reduction cooperative is a type of social enterprise, privately owned and managed, conducting economic activities in the competitive market, with the goals to achieve sustainable development in economically left-behind, resource-deficient, and segregated rural areas (Si et al., 2015; Song, Qi, Zhang, & Vernooy, 2014; Zhao & Yuan, 2014).

To provide a snapshot of this type of social enterprise, and explore the dynamics among social capital, social enterprise, and poverty reduction, a case study was conducted in 2017 and 2018 with a follow-up visit in early 2019 at a rural cooperative in Goldenbrook Village (all real names were removed to protect participants' confidentiality). The village is located in China's southwestern Guizhou Province, a province with one of China's lowest income per capita and most concentrated levels of rural poverty (Xing, Fan, Luo, & Zhang, 2009). Goldenbrook Village is geographically isolated by mountains and located 16 kilometers away from the urban center. The village has a population of 2,803 residents within 702 rural households. The village was assigned as a "poor village" status (*Pin Kun Cun* 贫困村) by both provincial and national standards in 1998. A total of 188 households were designated as poor rural households in the 2010s. Around 2010, the average household income at Goldenbrook Village was less than 2,000 RMB (around 295 USD) per month, which was below the 2,200 RMB (around 320 USD) national poverty line. Historically, the small-scale peasant economy at Goldenbrook Village had been low in productivity and profitability. Most villagers had long relied on growing corns to feed their families and sustain their basic needs. In recent decades, most of the working-age population migrated to urban areas for work and income leaving the elderly, children, and women at home. Because of its geographic remoteness and poor transportation condition in a mountainous area, Goldenbrook Village long lagged behind in industrial and economic development; villagers long suffered from persistent rural poverty.

Following the inductive qualitative research tradition, information reported here comes from field experience, participatory observation, documentation review, archival research, and semi-structured in-depth interviews with various key informants in the village. The interviewees were cooperative participants and community members who have insights about the cooperative, village history, and progress in poverty reduction and rural development. Interview guides include questions concerning individual's demographics and family socio-economic background, experiences of working with cooperative participants and multiple sectors, perceived benefits and challenges associated with the cooperative implementation, the assessment of the impact of the cooperative on families and the village, as well as perception and reflection.

The Goldenbrook Village Story

The Village and its Efforts of Poverty Reduction

Traditional approaches to tackling rural poverty at Goldenbrook Village mainly relied on public service providers, that is, the government. Guizhou Provincial Government and local City Government are the major public funders investing in infrastructure, healthcare, education, and basic social securities at Goldenbrook. As a leader of the City Poverty Alleviation Office stated,

> Previously, our poverty alleviation efforts were like blood-transfer .... We've been trying to tackle the hardest circumstances of rural poverty for so many years. In the beginning, we started by building infrastructures, ensuring electricity and water supplies, as well as renovating their houses. We connect the roads to these villages .... Using our jargon today, this is called "achieving the national poverty-reduction standard, securing food and wearing, and ensuring housing, education, and medication" ("一达标, 两不愁, 三保障").

With this, poor households received subsidies for renovating their houses, as part of the rural dilapidated house rehabilitation program demanded by the Ministry of Housing and Urban–Rural Development in China.

Walking in the Village, new concrete roads connect the village with the nearest inter-provincial highways; community sports facilities and newly renovated village center and residential houses suggest positive changes in the village's infrastructure development. A villager said,

> Public infrastructure, I can say that they are almost satisfactory. They are definitely much better than before .... The government is doing this "Roads to each Village" project (*Cun Tong Gong Lu*村村通公路), and the houses. I don't know what to say. These renovation projects, I can say they are just about right. For instance, some of them can get 70% of reimbursement for their house renovations.

While investments in infrastructure and public services have increased the living condition of villagers and supported basic agricultural and economic activities, they hardly generate sustainable economic opportunities for villagers in poverty. Under a series of "Targeted Poverty Alleviation" policies issued by the national government since 2013, an innovative approach – rural cooperative – has been adopted in poor rural areas nationwide including Goldenbrook Village. In 2016, the State Council in China issued guidance that supports poor villages to initiate rural cooperatives, develop rural entrepreneurship, and leverage e-commerce businesses to overcome extreme poverty (*Guidance on Leveraging E-Commerce to Support Poverty Alleviation*, 2016; Zhou et al., 2018). Given the larger policy context, local initiators, government agencies, private sector organizations, and local community members are involved in poverty-reduction cooperative projects from planning to the execution process.

Goldenbrook Village Cooperative was launched in 2013 with such institutional supports. Reputable village leaders and local villagers with experiences in entrepreneurship who had worked in more developed coastal regions in China became leaders of the cooperative. Leader of the Goldenbrook Cooperative, Zhao, is such an individual. A native of the Village, Zhao has worked as a migrant worker and entrepreneur in China's coastal province, Zhejiang for years before returning to the Village. Zhao, along with other four local rural entrepreneurs, initiated the development of kiwi farming at Goldenbrook. In 2013, they put down personal investment and planted 200 acres of kiwi trees as pilot fields, and Zhao and his rural partners became the "shareholders" of the cooperative. One of Zhao's business partners recalled,

> Our cooperative was started by a few rural entrepreneurs. They began to grow kiwi trees in 2013. They bought the tree plants by themselves back then. In 2014, we applied for central government funding and started our cooperative, because we had been a profiled as a poor village (*Pin Kun Cun* 贫困村).

Kiwi, a high-value crop, can be a great source of rural income for marginal farmers, thus giving Goldenbrook Village a great amount of hope to improve their livelihood and lift them out of poverty. The Goldenbrook Cooperative well exemplifies a social-business model. The local City Poverty Alleviation Office indicated that the Goldenbrook Cooperative began as a participatory initiative to tackle sustained rural poverty through the means of entrepreneurship and business. Stakeholders of the cooperative include participants across multiple sectors, such as local village officials, rural social entrepreneurs, and community members living below the poverty line. The Goldenbrook Cooperative registered at the local government as Specialized Farmers' Cooperative (*Nong Min Zhuan Ye He Zuo She* 农民专业合作社), distinguishing from non-governmental organizations or for-profit companies. This registration category in China allows the cooperative to engage in economic activities kiwi farming activities with the aim to tackle rural poverty through rural entrepreneurship and agricultural marketization.

Participation and Cooperative Development

Beginning with the pilot kiwi fields, to encourage local villagers to join the cooperative, Zhao led his fellow villagers at Goldenbrook to visit neighboring towns and learn from others' experiences in market-oriented initiatives for poverty reduction. These visits exposed local villagers to the mindset of making profits from agricultural activities, as an entrepreneurial way to escape sustained poverty. A member of Goldenbrook Cooperative recalled his experience seeing how people in neighboring villages marketized kiwi plants and sold them as profitable kiwi products:

> For the kiwi project, I was among the first group that visited other kiwi projects, and I was among the first one that joined the kiwi cooperative program. The first time that we visited, I saw that other people did it really well, with tens of thousands of acres of kiwi trees. We went to places ... in Sichuan Province and [the other] city. What we were, only a few thousand acres? ... But if we can let them (kiwi plants) grow gradually, they should develop quite well.

The success of the pilot kiwi fields gave Zhao and his fellows the confidence to scale up the kiwi business in Goldenbrook Village. In 2014, the Village Committee approved Zhao and the Goldenbrook Cooperative's initiative of kiwi farming. The Village Committee supported Zhao in applying for Poverty Reduction Funds from District level and Provincial level governments. Around the same time, Zhao was also elected by Goldenbrook residents to serve as the Village Committee Secretary, hoping that Zhao would lead local villagers to escape the long-term rural poverty and achieve common prosperity. The Goldenbrook Cooperative then received 1 million RMB funding from the district level government and additional 4 million RMB from the Provincial government.

These district and provincial governments' funding provided financial resources for villagers, from both low-income households and non-poor households, to join the cooperative, purchase kiwi plants, agricultural equipment, and fertilizers, and engage in the business of kiwi farming. Unlike the cooperative's initial investors for instance Zhao who did personal investment into the cooperative's assets, villagers were not required to contribute anything. As kiwi plants reach fruiting seasons in four to five years, the Goldenbrook Cooperative also provided agricultural technical support and sales and marketing assistance for its members. The Goldenbrook Cooperative organized weekly meetings so that the cooperative members were involved in a participatory decision-making process.

In 2017, most of the kiwi crop was sold in the nearest township and city, as kiwi production volume still remained low. During the field visit in August 2017, 270 rural households had joined the cooperative as freestanding members. Combining a kiwi business at Goldenbrook Cooperative and other poverty-reduction business projects, such as growing vegetables or raising hens, Goldenbrook Village had reduced the number of poor rural households from 188 to 27 in 2017. The village also received 500,000 RMB (about 73,529 USD) financial incentives from the Central Government Poverty Reduction Fund (*Tuo Pin Chu Lie Zi Jin* 脱贫出列资金). According to the leaders of Goldenbrook Cooperative, they expected an annual return of 40,000 to 50,000 RMB from each acre of kiwi plants, and about 20 million RMB revenues in total kiwi plants owned by the cooperative.

Building upon existing kiwi plants, Goldenbrook Cooperative members started to explore diverse pathways to further market their kiwi crops. The cooperative began to explore e-commerce sale channels in 2017, as they expected a greater amount of kiwi crops would be produced in coming years. In 2018, the cooperative signed an agreement with a private e-commerce company, providing support in e-commerce training, enlarging sales channels, branding, and marketing. The cooperative gradually grew kiwi plants at a greater scale, produced kiwi products with higher added-value like kiwi wine, and used branding techniques to sustainably grow into a marketized kiwi industry.

The Kiwi Network

The Goldenbrook Cooperative is in itself a success story of alleviating rural poverty through rural entrepreneurship from the ground up. Nonetheless, the success of this cooperative is highly contingent on a network built of public investors and business partners (see Fig. 9.1).

The cooperative, endorsed by the Village Committee, the lowest rural administrative unit in China's political hierarchy, has been able to be connected with various level governments and received funding, incentives, and various policy benefits. For instance, the Ministry of Finance in China, Provincial Government in Guizhou, and City Government allocate special Poverty Alleviation Funds (*Fu Pin Zhuan Xiang Zi Jin* 扶贫专项资金) to poverty-reduction cooperatives, such as the Goldenbrook Cooperative. The City Government also designates city government officials to serve as cadres in residence (*Zhu Cun Gan Bu* 驻村干部) at poor villages like Goldenbrook. International organizations including the World Bank also joined the efforts and participated in several poverty-reduction cooperative projects in western China including rural Guizhou, where the Goldenbrook Cooperative locates. International organizations and other public agencies provide support in financial resource, strategic planning, and technical expertise for poverty-reduction cooperatives. A cooperative leader explained the significance of public organization support as follows:

> We started the cooperative back then in order to boost our sales, and also develop our (grapefruit) industry. We gradually had some policy incentives for poverty-reduction, and they have helped us grow the industry. If we are on our own, we cannot do much. It was only under the guidance of the government that we did so many things.

The Goldenbrook Cooperative has established business partnerships with traditional commerce and e-commerce companies to sell their agricultural products. E-commerce companies involved in the Goldenbrook Cooperative include both

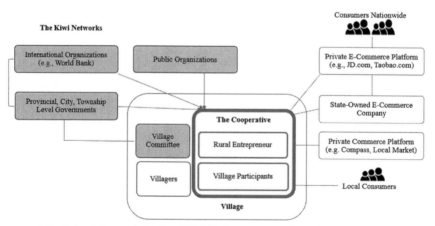

Fig. 9.1. Network Built of Public Investors and Business Partners. *Note*: The figure was developed by the author.

privately owned e-commerce companies and state-owned e-commerce companies. The private e-commerce platform, JD.com, is an example of a private partner. This e-commerce company provided funding and support to provide e-commerce training and services to poverty-reduction cooperatives in the area. Another privately owned e-commerce company helped Goldenbrook Cooperative and others develop brands, enlarge marketing and sales channels, linking these rural cooperatives to buyers in the national e-commerce marketplace. As one cooperative leader explained how private e-commerce companies were involved in this poverty-reduction cooperative model:

> As for "poverty reduction through marketization" (产业扶贫), we focus on their products. Products that help them reduce poverty. Take the blueberries from [the] Township as an example. If we hadn't helped them build up their brand or do marketing, locals might not have known that this place produces blueberries. That's the task we do in poverty reduction …. Our efforts in poverty alleviation (*Fu Pin* 扶贫) work through marketizing their (agricultural) products, and our focus is about selling the (agricultural) products that they (farmers) cannot sell (find sales channels).

Commercial partners are crucial in helping anti-poverty cooperatives better achieve success in a competitive market environment, particularly relying on e-commerce platforms.

State-owned e-commerce companies are fully funded by the government; however, they engage in commercial activities like selling agricultural products on multiple e-commerce platforms in the competitive market environment. For instance, a state-owned e-commerce company purchases agricultural products, including kiwis and grapefruits, from different cooperative businesses and sells these products in their online retail stores on e-commerce platforms like Taobao.com and JD.com. Because the state-owned e-commerce company is funded by the government, it has not only engaged in commercial activities but also provided such public services under the demand from its public sector funders. The state-owned e-commerce company also serves as service contractors when public organizations intend to provide training programs for poverty-reduction cooperatives. It contracts the task of building regional e-commerce centers in multiple townships, as a service purchased by the local city government. As a leader of this company explained:

> As for our e-commerce centers in [two] Districts, these are services purchased by the government. In some way, we are providing public services. For instance, poverty reduction is also a task we must fulfill, and we try to do as much as we can …. (We received) national funding for our programs, under the category of public service. Building e-commerce centers, providing training in e-commerce, and incubating talents (in e-commerce). These are some of the programs at our E-commerce Center.

With funding from public sector investors and marketization support from commercial partners, poverty-reduction cooperatives can grow in a favorable institutional environment and achieve both commercial and social goals.

The Cooperative: From a Social Capital Perspective

The cooperative in China has been greatly prompted as an innovation that combines the feature of a for-profit business entity and public goals for poverty reduction and elimination. From the social capital perspective, the cooperative has served as a connector and attracted individuals and organizations with diverse interests, resources, and power. The cooperative satisfies the government and public organizations by offering a business entity for implementing poverty-reduction policies thus funding and services would have recipients; it meets the demands from the community by making resources and information more accessible and available to the poor rural villagers, and helping develop rural entrepreneurship; it follows market rules but its unique social enterprise status also enhances the trust and bond with business partners. For instance, an e-commerce business leader explained,

Often, we only deal with cooperatives, and cooperatives will deal with their cooperative members. I only go to cooperatives for products, and I only sign contracts with them.

As one local government officer summarized:

> Cooperative is essentially ... an intermediary organization (Zhong Jie Zu Zhi 中介组织) in the rural cooperative economy. It connects with local villagers (Lao Bai Xing 老百姓) on the one side, and the market (Shi Chang 市场) on the other side. It can organize our villagers together. We've been trying to reduce rural poverty through developing local industries. From our experience, without capable rural leaders, rural entrepreneurs, or cooperatives, ... villagers in poverty cannot develop by themselves.

Examining the kiwi network, it is noted that the network transcended the power hierarchy; the cooperative-center network makes the poor no longer disconnected from the power. Resources, information, knowledge, and market know-hows which traditionally were reserved to political cadres, successful businessman, social elites, and the other "haves" now became available to rural poor villagers and the "have nots." The network was developed based on existing networks and *guanxi* within Goldenbrook Village, including the kin or extended family networks, the business networks that the rural entrepreneurs had accumulated, possessed, and mobilized, the social and political networks that the Village Committee has maintained. More importantly, the kiwi network expanded to and engaged national/international organizations and e-commerce corporations primarily due to a shared purpose – poverty reduction and elimination. The synergies of these network members did not naturally emerge just because rural poverty reduction is a shared and appealing purpose with some existing intrinsic interlinkages. While it is unclear whether the government provides direct incentives to non-government organizations and private corporations, series of central governmental policies did create a social-political environment that prioritizes pro-poor investments and pro-poor initiatives. Because of the shared purpose, members in the kiwi network do not usually take the traditional roles as favor givers and favor receivers; the flow of resources, knowledge, information, and market know-hows should not be perceived as favor transfers, as results of *guanxi* capital articulated in Bian's 2001) work. Indeed, the network is stronger bonded by a shared purpose and more sustainable as long as the shared purpose stayed valid.

It is interesting to note that the participation of the cooperative was not evidently built upon the general trust in the village or what have been widely considered as the important aspect of social capital, reciprocity; instead, poor villagers were convinced to join the cooperative in the hope that their participation would help increase family income. Meanwhile, it is also a village norm and/or expectation that the better-off individuals have the moral obligation to help the worse-off households within the village. Capable rural leaders, rural entrepreneurs, and village officials were indeed willing to personally take part in and invest in the poverty-reduction cooperative; they mobilized connections with the outer market, attracted funding and resources from public or private sector organizations, in order to build up community-based approaches to tackling community-wide poverty. Given these, the major components of social capital – network, trust, and reciprocity – as well as structural and cognitive aspects, have not been evenly functioning. Notably, social network is more important than trust and sense of reciprocity in poverty reduction. Unlike previous discussions that social capital is either enabling innovative collective actions to address poverty or facilitating innovative approaches, in China, collective actions – joining the cooperative, doing kiwi farming, and participating e-commerce – were, by and large the results of government's promotions and individual rural entrepreneurs' leadership; social capital in the rural village at its maximum served to facilitate the cooperative's operation and activities and had *not* enabled such collective actions. Saying this, it is the hope that the results of the cooperative, an expanded social network, as well as trusting relationships among the cooperative entrepreneurs, rural villagers, business partners, and public social organizations, would help sustain a dynamic economic entity in the rural area, generate additional innovative ways, nurture entrepreneurs, empower villagers to engage in the mainstream market and society for long-term development, decreased inequality, and enhanced overall wellbeing. The hope is big but potentially tangible.

Because of the cross-cutting social ties in the value chain of growing and selling kiwi products, the cooperative facilitated new social relationships among the poor and various groups and institutions that are otherwise disconnected. One defining feature of poverty is that one is excluded from certain social networks and institutions, resulting in economic and social marginalization. Effectively, the cooperative did mobilize the social capital embedded in the Goldenbrook Village. Engaging villagers in the market-based agricultural business nurtured conditions of personal and community networks, trust, and reciprocity crucial for rural poverty relief. Being able to learn and participate in the e-commerce that process both business-to-consumer and consumer-to-consumer sales is not only generating profit-making activities, but also empowering the villagers given that China's most recent and rapid development of e-commerce has reshaped and profoundly affected economic activities and changed people's everyday lives. However, the extent that the cooperative has transformed institutional arrangements and social relations in substantial ways remains questionable. Fully recognizing the strong political wish of promoting rural cooperatives to tackle poverty, it is noted that the market-based institutional arrangements and administrative power hierarchy did not change substantially in response to the organizational form- cooperative. In addition, unlike other country's practice of investing in social capital accumulation for poverty reduction (Rustiadi & Nasution, 2017), during the cooperative operation there was less emphasis on" to "the cooperative's operation emphasizes less on pro-poor activities to nurture and transform social relations for poor villagers, but more on encouraging the ownership of such social relations developed by the cooperative.

Conclusion

Poverty reduction and elimination are desired outcomes and enjoy a global priority. This chapter has discussed that the development of social enterprises in rural China links to state influence and local government's financial supports; the rural cooperative has played a significant role in shaping the practices social enterprises have engaged. Individual social capital at the village level is considered as a condition of shared destiny which is critical to the development and operation of such rural cooperatives. The snapshot of a rural village in southwestern China demonstrates the significance of building social networks across community, commercial, and public organizations in developing social capital and reducing rural poverty. Poverty relief practices at Goldenbrook Village differ from what has been observed in other countries, particularly the strong role of the government and the weak role of civil society, which offers insights into poverty relief efforts global wide.

Acknowledgments

Case study included in this chapter is supported by villagers, village officials, entrepreneurs, and informants working on this market-based initiative to reduce rural poverty. The authors gratefully acknowledge the support by all the participants involved in this study.

References

Abdul Hakim, R., Abdul Razak, N. A., & Ismail, R. (2010). Does social capital reduce poverty? A case study of rural households in Terengganu, Malaysia. *European Journal of Social Sciences*, 14(4), 556–566.

Almedom, A. M. (2005). Social capital and mental health: An interdisciplinary review of primary evidence. *Social Science & Medicine (1982)*, 61(5), 943–964.

Akçomak, I. S., & Ter Weel, B. (2009). Social capital, innovation and growth: Evidence from Europe. *European Economic Review*, 53(5), 544–567.

Becker, J., & Smith, D. B. (2018). The need for cross-sector collaboration. *Stanford Social Innovation Review*, (Winter), 2–3.

Bhatt, B., Qureshi, I., & Riaz, S. (2019). Social entrepreneurship in non-munificent institutional environments and implications for institutional work: Insights from China. *Journal of Business Ethics, 154*(3), 605–630.

Bian, Y. (1997). Bringing strong ties back in: Indirect ties, network bridges, and job searches in China. *American Sociological Review, 62*(3), 366–385.

Bian, Y. (2001). Guanxi capital and social eating in Chinese cities: Theoretical models and empirical analyses. In N. Lin, K. Cook, & R. S. Burt (Eds.), *Social capital: Theory and research* (pp. 275–296). New York, NY: Aldine De Gruyter.

Choudhury, M. A., & Hassan, A. (2014). The challenge in poverty alleviation: Role of Islamic microfinance and social capital. *Humanomics, 30*(1), 76–90.

Cleaver, F. (2005). The inequality of social capital and the reproduction of chronic poverty. *World Development, 33*(6), 893–906. https://doi.org/10.1016/j.worlddev.2004.09.015

Fotheringham, S., & Saunders, C. (2014). Social enterprise as poverty reducing strategy for women. *Social Enterprise Journal, 10*(3), 176–199.

Fox, J., & Gershman, J. (2000). The World Bank and social capital: Lessons from ten rural development projects in the Philippines and Mexico. *Policy Sciences, 33*(3–4), 399–419.

Găucă, O., & Hadad, S. (2013). Does civil society create social entrepreneurs?. *Annals of the University of Oradea, Economic Sciences, 22*(1), 650–658.

Guo, Y., Zhou, Y., & Liu, Y. (2019). Targeted poverty alleviation and its practices in rural China: A case study of Fuping county, Hebei Province. *Journal of Rural Studies.* https://doi.org/10.1016/j.jrurstud.2019.01.007

Hassan, R., & Birungi, P. (2011). Social capital and poverty in Uganda. *Development Southern Africa, 28*(1), 19–37.

Hämäläinen, T. J. (2007). *Social innovations, institutional change, and economic performance: Making sense of structural adjustment processes in industrial sectors, regions, and societies* (Vol. 281). Cheltenham: Edward Elgar Publishing.

Heiskala, R. (2007). Social innovations: Structural and power perspectives. In T. J. Hämäläinen & R. Heiskala (Eds.), *Social innovations, institutional change and economic performance* (pp. 52–79). Cheltenham: Edward Elgar Publishing.

Hong, L., Tisdell, C., & Fei, W. (2019). Poverty and its reduction in a Chinese border region: Is social capital important?. *Journal of the Asia Pacific Economy, 24*(1), 1–23.

Idris, A. J., & Agbim, K. C. (2015). Effect of social capital on poverty alleviation: A study of women entrepreneurs in Nasarawa State, Nigeria. *Journal of Research in National Development, 13*(1), 208–222.

Johnson, J. A., Honnold, J. A., & Threlfall, P. (2011). Impact of social capital on employment and marriage among low income single mothers. *Journal of Sociology & Social Welfare, 38*, 9.

Jones, N. (2010). Investigating the influence of social costs and benefits of environmental policies through social capital theory. *Policy Sciences, 43*(3), 229–244.

Kawachi, I., & Berkman, L. (2000). Social Cohesion, Social Capital, and Health. In *Social Epidemiology*. Oxford University Press.

Kerlin, J. A. (2009). *Social enterprise: A global comparison*. Lebanon, NH: UPNE.

Klein, J. L., Fontan, J. M., Harrisson, D., & Lévesque, B. (2012). The Quebec system of social innovation: A focused analysis on the local development field. *Finisterra-Revista Portuguesa de Geografia*, (94), 9–28.

Koka, B. R., & Prescott, J. E. (2002). Strategic alliances as social capital: A multidimensional view. *Strategic Management Journal, 23*(9), 795–816.

Lin, N. (2001). *Social Capital: A Theory of Social Structure and Action*. Cambridge University Press. https://doi.org/10.1017/CBO9780511815447

Lu, H., Trienekens, J. H., Omta, S., & Feng, S. (2010). Guanxi networks, buyer–seller relationships, and farmers' participation in modern vegetable markets in China. *Journal of International Food & Agribusiness Marketing, 22*(1–2), 70–93.

Ma, Z. (2002). Social-capital mobilization and income returns to entrepreneurship: The case of return migration in rural China. *Environment and Planning A, 34*(10), 1763–1784.

Mumford, M. D. (2002). Social innovation: Ten cases from Benjamin Franklin. *Creativity Research Journal*, *14*(2), 253–266.
Oosterlynck, S., Novy, A., & Kazepov, Y. (2019). *Local social innovation to combat poverty and exclusion: A critical appraisal*. Bristol: Policy Press.
Osei, C. D., & Zhuang, J. (2020). Rural poverty alleviation strategies and social capital link: The mediation role of women entrepreneurship and social innovation. *SAGE Open*, *10*(2), https://doi.org/10.1177/2158244020925504
Paunescu, C. (2014). Current trends in social innovation research: Social capital, corporate social responsibility, impact measurement. *Management & Marketing*, *9*(2), 105.
Phillips, B. N., Robison, L. J., & Kosciulek, J. F. (2014). The influence of social capital on starting wage for people with and without disabilities. *Rehabilitation Counseling Bulletin*, *58*(1), 37–45. doi:10.1177/0034355214524834
Piven, F. F., & Cloward, R. (2012). *Regulating the poor: The functions of public welfare*. New York, NY: Vintage.
Putnam, R. (1993). The Prosperous Community: Social Capital and Public Life. *The American Prospect*, 13, 35–42.
Puttnam, R. (2002). *The role of social capital in development: An empirical assessment*. Cambridge: Cambridge University Press.
Rustiadi, E., & Nasution, A. (2017). Can social capital investment reduce poverty in rural Indonesia?. *International Journal of Economics and Financial Issues*, *7*(2), 109.
Scarlato, M. (2013). Social enterprise, capabilities and development paradigms: Lessons from Ecuador. *The Journal of Development Studies*, *49*(9), 1270–1283.
Seelos, C., & Mair, J. (2005). Social entrepreneurship: Creating new business models to serve the poor. *Business Horizons*, *48*, 241–246.
Si, S., Yu, X., Wu, A., Chen, S., Chen, S., & Su, Y. (2015). Entrepreneurship and poverty reduction: A case study of Yiwu, China. *Asia Pacific Journal of Management*, *32*(1), 119–143.
Song, Y., Qi, G., Zhang, Y., & Vernooy, R. (2014). Farmer cooperatives in China: Diverse pathways to sustainable rural development. *International Journal of Agricultural Sustainability*, *12*(2), 95–108.
Staveren, I. v. (2003). Beyond social capital in poverty research. *Journal of Economic Issues*, *37*(2), 415–423.
Vorhies, V., Davis, K. E., Frounfelker, R. L., & Kaiser, S. M. (2012). Applying social and cultural capital frameworks: Understanding employment perspectives of transition age youth with serious mental health conditions. *The Journal of Behavioral Health Services and Research*, *39*(3), 257–270.
Warren, M. R., Thompson, J. P., & Saegert, S. (2001). The role of social capital in combating poverty. *Social Capital and Poor Communities*, *3*, 1–28.
Xing, L., Fan, S., Luo, X., & Zhang, X. (2009). Community poverty and inequality in western China: A tale of three villages in Guizhou Province. *China Economic Review*, *20*(2), 338–349.
Yu, X. (2011), Social enterprise in China: Driving forces, development patterns and legal framework, *Social Enterprise Journal*, *7*(1), 9–32.
Zhang, N. (2011). The impact of guanxi networks on the employment relations of rural migrant women in contemporary China. *Industrial Relations Journal*, *42*(6), 580–595.
Zhang, Y., Zhou, X., & Lei, W. (2017). Social capital and its contingent value in poverty reduction: Evidence from Western China. *World Development*, *93*, 350–361.
Zhao, L., & Yuan, P. (2014). Rural cooperative in China. *Chinese Economy*, *47*(3), 32–62.
Zhou, M., & Kim, S. S. (2006). Community Forces, Social Capital, and Educational Achievement: The Case of Supplementary Education in the Chinese and Korean Immigrant Communities. *Harvard Educational Review*, 76(1), 1–29. https://doi.org/10.17763/haer.76.1.u08t548554882477
Zhou, Y., Guo, Y., Liu, Y., Wu, W., & Li, Y. (2018). Targeted poverty alleviation and land policy innovation: Some practice and policy implications from China. *Land Use Policy*, *74*, 53–65.

Chapter 10

Conclusion: A Shifting Recognition of Global Civil Society?

Roopinder Oberoi, Jamie P. Halsall and Michael Snowden

Abstracts

In the final chapter of this edited book, the authors provide a summary of the key messages of civil society in a globalized world. To do this, the authors firstly discuss the future direction of civil society, and then examine the enhancement of social movements in contemporary society. In the final part of this chapter, the authors provide some observations regarding the recent global health crisis (COVID-19) and why civil society is vitally important in a globalized world.

Keywords: Civil society; COVID-19; global; networks; social movements; technology

1. The Future Role of Global Civil Society

Global civil society, drawing upon the classic illustrations of Edwards (2011) and Keane (2003), can be described as a collective delineated societal space that sits between government, market and the family unit that hosts similar interests, values and goals. However, it is not, as traditionally presented within the literature, solely the domain of western cultures. Examples of these groups, as illustrated by the World Economic Forum (2013, p. 8), include:

- NGOs, non-profit organizations and civil society organizations (CSOs) that have an organized structure or activity, and are typically registered entities and groups.
- Online groups and activities including social media communities that can be "organized" but do not necessarily have physical, legal or financial structures.

- Social movements of collective action and/or identity, which can be online or physical.
- Religious leaders, faith communities, and faith-based organizations.
- Labour unions and labour organizations representing workers.
- Social entrepreneurs employing innovative and/or market oriented approaches for social and environmental outcomes.
- Grassroots associations and activities at local level.
- Cooperatives owned and democratically controlled by their Members.

Globally, CSOs such as Amnesty International, Greenpeace, Unicef and the World Wildlife Fund have become increasingly involved in global affairs and played a role in law and policymaking, agenda setting and diplomacy in tackling global social, political and environmental issues.

The COVID-19 pandemic has had an immeasurable and catastrophic effect on global society and groups; it has in one way or another affected every individual's life. The pandemic has presented global society with a distinct challenge in order to safeguard humanity. This is emphasized in the recent "State of Civil Society" (CIVICUS, (2021) report, which states that global civil society has a vital role to play in reconstructing the post COVID-19 world. The COVID-19 pandemic and the necessary lockdowns imposed by countries worldwide are having a significant impact on social and economic life, including, for example, the rights of excluded vulnerable groups and personal civic freedoms. Snowden, Oberoi, and Halsall (2021) emphasize that the COVID-19 pandemic signals the need to reset social, economic and political structures. Furthermore, the UN's Framework for the Immediate Socio-Economic Response to the COVID-19 Crisis warns that:

> The COVID-19 pandemic is far more than a health crisis: it is affecting societies and economies at their core. While the impact of the pandemic will vary from country to country, it will most likely increase poverty and inequalities at a global scale, making achievement of SDGs even more urgent. Without urgent socio-economic responses global suffering will escalate, jeopardizing lives and livelihoods for years to come. (UNDP, 2020)

CIVICUS (2021) in their recent analysis of the civic society assert that the socio-economic and political problems highlighted by the pandemic are enduring, and post COVID recovery plans must be inclusive of agencies such as charities, NGOs and civic campaigners. Globally, civil society has proved its worth during the pandemic, has made a substantive contribution to the global social fabric, and has presented a distinct source of resilience. CIVICUS (2021) argue that civil society should be encouraged to grow rather than inhibited, and should be nurtured rather than repressed. Third Force News (2021), representing the voice of the "third sector" in Scotland, argue that civil society has been mobilized to instigate change globally. Clearly, civil society should be enabled to fulfill its potential in service provisions, but also in its traditional role of enabling collective decision making to develop awareness of issues and to further the scrutiny of polices and decisions made by governments.

While civil society must be enabled to fulfill its potential, achieving this is a challenge. The notion of global civil society is difficult to define, with some disagreement evident when attempting a definition (Keane, 2003; Edwards, 2011); this multifaceted and contested concept causes confusion and a lack of clarity when determining impact. Gómez (2018) conducted an in-depth systematic review of the notion and impact of the civil society on policy. Gómez reports that most research focuses on agenda setting and policy implementation and fails to account for all stages of the policymaking process and the role civil society plays in the process. However, Gómez does concur with the generally accepted assertion that civil society does have influence. Nonetheless, civil society's impact has been demonstrated clearly in response to the COVID-19 pandemic. While much of the impact of civil society is unreported, the Solidarity in the Time of COVID-19 report published by CIVICUS (2020) provides clear evidence of civil society responses to the pandemic and their impact.

The CIVICUS (2020) report illustrates impact by drawing upon global examples of how civil society has met the basic human needs of food and safety using the following seven strategies:

1 Providing personal protective equipment and financial aid, maintaining health and social care provision, and the provision of mental well-being support.
2 Promoting and sharing information, by acting as a hub to disseminate accurate information; for example, by providing access to accurate information in appropriate languages and formats that can be understood.
3 Providing remote services; while digital technology was used for sharing information, it also became an important tool for service provision – the provision of online and phone support enabled many services to continue when face-to-face support was no longer possible.
4 Monitoring and defending human rights.
5 Influencing and engaging with states; for example, civil society urged that international guidance should be followed so that elections could be held safely, and people could vote in confidence, which resulted in delayed elections in Malawi and the Dominican Republic.
6 Public campaigning – in Brazil, a CSO coalition campaigned for the introduction of a minimum income during the pandemic; more than 500,000 people supported the campaign and secured a law approving the scheme.
7 Nurturing community leadership – investing in community leadership and volunteering enabled local knowledge and resilience; for example, in Malaysia, a coaching scheme was implemented for community leaders to develop skills that enabled them to connect with the platforms offering support and which enabled them to articulate their communities' needs. For example, in the Democratic Republic of Congo, in response lockdown poverty, the BIFERD organization trained more than 50 local volunteers to develop negotiation and advocacy strategies to support communities in lockdown.

CIVICUS (2020) provides detailed case studies illustrating impact at local, national and global levels. Civil society, as a consequence of the COVID-19

2. Civil Society and Social Movements

Over the past decade, there has been an extraordinary level of mobilization of various types of protest movements globally, from the most recent Black Lives Matter protests in the summer of 2020 in the USA, to Latin America, to the Arab Spring, to the "occupy movements" in the USA and Europe 2009–2010, to democracy protests in Hong Kong in 2019. The transnational networks of "self-representation" grant a voice for the marginalized who may be unheard due to local inaccessibility and indifference. In multiple ways therefore, global civil society has formed, fashioned and expanded a "new" space to reinstall voices, concerns and justice as inspiration and arbiter of laws. The sensed unfairness draws on the knowledge of grievances by individuals in comparable circumstances wherever they are in the world as long as a reason of the wrongdoing is upheld in folk memory or historical record.

There are ample instances of very boisterous discontentment with the neoliberal agenda and its wicked effects, which offers substantiation to the ascendency of some nascent and vigorous transnational alliances. These links and movements have stirred civic contest and captivated bigger crowds, unswervingly committed to challenging current agendas and organizations. We are witnessing heightened global coalitions aiming to draw the attention of governments in order to alter the structures and institutions that fail to assist the masses or openly violate the rights of common citizens. The public no longer remain silent, quiet down or halt their presumptions. Rather, they can demonstrate/mobilize their discontent, protesting and dissenting in novel and innovative ways: on social media, through their cell phones and cyberspace networks and on the ground. Modern information and communication platforms have emboldened civil societies and the public to consider that they can transform things, topple regimes, make systems better and insist on the means and apparatuses that give them a legitimate say; they can demand that they are both heard and attended to, and install movements and strategies that help them and a wide swath of society, not just the elite 1% (of the population). New high-tech developments have changed social ties, particularly the meaning of the term co-presence. The label "swarm" has been used to refer to new horizontal forms of CSO that are highly decentralized, flexible and multidimensional, associated with and organized in cyberspace (Taylor, 2004).

Politics and the political ideas that stimulate and undergird civil society are shifting, and the involvement of modern technology is only aggravating the trend. As we advance into the third decade of the twenty-first century, an extensive alteration in political culture is becoming more apparent. There are innovative approaches and new methods of contesting and challenging power, and new models and analytic contexts are required so as to comprehend global social movements. There are global movements, transnational actions, democratic and membership philosophies that are bubbling and springing up everywhere.

Novel consciousness, judgment and praxis of global civil society movements is sweeping through Asia, the Middle East, the USA, Latin America and Europe. Within western liberal economies, the "occupy movement" became an iconic marker of this contemporary cycle of economic contention. The slogan 1% and 99% caught the imagination of the masses facing the brunt of recession and economic downturn. Enthused by Tahir Square and Iceland, the Spanish Indignados and the 15M movements in Portugal and Spain, New York's Occupy Wall Street stirred dissents and occupations in over 900 cities across more than 80 states. Across the globe, the public took to the streets to dissent against skewed socio-economic and political developments in the wake of the global 2008 recession and the banking debacle, appealing to the new repertoires of contention or re-explaining older forms of demonstration such as occupation of public space and encampments (Vanden, Funke, & Prevost, 2017, p. 1). Similarly, Black Lives Matter emerged as a reaction to the ongoing police brutality against black people in the USA, itself a symptom of much deeper injustices the poor and those of color face in the USA in everyday life. According to Manuel Castells (2015):

> It began on the Internet social networks, as these are spaces of autonomy, largely beyond the control of governments and corporations that had monopolized the channels of communication as the foundation of their power, throughout history .... They came together. From the safety of cyberspace, people from all ages and conditions moved toward occupying urban space, on a blind date with each other and with the destiny they wanted to forge, as they claimed their right to make history – their history – in a display of the self-awareness that has always characterized major social movements. The movements spread by contagion in a world networked by the wireless Internet and marked by fast, viral diffusion of images and ideas. (p. 2)

Furthermore, Melucci (1980) has noted that new social movements are rising not primarily from the relations or means of creation and delivery of resources as perceived earlier, but rather in the context of construction and the whole ecosphere. Therefore, CSOs and social movements are moving from exclusively focusing on economic relations to the socio-cultural creation of symbols and identities. The current social movements discard the acquisitive and economic positioning of consumerism in capitalist systems by enquiring about the contemporary views that connect the quest of contentment and accomplishment closely to progress, growth and improved efficiency by an alternative endorsement of ideals and empathies in relation to the social order. For instance, the ecological crusade of the 1970s, which began in North America, spread throughout the world and has brought a "dramatic reversal" in how we contemplate the connection between economy, society and ecology.

Additionally, new social movements are positioned in civil society or the cultural domain as a priority for united action rather than contributory action in the state, that Claus Offe typifies as "bypass[ing] the state" (REF). The new-fangled social movements are difficult to describe, as they display heterogeneity of concepts and ideals, and often tend to have realistic positionings and pursue institutional restructurings that broaden the structures of participants in deciding the course of action (Larana, 1992; Offe, 1985). These actions point toward a "democratization dynamic" of average life and the enlargement of civil versus political dimensions of the social order (Larana, 1992). The reallocation toward the "cultural turn" was accomplished by highlighting the latest social movements as products of post modernity. The "hyper-individualism" that typifies the capitalist market system tenders disapproval for shared accomplishment and offers little to embrace communities collectively in the face of rising personalized pecuniary and collective disquiet. Hence, new-fangled social movements appeared from the disintegration of politics and mirrored a profound disenchantment with institutional and formalistic politics the waning of the collective setting of groups and occupations as locations for political mobilization, and the growing standing of culture as the domain through which individualities and groups are shaped, created and stabilized (Larana, 1992).

Social movements are accordingly rendered as "global fluids" that move persistently in networks and grids and take the form of an unstructured nebula with blurry outlines and a mutable future (Melucci, 1996). Moreover, Taylor (2004) gives example of:

> networking switching that involves the movement of people, objects and images that coalesce, disperse, concentrate and dissolve and thereby switch the point of attack through the flooding of spaces. Complex social movements are conceptualized as leaderless, non-organization. (p. 23)

The contemporary ascendency in the influence of global civil society is linked to the revolution of information, communication and technology. Cyberspace is revolutionizing civil society advocacy and is enabling the creation of networks and coalitions. The term "dot cause" applies to any citizen assemblage that encourages a societal cause and essentially mobilizes backing through its internet site. The constant change of communication know-how in the digital era encompasses the scope and spread of messaging on social media to all spheres of public life in a system that is simultaneously global and local, general and personalized, in an ever-changing form. The method of making meaning is characterized by boundless variety. There is, though, one characteristic shared by all procedures of emblematic construction: they are mainly reliant on the communications and references shaped, structured and disseminated in cyberspace communication networks. Even though citizens construct their own connotations through their understanding of communicated resources on their terms, this rational processing of ideas is often preconditioned by the communication setting. Recently, the upsurge of "mass self-communication," that is, the usage of cyberspace networks as podiums of digital messages, has caused a vital transformation of the communication infrastructure. Mass messaging has the potential of reaching an array of receivers, and of linking to boundless networks that diffuse digitized data in the ecosphere. This sort of mass communication is based on horizontal networks of collaborative communication that are difficult for regimes to control; it also offers a high-tech stage for the manufacture of the social actors' originality, be it distinct or cooperative, apropos the formations of the social order. This is the reason why regimes are becoming wary of tech giants like Twitter and Facebook, and why organizations have a love/hate rapport with them. Communication can be viewed to operate as an infrastructural dimension with the capacity to outline and shape social relationships across the disjointed landscape. The critical features of on- and offline communication tools are immediately noticeable when observing the indicators or advents of contemporary movements (Castells, 1996, 2015).

One lesson evolving globally is that the way forward is a better state–CSO partnership in the distribution of basic services to citizens. The philosophy that encouraged minimal government involvement and promoted market-based resolutions to service provision is conspicuously receding, and there is increasing reappraisal of the critical role of the state – especially during the current COVID-19 pandemic. As a consequence, CSOs seem to be facing numerous vital prospects and contests. In relation to effectiveness, enhanced economies of scale in health supplies are one potential benefit for CSOs in their superior teamwork with regimes. There is also the likelihood that better CSO–government partnerships could lead to the improved sustainability of CSO programs. Universally, CSOs face intricate choices and challenging demands when harmonizing diverse activities. The key contemplation for different CSOs is where they are likely to have maximum impact. There is a requirement for dedicated CSOs with a distinct advocacy role at the nationwide level, and there are countless CSOs whose involvement, proficiency and impact lies in local-level provision. The CSO sector as a whole must safeguard both methods.

3. Some Observations

The book was compiled during the coronavirus pandemic and, as editors, we could witness the acute pressure and tall expectations from regimes around the globe to alleviate the disruption, hurt and suffering the pandemic was causing. During the course of the last year and a half, much has been debated on a "return to big government." The attention on state responses is definitely logical, as people looked to the authorities for real help and aid and, repeatedly, this assistance actually made the critical difference between life and death. Thus far, the COVID-19 pandemic has had a deep effect on government policies, business strategies and on societies at large. The disaster has played out at the global and national levels, and, correspondingly, at community and civil society levels. To a certain degree amid the emphasis on governments' pandemic responses, the coronavirus actually sharpened and intensified the significance of organized civil society action.

Globally, the mandate for civic engagement has increased, and innovative avenues are opening up for CSOs to play significant and multilevel roles during the crisis. The COVID-19 pandemic has placed implicit and explicit pressure on global civil society, unleashed by the kernel of civic empowerment that compelled

CSOs to extend their presence in local communities. In some nations, civil society activism moved up a gear and undertook tougher approaches, as during the pandemic, governments tried to drown out the critical voices of civil society. The COVID-19 pandemic has heightened the demand for, and augmented the supply of, civic activism, along with the need for CSOs to push back against punitive regime restrictions. All in all, COVID-19 has been a bugle call for global civil society. The pandemic has placed substantial stresses not only on administrations but also on societies around the world.

References

Castells, M. (1996). *The Rise of the Network Society: The Information Age: Economy, Society and Culture*, Oxford: Blackwell.

Castells, M. (2015). *Networks of outrage and hope social movements in the internet age.* Cambridge: Polity Press.

CIVICUS. (2020). Solidarity in the time of COVID-19: Civil society responses to the pandemic. Retrieved from https://www.civicus.org/documents/reports-and-publications/SOCS/2020/solidarity-in-the-time-of-COVID-19_en.pdf. Accessed on August 19, 2021.

CIVICUS. (2021). The state of civil society. Retrieved from https://civicus.org/state-of-civil-society-report-2021/wp-content/uploads/2021/05/CIVICUS-State-of-Civil-Society-Report-ENG-OVERVIEW.pdf. Accessed on August 19, 2021.

Edwards, M. (2011). *The Oxford handbook of civil society*. Oxford: Oxford University Press.

Gómez, E. J. (2018). Civil society in global health policymaking: A critical review. *Global Health, 14*, 73. https://doi.org/10.1186/s12992-018-0393-2

Keane, J. (2003). *Global civil society*. Cambridge: Cambridge University Press.

Larana, E. (1992). Student movements in the U.S. and Spain: Ideology and the crisis of legitimacy in post-industrial society. *Paper presented at the international conference on culture and social movements*, University of California, San Diego, June 17–20.

Melucci, A. (1980). The new social movements: A theoretical approach. *Social Science Information, 19*, 199–226.

Melucci, A. (1996). Challenging codes: Collective action in the information age. Cambridge University Press.

Offe, C. (1985). New social movements: Challenging boundaries of institutional politics. *Social Research, 52*, 817–868.

Snowden, M., Oberoi, R., & Halsall, J. P. (2021). Reaffirming trust in social enterprise in the COVID-19 era: Ways forward [Special issue]. *Corporate Governance and Sustainability Review, 5*(1), 120–130. https://doi.org/10.22495/cgsrv5i1sip3

Taylor, R. (Ed.). (2004). *Creating a better world interpreting global civil society*. Bloomfield, CT: Kumarian Press.

Third Force News (TFN). (2021). Protests are the new normal as civil society takes lead role in changing inequality. Retrieved from https://tfn.scot/news/protest-are-the-new-normal-as-civil-society-takes-lead-role-in-changing-inequality. Accessed on August 20, 2021.

UNDP. (2020). COVID-19: Socio-economic impact. Retrieved from https://www.undp.org/coronavirus/socio-economic-impact-COVID-19. Accessed on August 19, 2021.

Vanden, H. E., Funke, P. N., & Prevost, G. (Eds.), (2017). *The new global: Politics global social movements in the twenty-first century*. London: Routledge.

World Economic Forum. (2013). The future role of civil society. Retrieved from http://www3.weforum.org/docs/WEF_FutureRoleCivilSociety_Report_2013.pdf. Accessed on August 18, 2021.

Index

Note: Page numbers followed by "*n*" indicate notes.

Academic new syllabi of future, 56–59
Accountability A/IS, 75, 121
Acquired Immunodeficiency Syndrome (AIDS), 101
Actors, 36–37
Administrative decision-making, 138
African Development Bank, 55
Agricultural marketization, 162
Agricultural products, 165
"AI2" design, 72
Algorithmic governance, 65, 139
Algorithmic systems, 138
Altruistic behaviors, 38
Alzheimer's Society, 21–22
Amnesty International, 172
Anglo-American populism, 81–83
Apple organization, 72
Artificial intelligence (AI), 48, 52–56, 64–65, 121, 130, 142
    comments AI governance, 138–141
    for governance, 148
    governance systems, 125
    impact on social capital, 138–141
    main opportunities and risks emerging from, 54
    systems, 72–74, 148–149
    systems impact on community social capital, 121
Asian Development Bank, 55
"Asymmetric transactions", 157
Atlantic Forest Biome, 106
Augmented reality, 48
Australia's "neoliberal" experience, 82
Australian Commonwealth Department of Human Services and Centrelink's online system, 140
Australian economic stimulus, 86
Australian Economy, re-opening, 88
Autocracies, 8
"Autocratic capitalism", 90
Automation, 138
Autonomous vehicles, 65
Awareness of misuse A/IS, 75, 121

"Ba" (shared context), 70
Big data, 48, 52, 73–74, 143
"Big Data Sets", 141–142, 148
Bilateral and multilateral development partners (BMDP), 52–56
Biotechnologies, 48
Black Lives Matter protests (2020), 174
Black Power movement, 104
Blockchain, 48
Bonding social capital, 16
"Bottom up" approach, 139
Branding, 69
Brave New World (Huxley), 142
Brazil
    civil society and environmental protection, 106–112
    civil society in, 97–98, 102–103
    empowerment of civil society, 101–102
    evolution of civil society in Brazil, 99
    importance of 1988 FC, 99–101

managing civil society
organizations, 105–106
organization and professionalism
of civil society, 104–105
Brazil, Russia, India and China
countries ("BRIC"
countries), 68
Brazilian environmental legislation, 110
Brazilian Foundation for
Conservation of Nature
(FBCN), 106–107
Brazilian Institute of Environment
and Renewable Resources
(IBAMA), 110
"Brazilian model", 98
Brazilian Society for Progress of
Science (SBPC), 99
Brexit, 133
campaign, 81
focused on "economic migrants", 134
policy, 15
Bridging social capital, 16–17, 19
Budget deficits, exploding, 86
Building culture of integrity in
organizations, 120–127
Businesses organizations, 121

Cannes Film Festival, 16
Capital types and interrelationships,
15–16
Capitalism, 90
Case study approach, 10
Catalysts for social transformation, 31
Charitable Organizations,
China's poverty relief
Goldenbrook Village Story, 160–162
innovation, social enterprise, and
social capital, 158–159
Kiwi network, 163–166
participation and cooperative
development, 162–163
social capital in use, 156–157
from social capital perspective,
166–168
social enterprise and poverty
reduction in China, 159–160

CIOs, 139
"Citizenship Constitution", 99
City Government, 164
Civic actors, 6
Civic participation, 100, 104
in Brazil, 101
in environmental issues, 107–108
institutionalization of, 101
Civil society, 1–2, 47
in Brazil, 10, 97–98, 102–103
empowerment of, 101–102
engagement, 104
and environmental protection,
106–112
evolution in Brazil, 99–106
managing civil society
organizations, 105–106
mobilization, 98
organization and professionalism
of, 104–105
and social movements, 173–177
Civil society organizations (CSOs), 6,
47–48, 52–56, 171–172, 177
"Clap for the NHS", 17, 19
"Click-thru", 127, 144
Climate change, 136
Co-operative social capital, 16
Collaboration, 5–9, 149
typology, 149
Collaborative advantage, 134
Collaborative knowledge creation, 24
Collaborative leadership model, 136
Comirnaty, 83
Commercial AI systems, 72
Commercial partners, 165
Communication, 176–177
systems, 16
technologies, 3
Community
community-based approach, 159
community-based developments, 159
councils, 102–103
development, 31
groups, 47
involvement, 25
social capital, 32

Comorbidities, 14
Comparative advantage, 134
Comparative advantage, Competitive advantage, and Collaborative advantage (three Cs), 134
Competence A/IS, 75, 121
Competitive advantage, 134
Conceptualization, 25
Confidence, 87
Contemporary ascendency, 176
Contestations, 5–9
Context, 38
Convergence of agendas, 109
Cooperative in China, 166–168
Cooperatives, 102–103
Coronavirus, 14
  coronavirus-related activism, 6
  crisis, 138
  disease, 5
Corporate social responsibility (CSR), 39
Cosmopolitan citizenship, 136
COVID Alliance for Social Entrepreneurs, 38
COVID-19 Vaccines Global Access (COVAX), 6
COVID-19, 6, 137
  combination of dementia with, 22
  crisis, 15
  deadly second wave in India, 8
  economic impact of, 85–86
  and global civil society, 177
  impact on already-under-pressure emergency services, 18
  impact on neoliberalism, 80
  and modern monetary theory, 87–88
  pandemic, 21, 64, 130, 134, 172
  social distancing, 16
  UN's Framework for the Immediate Socio-Economic Response to, 172
  virus, 127, 144
Crisis, 8
Cryptocurrency, 48

Cultural capital, 15
Customer
  capital, 67
  relationship management, 75
Cyberspace, 176

Data, Information, Knowledge, Wisdom pyramid (DIKW pyramid), 66
Data agency A/IS, 74, 121
"Data for-profit model", 53
Data science, 74
"Decentralised smart manufacturing", 49
Decision-making process, 140
Deforestation, 110
Delta variant, 14
Democracy, 8, 90
"Democratic catalyst", 2
Democratic regime, 98
Democratization, 98, 108
Democrats "stole" election, 130
Deterritorialization, 48
Dialoguing Ba, 71
Digital technology, 173
"Distant" leadership, 130
Diverse communal forms of social capital, 150
Diverse organizations, 126
Divisiveness, 21
Do-It-Yourself (DIY), 150
"Dot cause", 176
Dynamic social movements, 4

E-business proactiveness, 24
E-commerce
  center, 165
  companies, 164
  platforms, 165
Earth Summit, 98, 109, 110
Economic impact of COVID-19, 85–86
"Economic migrants", 134
"Economies of flows", 135
Economists, 157
Economy, health *vs.*, 86–87

Education, 57
  motivational multiapproach collaborative rationale in, 58
Effectiveness, 111–112
Effectiveness A/IS, 75, 121
Egoistical behaviors,
Eldonian Community, 16
Emergency first responders, 18
Emergency social capital, 16
Empowerment of civil society, 101–102
Enterprise resource planning (ERP), 75
Entrepreneurship, 31
Environmental Crime Law, 110
Environmental degradation, 109n5
Environmental movements in Brazil, 107–108
Environmental organizations, 109
Environmental protection, 98
  civic participation in environmental issues, 107–108
  civil society and, 106
  environment and growth, 109–111
  FBCN, 106–107
  organization, effectiveness, spatial scale and reach, 111–112
Environmental qualities, 16
Ethical capital, 122
European Bank for Reconstruction and Development and Inter-American Development, 55
European City/Capital of Culture, 16
European Union (EU), 49, 133
Events, 38
Ex post failure, 80
Exercising Ba, 71
Explicit knowledge, 66, 70
Extra-activist movements, 109

Facebook, 72, 130, 176
Faith institutions, 8
Faith-Based Organizations, 47
"Fake news", 69–72, 127, 144
False dichotomy, 87
"Favor exchanges", 157

Federal Constitution (FC), 98n2
Federal Decree-Law, 108
Fifth Industrial Revolution (IR5. 0), 46–47
  academic new syllabi of future, 56–59
  IR 5. 0 and human social capital, 48–52
Financial Crisis, 88
Financial support, 25
Firm, 67
First industrial revolution, 48
Formal rules, 37
Fourth industrial revolution (IR 4. 0), 48–49, 52
Framework Programmes, Responsible Research and Innovation, 50
Fundamental human data rights, 53

Gaúcha Association for the Protection of the Natural Environment (AGAPAN), 107
Geopolitical manifestation, 81
Global Alliance for Vaccination and Immunization (Gavi), 6
Global civil society, 3–5, 48, 53, 55
  future role of, 171
  and pandemic, 5–9
  paradigms of, 5
Global climate crisis, 56
Global consumption, economic growth underpinned by rising debt levels, 132–138
Global digitization, 68
Global economy, 3, 132
Global Financial Crisis (2008–2009), 81
Global financial markets, 3
Global pandemic, 9
Global society, 134
Global supporters of civil society, 8–9
Globalization
  empowerment of, 3
  rapid development of, 4

Gofundme type of charitable campaigning, 131
Goldenbrook Cooperative, 163–164
Goldenbrook Village Cooperative, 161
Goldenbrook Village Story, 160
  village and efforts of poverty reduction, 160–162
Google, 72, 121
"Googling", 71–72
Governance
  of enterprises, 71
  in era of "fake news", 69–72
  systems, 69
  and trust, 89–90
Government, 7
  across world engaged with UN, 4
  administrations, 6
  COVID-19 responses, 6
  disaster responses, 5
  governments organizations, 121
  leaders, 129
  political responses by, 8
"Government-regulated model", 53
Grapefruits, 165
"Great man" theory, 127, 144
Great Recession, 88
Green norms, 122
"Green-ness", 122, 125
Greenpeace, 172
Gross domestic product (GDP), 86
Guanxi concept, 157
"Guidance on Leveraging E-Commerce to Support Poverty Alleviation", 159
Guizhou Provincial Government, 160

#Black Lives Matter movement, 133
Health *vs.* economy, 86–87
Healthy work force, 18
"Hereditary Genius", 127, 144
"Heroic" style of leadership, 129–130, 146
High-resolution satellite imagery, 54–55
Higher education, 59
HIV/AIDS crisis, 23
Home schooling resources, 133
HR decision-making systems, 126
Human behavior, 125
Human capital, 15–16, 67
Human rights A/IS, 74, 121
Human skills, 59
Human social capital, IR 5. 0 and, 48–52
Human to Human education (H2H education), 57, 58
Human to Technology (H2T), 57, 58
Hybrid cosmopolitan–localist model, 137
"Hyper-individualism", 175

Idea, 37
In-depth systematic review, 173
Inclusive social capital, 143–148
Inclusive socio-digital capital, 143
Indigenous Groups, 4747
Industrial capital, 15
Industry Revolution (IR), 2, 46
  first industrial revolution, 48
  second industrial revolution, 48
  third industrial revolution, 48
Information, 37, 66, 139, 166
  asymmetric, 53
  customer, 141
  filtering, 148
  flows, 147
  personalization of, 74
  promoted and shared information, 173
  structured, 54
  type, 148
Information and communication technology (ICT), 65, 131
Innovation, 32
  and social enterprise, 158–159
  for social impacts, 31
Institutional arena, 102
Institutional involvement, social capital and, 34–36
Institutionalization
  of civic participation, 101–102
  of social participation, 99

Institutions, 34, 37
Intangible assets, 67
Integrity in organizations, building culture of, 120–127
Intellectual capital (IC), 66, 67
Interculturalism, 59
Interlocking system of macroeconomic policies, 33
International consultation, 52
International Finance Corporation (IFC), 55
International Labour Organisation (ILO), 49
International Organization for Migration (IOM), 133
International organizations, 4, 164
Internationalization, 48
  of Brazilian civil society, 109
  of civil society, 109
Internet, 3
Internet of things (IoT), 48, 133

JD. com (private e-commerce platform), 165

Kiwi (high-value crop), 162
Kiwi network, 163–166
  network built of public investors and business partners, 164
Knowledge, 66–67
"Knowledge conversion", 70
Knowledge management (KM), 65, 67–68
"Knowledge society", 65

Labor Unions, 47
Leadership, 127–129, 144–145
  of cooperatives research, 126
  role in building, maintaining, and developing social capital, 127–130
LGBTQI+ movement, 104
Liberal Coalition governments, 82
Liberalization, 48
Liverpool Biennial, 16
Liverpool City Council, 19

Local City Government, 160
Local community, 159
  members, 160
Local social capital, 16
Localism, 9

Machine learning system, 146
Macro-levels
  leadership role in building, maintaining, and developing social capital at, 127–130
  of strategic vision and purpose or mission, 122
Macroeconomic policies, 33
Make America Great Again (MAGA), 80
Marketized kiwi industry, 163
Mass messaging, 176
"Mass self-communication", 176
Meso-level
  of community systems focus, 122
  leadership role in building, maintaining, and developing social capital at, 127–130
Micro-level for individuals, 122
Military regime, 98
Ministry of Finance in China, 164
Modeling organizational knowledge, 65–69
Modern Monetary Theory (MMT), 87–88
Movement of People Affected by Dams (MAB), 107
Multiculturalism, 58
Mutual trust, 17

National Audit Office, 15
National Constituent Assembly (NCA), 98
National Health Service (NHS), 17
National Policy for Water Resources, 110
Nationalism, 81–83, 90–91
"Nearby" leadership, 130

Neighborhood associations, 102–103
Neoconservative "soulmates", 81
Neoliberal Capitalism, 15
"Neoliberal" domestic policies, 80
Neoliberalism, 10, 34, 80, 90
  COVID-19 and modern monetary theory, 87–88
  COVID-19 health impacts and responses, 83–85
  economic impact of COVID-19, 85–86
  geopolitical manifestation, 81
  health vs. economy, 86–87
  heritage and legacy, 80
  importance of social capital, 88–89
  neoconservative "soulmates", 81
  neoliberal society and government, 80–81
  neoliberalism, capitalism and democracy, 90
  populism and nationalism, 90–91
  post-COVID-19 scenarios, 89–90
  resurgent Anglo-American populism and nationalism, 81–83
Network(s), 37
  enterprise, 3–4
  social capital, 16
Networked society, 3
  AI, 64–65
  AI systems, 72–74
  modeling organizational knowledge, 65–69
  trust and governance in era of "fake news", 69–72
Networking, 4, 19
Non-AI marketing, 139
Non-conscious cognition, 142, 149
Non-governmental organizations (NGOs), 8, 47, 69, 102, 121, 128, 171
Non-local social capital, 16
Non-profit organizations, 171
Novelty, 32
"Nudging" process, 139, 142

"Occupy movements", 174–175
Online groups, 171
Organization for Economic Cooperation and Development (OECD), 49, 51, 126, 143
Organization of Lawyers of Brazil (OAB), 103
Organizational knowledge modeling, 65–69
Organizational support, 25
Organizations, 4, 64, 111–112, 127–128, 145
  of civil society, 104–105
  types, 102–103
Originating Ba, 71

Pandemic, global civil society and, 5–9
Participation and cooperative development, 162–163
"Participatory budget" initiative, 101
Patriarchal feudal society, 20
Personal protective equipment (PPE), 15, 38, 173
Personalization of companies targeting, 139
"Perspective-taking", 71
Pfizer/BioNTech, 83
Political faith in civil society, 2
Political ideologies, 1
Political instability, 82–83
Political organization model, 100
Political responses, 8
Populism, 90–91
"Post-bureaucratic" agenda, 30
Post-COVID-19 scenarios, 89–90
Post-Keynesian, 87–88
Poverty reduction, 157
  in China, 159–160
  funds, 163
  through marketization, 165
  poverty-reduction business projects, 163
  poverty-reduction cooperatives, 159
  poverty–reduction cooperative model, 165

Pre-COVID-19 "baseline", 83
Private corporate technology, 32
Private e-commerce platform, 165
Private partner, 165
Private sector, 80
Pro-social behavior, 38
Professional Associations, And Foundations, 47
"Professional" groups, 70
Professionalism, 18
  of civil society, 104–105
"Prosumers", 69
"Prosumption", 151
Protest movements, 173–174
Provincial Government in Guizhou, 164
Public policy
  for social innovation, 32
  social value creation in, 36–40
Public Services (Social Value) Act (2012), 39

Reaganomics, 80
Remote services, 173
Restrictive rules, 8
"Roads to each Village" project, 161
"Robots", 147
Rural cooperatives, 161
Rural entrepreneurship, 162
Rural poverty, 159
Rural poverty reduction, 166

Safety, 87
Sao Francisco River, 111
Second industrial revolution, 48
Sensitive design, 50, 56
Severe Acute Respiratory Syndrome Coronavirus 2 (SARSCoV-2), 127, 144
"Shareholders", 162
Sikh communities, 8
"Smart factories", 49
Smart manufacturing, 50
"Social bargain", 90

Social capital, 10, 14–15, 30–34, 121–122, 144, 156–158
  3D culture of integrity, 125
  academic perspectives on, 35
  AI impact on, 138–141
  AI systems impact on, 121
  building culture of integrity in organizations, 120–127
  comments AI governance, 138–141
  creation, 20
  culture and ethical dimensions, 123–124
  evolution and complexity of systems, 141–143
  examples of social capital creation in different societies, 21–24
  green norms, 122
  hierarchy to heterarchy, 130–132
  importance of, 88–89
  inclusive social capital, 143–148
  innovation, social enterprise, and, 158–159
  and main components, 16–20
  mediated data and voice, 148–151
  nurture social capital for future, 24–25
  perspective, 166–168
  role of leadership in building, maintaining, and developing social capital, 127–130
  social capital and institutional involvement, 34–36
  social value creation in public policy, 36–40
  SWOT analysis of, 20–21
  theory, 156
  types of capital and interrelationships, 15–16
  unequal social capital burdens, 132–138
"Social cohesion", 85
Social enterprise, 10, 30–34, 159
  in China, 159–160
  strategy, 159
  tool, 159

Social entrepreneurs, 32–33, 158
Social entrepreneurship, 31, 33
"Social environmentalism", 105
Social innovation, 30–34, 158
Social innovator, 158
Social insurance schemes, 33
Social life, 17
Social media, 65, 127
  communities, 171
  influencers, 72
Social movements, 175–176
Social movements, civil society and, 173–177
Social networks, 33, 130, 143
Social norms and values, 122
Social organizations, 32
Social participation, 99
"Social purpose organisations", 31
Social research, 127
Social systems, 126
Social value creation, 39
  in public policy, 36–40
Social wellbeing, 18
Socialization, 59
Socialization, externalization, combination and internalization model (SECI model), 70
Society, 80
Socio-digital technology, 64, 66, 121
Socio-technical capital, 126
Socioenvironmental degradation, 111
Solidarity, 9
Space traveling, 48
"Speed networking", 131
State capital, 15
"State of Civil Society", 172
State-owned e-commerce company, 165
Strategic Direction, 131
Strengths, weaknesses, opportunities, threats analysis (SWOT), 10
  analysis of social capital, 20–21
Stress factors, 7
Structural capital, 67
Supply chain management, 75
"Supraterritorial" character, 48

Sustainable development goals (SDGs), 39
System justification theory, 129, 146
Systemizing Ba 71
Systems thinking, 91

Tacit dimensions of organizational knowledge, 70
Tacit knowledge, 66
Tandem solutions, 56–59
Taobao. com (e-commerce platforms), 165
"Targeted Poverty Alleviation" plan, 159, 161
Tax evasion, 72
Tax-financed services, 33
"Tech-ethics", 55
Technical knowledge, 109
Techno-corporatism, 56
"Technologic man's petulance", 56
Technological development, 50, 55, 68–59
Technological threat, 57
Technology, 56–57, 173, 174, 176
Thinking About You (Tay), 73
Third industrial revolution, 48
Three–dimension (3D)
  culture matrix, 125
  culture of integrity, 125–126
  perspective, 122
  printing, 48
Three-dimensionality, 122
Total societal impact (TSI), 39
Traditional CSOs, 9
"Transborder" character, 48
Transformation of social relations, 158
Transnational NGOs, 109
Transparency, 75, 121
"Transworld" character, 48
Trussell Trust, 18
Trust, 17, 87
  in era of "fake news", 69–72
  governance and, 89–90
"Truth decay", 127
Tumultuous change, years of, 82–83
Twitter, 176

UK vaccination program, 15
UNICEF, 172
United Nations (UN), 4
United Nations Educational, Scientific and Cultural Organization (UNESCO), 50

Venice Bienniale (*see* Liverpool Biennial)
Veracity, viability, value (three Vs), 149
Vertical alignment, 122
Village Committee, 164
Virtual activities, 22
Virtual reality, 48
Virtual teams, 131
Volatile Uncertain Complex and Ambiguous business environments (VUCA business environments), 65

Voluntarism, 4, 17

Well-being A/IS, 74, 121
Well-functioning computer-mediated team, 131
Westernization, 48
"Work Choices", 82
Working processe of cooperatives research, 126
World Bank, 164
World Economic Forum, 48, 171
World Health Organisation (WHO), 14, 127, 144
World Wide Web, 3
World Wildlife Fund, 172